Praise for Ann Douglas and her previous books

The Mother of All Pregnancy Books

"The perfect book to address all your pregnancy concerns."

—Todaysparent.com

"Comprehensive, informative, up-to-date, and brazenly neutral. . . . A must-have primer."

—*Toronto Star*

"Not preachy and bossy. . . . It's upfront and fun."

—*Toronto Sun*

"A book that lives up to its name. . . . Incredibly comprehensive yet easy to follow."

—*Chicago Tribune*

"The must-read pregnancy book! Ann Douglas has created the most comprehensive guide to pregnancy we've ever seen."

—Denise and Alan Fields, authors, *Baby Bargains*

"Non-bossy, fresh, and fun . . . with a uniquely Canadian spin."

—*The Hamilton Spectator*

The Mother of All Baby Books

"Ann Douglas, Canada's own Dr. Spock, gives us the manual Mother Nature forgot to include."

—*Flare Pregnancy*

"Ann Douglas is the kind of savvy and reassuring guide that you'll want by your side as you embark on the monumental journey into motherhood."

—Cecilia A. Cancellaro, author of *Pregnancy Stories: Real Women Share the Joys, Fears, Thrills, and Anxieties of Pregnancy from Conception to Birth*

The Unofficial Guide to Having a Baby

"Probably the best reference book on the market, giving non-judgmental and fairly exhaustive information on [a variety of] hot-button topics. . . . The book lays out as much information as possible and leaves the decision-making to the parents—a surprisingly rare gambit in the bossy world of pregnancy books."

—Amazon.com Parenting Editor

"The childcare bible."

—*Chicago Tribune*

Baby Science

"With candid photos and a warm, conversational style, *Baby Science* describes the first extraordinary year of life."

—Children's Book of the Month Club

Parenting Through the Storm

"This deeply personal account will move, support, and inspire parents who feel lost in dealing with challenging children."

—*Publishers Weekly*

"Ann Douglas writes with hard-won wisdom, honesty, and vulnerability."

—Sasha Emmons, Editor-in-Chief, *Today's Parent*

"This book is like a big supportive hug when parents need it most."

—Heidi Bernhardt, President and Executive Director, Centre for ADHD Awareness Canada

"With her new book *Parenting Through the Storm*, Douglas becomes an important voice in the national conversation on youth mental health."

—Marc and Craig Kielburger, Postmedia News

"A true gift to parents."

—Claire Lerner, Senior Parenting Strategist, ZERO TO THREE

THE MOTHER OF ALL

TODDLER

BOOKS

THE MOTHER OF ALL
TODDLER
BOOKS

The All-Canadian Guide to Your Child's
Second and Third Years

ANN DOUGLAS

Collins

HarperCollins books may be purchased for educational, business, or sales
promotional use through our Special Markets Department.

HarperCollins Publishers Ltd
Bay Adelaide Centre, East Tower
22 Adelaide Street West, 41st Floor
Toronto, Ontario, Canada
M5H 4E3

www.harpercollins.ca

Library and Archives Canada Cataloguing in Publication
information is available upon request.

ISBN 978-1-44342-797-5

Printed and bound in the United States of America
LSC/H 9 8 7 6 5 4 3 2 1

Medical Disclaimer:

To Julie, Scott, Erik, and Ian, with love and gratitude
for everything you taught me about the sometimes tumultuous
but always terrific toddler years.

Contents

THE MOTHER OF ALL

TODDLER

BOOKS

Introduction

You've just been through an intensive year-long training program designed to build your patience, increase your stamina, and test your ability to survive with little or no sleep. The goal of all this training? To prepare you for The Mother of All Challenges—surviving the toddler years!

While raising a toddler certainly isn't for the faint of heart or the squeamish, it isn't nearly as difficult as some people would have you believe. The very same people who had you scared silly about going into labour are doing a similar number on you right now, convincing you that parenting a toddler is guaranteed to be an exercise in torture. Their eyes positively gleam as they bombard you with hair-raising tales of temper tantrums, hunger strikes, and the perils of potty training. The end result? You're left with this sinking feeling that you've just signed up to be a contestant on the most frightening reality television show to date: Toddler TV!

Fortunately, the scaremongers are about to fall off your radar screen for the next 10 years or so, patiently biding their time until they can terrorize you with even scarier tales about teenagers. Until that happens, tune them out. After all, you've already figured out that their stories about 15-pound newborns, 96-hour labours, and foot-long episiotomy scars were, well, a little overblown. So it hardly makes sense to buy into their toddler tall tales, now does it?

A Toddler by Any Other Name

Before we get too much further into the book, we'd better tackle an important terminology issue: the definition of the word *toddler*.

If you pick up an armful of parenting books, you'll see that child development experts aren't exactly in agreement about the term. Some experts insist that toddlerhood begins at age 12 months; others don't grant a baby toddler status until age 18 months or until he's actually walking. But where the *real* disagreement arises is in deciding when to mark an end to the toddler years. Some experts claim that toddlerhood lasts until a child starts school (around age five). Others argue that the toddler years come to an end as soon as a child turns three, at which point he becomes a preschooler (ages three and four).

I tend to buy into this last school of thought. The reason is simple: I can't imagine lumping one-year-olds and four-year-olds together into the same category. It's hard enough to talk about one- and two-year-olds in the same breath, given the lightning speed at which developmental breakthroughs occur during the toddler years. I mean, preschoolers are practically civilized beings in many ways, while toddlers—toddlers— well, let's just say toddlers are not. So there you go: that's my rationale for focusing on one- and two-year-olds in this book and leaving the three- and four-year-olds for other parenting books to tackle!

Made in Canada

Now that we've pinned down the definition of a toddler, let's get another important bit of housekeeping business out of the way: my rationale for writing a Canadian toddler book.

As you've no doubt gathered by now, the vast majority of toddler books—and parenting books in general—are written by American authors. While some might argue that there's no need for an all- Canadian parenting resource, I happen to disagree. If you flip through a typical American parenting book, you'll find pages and pages of material that simply doesn't apply to Canadian parents, like tips on shopping for juvenile products that may not even be available in this country. (Baby walkers, for example, are banned in Canada but still widely available for sale south of the border.) Even the chapters that are relevant to Canadian parents suffer from a major shortcoming: the expert sources cited time and time again in the book are almost exclu- sively American.

What Canadian parents need is a book that reflects the reality of raising a toddler in Canada—a book that zeroes in on the unique chal- lenges that Canadian parents face (the doctor shortage that plagues many communities across the country, for example) and that contains up-to-the-minute advice from such respected Canadian health authorities as the Canadian Paediatric Society and Health Canada. (Believe it or not, health authorities on both sides of the border don't always see eye to eye on key pediatric health issues.)

Of course, it wouldn't be possible—or even advisable—to write a book that completely ignores what's happening south of the border. After all, many noteworthy breakthroughs in pediatric health and child development research in recent years have occurred in research laboratories beyond our borders. What Canadian parents need, however, is a book that looks at that information through Canadian eyes and interprets it for a Canadian audience.

My publisher and I think we're on to something with this all-Canadian focus. After all, the response to the first two books in this series—*The Mother of All Pregnancy Books* and *The Mother of All Baby Books*—has been nothing short of phenomenal. But enough with the flag waving for now! Let me tell you a bit about what *The Mother of All Toddler Books* has to offer.

A One-of-a-Kind Toddler Book

As you've no doubt noticed by now, books about toddlers tend to fall into one of two distinct categories: books that focus on toddler behaviour and books that focus on toddler health. *The Mother of All Toddler Books* covers both topics in exhaustive detail, doubling as a parenting book and a pediatric health reference book. (Hey, we didn't call it *The Mother of All Toddler Books* for nothing!)

If you take a quick flip through the book, you'll find a smorgasbord of valuable information, including:

- a frank discussion of the joys and challenges of parenting a toddler;
- detailed information about the key developmental milestones for the toddler years;
- parent-tested advice on coping with temper tantrums, biting, and other challenging toddler behaviours;

- the facts about discipline: what works and what doesn't—for both you *and* your toddler;
- the facts about how your toddler's play style will evolve over the next two years;
- money-saving tips on choosing toys and other play materials that will deliver the most bang for the buck, both developmentally and budget-wise;
- nitty-gritty advice on coping with all the toddler-related clutter in your life: storing toys, organizing art supplies, and so on;
- the secrets to serving up nutritious, toddler-pleasing meals;
- important information about choking, food allergies and intolerances, vitamin supplements, and other food-related health concerns;
- tried-and-true methods of coping with bedtime fears, night terrors, the transition from crib to bed, and other nighttime parenting challenges;
- sure-fire strategies for helping your toddler to brush his teeth, wash his hair, and otherwise keeping the dirt and grime at bay;
- parent-proven advice on choosing clothing and doing battle with the most common types of toddler-related stains;
- potty training dos and don'ts from parents who've weathered this particular toddler rite of passage, including insider tips on making potty training easier and less stressful for yourself and your toddler;
- practical guidelines for managing fevers and dealing with other toddler-related health concerns that can have you hitting the panic button (and/or Google!) at 3 a.m.;
- the facts on ear infections and antibiotic use;
- detailed information on potentially life-saving first-aid procedures;
- highly comprehensive safety checklists designed to help you toddler-proof each room in your home;
- a detailed glossary of pediatric health and child development terms.

As you get deeper into the book, you'll also notice that I've made a conscious effort to switch things up when it comes to using gender pronouns. I alternate between assuming that your toddler is a girl and assuming that your toddler is a boy. I did this for reasons of equality— so don't assume that I'm implying that a particular chunk of the book applies exclusively to toddlers of a particular gender (unless, of course, there was a specific reason for doing so, in which case I've made an effort to be explicit about it).

Now back to talking about what makes *The Mother of All Toddler Books* really special are the contributions of the more than 100 Canadian parents who agreed to be interviewed for this book. I pulled together their best advice on weathering the biggest challenges of the toddler years and sprinkled their funniest and most touching anecdotes throughout. It's their from-the-trenches words of wisdom that really bring the book to life. After all, who better to turn to for advice on potty training than a parent who's just cleaned up a toddler's third puddle of the day?

As you've no doubt gathered by now, *The Mother of All Toddler Books* is unlike any other toddler book you've ever encountered. It's comprehensive, it's fun to read, and—best of all—it's 100 percent Canadian-made!

I hope you enjoy the book.

ANN DOUGLAS

P.S. Have some thoughts on how I could improve this book? My editors and I would love to hear from you. You can contact us via the website for this book (www.having-a-baby.com).

CHAPTER 1

The Truth about Toddlers

"People always warn you about the terrible twos. I prefer to call them the terrific twos."

—JULIE, 30, MOTHER OF ONE

"I think the term 'terrible twos' is dreadful because it puts a negative twist on a beautiful experience. Why not call them 'the wonder years' instead? My son is in a daily state of wonder."

—KIMBERLEE, 28, MOTHER OF TWO

Welcome to the toddler years—that exciting tightrope walk that bridges the gap between babyhood and the preschool years. As any veteran parent can tell you, the toddler years are the best of times *and* the worst of times in one exciting yet exhausting package. There will be days when you're so head-over-heels in love with that wide-eyed, chubby-cheeked toddler that the mere thought of him ever growing up and moving away will bring tears to your eyes. And then there will be days when you seriously question whether you have what it takes to raise this high-energy and emotionally volatile human being!

In this chapter, we're going to talk about how you may be feeling as your baby celebrates that milestone first birthday—whether you're more inclined to fumble for a tissue box or pour yourself a glass of champagne. Then we'll look at how parenting a toddler is different from parenting a baby. (I know, I know: just when you had the baby thing down pat, Mother Nature had to go and throw you a curveball!) Finally, we'll wrap up the chapter by zeroing in on the stuff you *really* need to know: the joys and challenges of raising a toddler.

From Baby to Toddler

There's no doubt about it: your child's first birthday is a major milestone for him and for you. How you feel about reaching this milestone will largely be determined by your parenting experiences during your baby's momentous first year of life. If you have fond memories of toting a happy, gurgling baby around in a baby carrier, you may be reluctant to say goodbye to those baby days; if, on the other hand, you keep having flashbacks to all those endless nights spent pacing the floor with a highly displeased and/or squalling infant, you may be positively overjoyed to leave the baby stage behind.

"I was happy to have the first year over with," confesses Christy, a 38-year-old mother of two. "For me, it was one of the toughest years I had ever been through. I find having a baby a lot of work with very little reward."

"I personally found it a struggle when my daughter was a baby," adds Suzette, a 29-year-old mother of two. "She didn't sleep well, I was exhausted, and I felt very guilty because I didn't think I was living up to what society expected me to be as this baby's mother. Once she became more mobile and more communicative, I found her much easier to interact with. Not all mothers do well with the baby stage, and I was one of them."

Parents of higher-order multiples—triplets, quadruplets, and more—may be particularly eager to watch their babies celebrate that momentous first birthday. Yvonne—a 36-year-old mother of six—remembers feeling a tremendous sense of relief when her quintuplets reached that stage: "It was a huge milestone for us to know we'd made it through that first year. I'd been told by other mothers of higher-order multiples that nothing is as hard as the first year."

Of course, not every parent feels totally euphoric about having their baby's first birthday roll around. Many experience a mix of emotions:

excitement about watching their child move on to the toddler stage, but sadness at leaving those special baby days behind. "I felt an incredible sense of joy and awe watching my daughter gazing at her birthday candles," recalls Laura, a 33-year-old mother of one. "I was very excited about her moving into her toddler years. She was already walking and speaking and I couldn't wait for her to start telling me how she felt about her day. And yet, at the same time, I was feeling a little sad. Over the course of a year, she had grown up so much." Karen, a 33-year-old mother of three, echoes those sentiments: "I experienced a few moments of sadness as Alexis turned one, realizing that the completely dependent stage was over for good. She would never again need me in that baby way. And from this point forward, she would need me even less in her eagerness for independence."

Watching your child blow out the candle on his birthday cake can be particularly poignant if you feel fairly certain that you aren't going to be having any more babies. Catherine, a 32-year-old mother of four, explains: "When the twins' first birthday came up, I remember watching them making a mess in their high chairs, thinking to myself, 'We made it!' I was so proud at that moment to know that they were healthy and well. But I also had a nice long cry that night when all our guests had left, knowing that these were the last babies I would ever have. I would never again have a baby, nurse a baby, and do all those things that mommies do with their newborns. That was difficult—and yet, at the same time, I knew we were entering a whole new stage of life. Our youngest children were now entering the toddler years and things would get easier (or at least we hoped they would!) and our life would now revolve around all the fun things you can do with older kids. And so I wrote a little goodbye note in each of my twins' diaries that night, saying goodbye to their babyhood and welcome to the big kid years. I was proud to have known them as babies, and would be even prouder to help them grow into strong, good-hearted boys and men."

While you may find yourself feeling a little wistful as your child's babyhood comes to an end, it's important to remind yourself that equally magic moments await you and your child in the months—and years—to come. "Sometimes I think to myself, 'This is incredible. I wish I could freeze time right here,'" says Kimberlee, a 28-year-old mother of two. "And, of course, time rolls on and once again it seems perfect."

"I was thrilled to celebrate my daughter's first birthday. I think I felt somewhat heroic. I had survived! With my son, who will likely be my last child, I found myself in tears when the company cleared and the house was quiet again. I'm not quite as enthusiastic about the passing of time now."

—KIMBERLEE, 28, MOTHER OF TWO

Helena, a 32-year-old mother of one, agrees that it's important to focus on what lies ahead: "I think that if you always look back, then you don't enjoy what you have—and toddlerhood has its wonderful moments, too."

It's also important to resist the temptation to relentlessly fast-forward through the present, in an effort to arrive at some mythical future day when parenting is supposedly easier. Frankly, that's a bit of a mirage. Every stage of parenting has its joys and its challenges—and there's no such thing as "the perfect age" when you're a gloriously imperfect parent raising gloriously imperfect human beings. So rather than postponing your enjoyment of parenting until some hypothetical future day when everything about your parenting life is perfect, why not challenge yourself to find the stuff that's worth celebrating about today. Because there's always *something* worth celebrating . . .

Getting Psyched for Year Two

There's no denying it: the rules of the game have just changed forever. You're no longer responsible for caring for a baby; you've just become the parent of a toddler. Here's the scoop on how your role as a parent is likely to change during the exciting and sometimes exhausting months ahead.

You'll spend less time taking care of your child's physical needs and more time attending to his other needs. While you won't have to attend to your child's physical needs to quite the same degree as you did when he was a baby (he'll become more skilled at feeding himself during the months ahead, and—if the potty training gods are with you—he may even show some interest in toilet training within the next year or two), you'll spend a lot of time and energy trying to satisfy his almost insatiable hunger for new experiences. While many parents find this to be the most enjoyable aspect of raising a toddler, others find the pace to be a little overwhelming. "I'm at a constant loss as to how to keep my two-and-a-half-year-old son stimulated," confesses Elizabeth, a 27-year-old mother of three. "Some days, it's tempting to just leave him in front of the TV, especially when there are things around the house that need to be done and other children to tend to. I think we've done every activity ever invented a hundred times." The good news (for you and for your massively curious toddler) is that there are all kinds of simple and inexpensive ways to keep your toddler entertained—and without feeling like you have to take on the role of round-the-clock entertainment director. More about that in Chapter 4.

"I definitely prefer the toddler stage over the baby stage. The toddler stage gives you the opportunity to teach and guide your child through so many things. You can play and engage a toddler in so many activities and then enjoy them along with your child. The baby stage doesn't offer the same opportunities, and sometimes you feel like nothing more than a slave to the baby's schedule and needs."

—TANYA, 30, MOTHER OF TWO

The way you relate to your child will change. "Parenting a baby is so much about keeping them safe and dry and fed and happy," says Lisa, a 36-year-old mother of two. "Parenting a toddler is about that and so much more. It's about helping them take those steps away from you—both literally and figuratively. It's about watching to see what interests them most and then helping them to explore that more." Karen, a 33-year-old mother of three, agrees that there are many new challenges associated with parenting a toddler: "Parenting a baby is about giving time, giving love, giving energy, giving of self. Parenting a toddler is harder because you're giving space. Space for that toddler to attempt and fail and attempt again. Space to learn. Space to explore. Space to grow."

You'll get a clearer sense of your child's personality. Your child's had a personality of his own right from day one, of course, but it's during the toddler years that you start to get a strong sense of who he is as a person—whether he's a natural-born adventurer or someone who is a bit more cautious about meeting new people or tackling new experiences. As Heather, a 23-year-old mother of two, notes: "I prefer toddlerhood because I love watching my son's little personality blossom. Toddlers truly become 'little people.'" And once you have an idea about what makes your child tick, you can start figuring out which types of parenting strategies will bring out the best in him. After all, there's no such thing as "one size fits all" in the often weird but generally wonderful world of parenting.

You'll be able to download some of your childrearing responsibilities to other people. While babies tend to view anyone other than mom as second-rate, toddlers are ready to open their hearts to a growing number of people. And it's not just moms who are relieved to share star billing in their toddlers' hearts: partners enjoy assuming their new role at centre stage, too. As Kelly, a 31-year-old mother of two, explains: "Now that my twins are toddlers, my husband feels more like a parent and less like 'Mommy's assistant.'"

You may feel more confident in your parenting abilities. It's not just your partner who is likely to be feeling more confident about this parenting thing: chances are you are, too. After all, you've survived a whole year of baby boot camp. Your confidence can also be boosted by the simple fact that your child suddenly seems a whole lot less breakable. As Helena, a 32-year-old mother of one, puts it: "Toddlers seem sturdier—not as fragile as babies."

You may feel increased pressure to do a good job as a parent. Being a parent is hard work—the most difficult job in the world, in fact. And what makes it even tougher is knowing that you're under constant scrutiny from others around you—scrutiny that tends to intensify during the toddler years. "If your baby starts crying at the mall, most people smile sympathetically and say, 'Someone needs a nap,'" explains Terri, a 34-year-old mother of three. "But if that same child is a little older, people give you a look that says, 'What a brat!' Dealing with a toddler's emotional outbursts is difficult enough without the glares and stares of strangers." Or with the knowledge that your toddler's very public meltdown could be immortalized on YouTube by some not-so-well-meaning stranger with a penchant for parent shaming. And then, of course, there are the judgmental comments from other parents—something that only serves to make parenting harder. That's why Maria works hard at cutting other parents a bit of slack. "I don't want to be judged, so I try not to judge other parents," the 32-year-old mother of two explains. "Everyone has bad days. Parents have to learn to give other parents a break. There are enough other people out there putting pressure on us and our kids to measure up. We need not eat our own."

"The move from babyhood to toddlerhood is difficult from a social perspective. Babies are welcome almost anywhere. Everyone wants to see and hold them. Toddlers, on the other hand, are sometimes seen as a nuisance."

—JOAN, 35, MOTHER OF FIVE

You'll get a taste of your "old life" again. After a year of stumbling around in a sleep-deprived fog, you'll finally get a taste of some of the perks that come along with parenting a slightly older child—small but sanity-preserving things like sleeping for more than two to three hours at a stretch and eating your dinner while it's still warm. If you've got a particularly vivid imagination and/or are into self-delusion, you may even be able to convince yourself that you've got your old life back. (But, frankly, for most of us, that's a bit of a stretch.)

As you can see, there will be plenty of noteworthy changes during the months ahead as your baby makes the transition from baby to toddler—proof positive that becoming a parent is the ultimate personal growth experience! Now let's talk about how some of those changes are likely to play out in the months to come.

The Challenges and Joys of Raising a Toddler

You've no doubt heard plenty about the challenges of raising a toddler: after all, that's the stuff of which parenting blog posts and viral videos are made. What you might not have heard as much about are the joys of parenting a toddler—something that should go a long way toward explaining one of the greatest mysteries of our time: why some parents sign up for more than one tour of duty through toddlerhood! But just so that we can hold on to that mystery a little longer, we're going to tackle this thing in reverse order, starting out with the challenges and then working our way back to the joys. (What can I say? I've always been a sucker for happy endings.)

The challenges

As promised, here's a whole laundry list of reasons why parenting a toddler is not for the weak of heart—to say nothing of the weak of stomach!

Toddlers are fiercely independent. Toddlers are big on doing things for themselves. But whether they're prepared to admit it or not, they still need a lot of help from us. Of course, that help isn't always welcome or accepted with grace: "My two-year-old is very independent and wants to do everything himself," says Tanya, a 30-year-old mother of two. "Any assistance you give that wasn't requested leads to a huge fit."

> "It's not all sunshine and roses. The temper tantrums can be horrendous. Trying to reason with a 12-kilogram time bomb in the middle of a packed shopping mall can be a very delicate operation."
>
> —MYRNA, 34, MOTHER OF ONE

Toddlers are easily frustrated. At the root of this frustration is the fact that their abilities can't keep pace with their ambition: your toddler is determined to make a tower with his blocks and becomes enraged when he lacks the manual dexterity to do so. The upside to this drive to achieve is the fact that toddlers are extraordinarily persistent. One day soon your toddler will amaze you with his tower-building abilities.

Toddlers are highly volatile. It takes years for children to learn how to manage their emotions, and toddlers simply aren't capable of that yet. Their brains are still very much works-in-progress. As Terri, a 34-year-old mother of three, puts it: "If someone had told me that toddler-hood was like PMS, mood swings and all, I think I would have had a better idea of what to expect." Reminding yourself that your toddler is doing the best that he can with the skills and abilities he has right now can make it easier to cope with your toddler's emotional out-bursts. Instead of expecting him to behave like a much bigger kid than he actually is (something that simply serves to make life harder for both of you), you can simply focus on remaining calm yourself. It's a powerful strategy that reaps parenting dividends both in the moment and beyond. Not only will he calm down sooner as a result of being able to turn to you for emotional anchoring, your calming presence will, over time, help him learn how to regulate his emotions on his own. This is because co-regulation (relying on another person for help in managing your thoughts, feelings, and behaviour) lays the foundation for self-regulation (learning how to manage your thoughts, feelings, and behaviour on your own). It's a powerful two-step process and the strong attachment you've been forging with your child all along is the anchor that makes this powerful social-emotional learning possible. More about this in Chapters 2 and 3.

Toddlers are highly impulsive. Rather than slowing down long enough to weigh the pros and cons of eating dirt or climbing on top of the TV, toddlers just do it. Hey, it's how their brains work: not only do they prefer to learn by doing, they are very much rooted in the here and now. That's why you have to keep such a tight watch on them: they can get themselves into trouble when you're not looking—and sometimes even when you are!

Toddlers operate on their own time clock. "Toddler time" can either be extremely fast (when your toddler is magnetically pulled toward the closest hazardous object) or painfully slow (when he shrieks "Me do it!" when you're trying to get him dressed in a hurry). When your toddler dawdles over breakfast, he isn't the least bit worried about whether he's going to make you late for work: he's having too much fun floating his crusts in his milk! Here's the thing: your wants and needs don't even show up on your toddler's radar screen. At this stage in his development, it's all about him. So if you try to rush your toddler, you'll only end up frustrating yourself and him. "The biggest challenge for me is to give my toddler the time he needs to stop and smell the roses," admits Maria, a 32-year-old mother of two. "Too many times I'm after him to move faster, go quickly, hurry up, don't dilly-dally. But all he wants to do is explore. Who can blame him? His world is fascinating to him and he's just now learning how to communicate all the wonders of the world through words and actions. I need to stop and let him just be a toddler, stop and let him take his time, stop and let him explore and learn."

Toddlers have a limited attention span. They don't stick with any one task for very long. "Once children move into toddlerhood, the days seem to get divided into smaller and smaller chunks," explains Jo-Anne, a 43-year-old mother of seven. "Toddlers want to do everything, but only for a short time. Time moves incredibly quickly and the pace can be exhausting."

Toddlers are highly egocentric. They have not yet learned how to take other people's thoughts and feelings into account, and they're driven to find out just how much power they have over other people by constantly testing the limits. The child development experts stress that a toddler's extreme self-centredness is actually a good thing: it means that your toddler is developing a strong sense of himself. He's figured out that he's a separate human being (as opposed to merely an extension of you) and that he is capable of making things happen for himself. It's exciting, yes, but exhausting, too—both for you *and* for him.

Toddlers demand your undivided attention. Forget about breaking eye contact long enough to scroll through your Facebook feed: your toddler wants you to make eye contact with him every single second of the day! And as for heading down the hall to use the washroom on your own—you really *are* a dreamer, aren't you? While it feels pretty amazing to be the centre of someone's universe, it can also be more than a little draining. I swear, parenthood is the only job on the planet that doesn't guarantee you a coffee break or a lunch hour! Of course, there's a reason your toddler wants you to be tuned into his needs 24/7: knowing that he can turn to you for love and support at any time is what gives him the courage to begin to explore his tiny corner of the world. He can be brave and fearless because he knows he has a safe place to turn for comfort and reassurance. That safe place is you.

The joys

Fortunately, it's not all gloom and doom on the toddler front. Raising a toddler can also be tremendously rewarding. Here's why:

Toddlers are highly affectionate. They're generous with their heartfelt hugs and wet kisses. And when they manage to utter their first soulful "I love you"—well, that's pretty much as good as life gets. "Toddlers bring more joy simply because they give love back," says Janie, a 33-year-old mother of one. "Babies are a bit of a one-way street in that regard."

Toddlers are fun to be with. Whether they're stringing words together with hysterical results or hamming it up for the camera, it can be a lot of fun to spend time with a toddler. "I know how to make my daughter laugh and jump and dance," says Debbie, 33, mother of one. "She always wants to play and it's easy to make almost anything into a game."

Toddlers have a passion for learning. They're eager to explore every inch of their world. "Madison learns something new every hour of the day," insists Sidney, a 33-year-old mother of one.

toddler love

"The two-year-old . . . loves deeply, tenderly, extravagantly and he holds the love of his parents more dearly than anything in the world."

—SELMA H. FRAIBERG, *The Magic Years*

Toddlers find joy in little things. "One of the biggest joys is seeing the world through a toddler's eyes," says Terri, a 34-year-old mother of three. "Things that seemed so ordinary suddenly become new and exciting. This is the first year my one-year-old has taken notice of the leaves falling from the trees. It gives me a chance to teach him about the changing of the seasons. I can't wait for the first snowfall so that I can see the look on his face."

Toddlers are learning how to communicate. This is the age at which language development really explodes. "For me, the biggest joy of parenting a toddler is being able to communicate with your child," says Janet, a 34-year-old mother of one. "When Malorie was a baby, she was able to communicate her basic needs, but I had no idea what she was thinking about. Now that she can speak, she's able to tell me about the hundreds of little discoveries she's making each day. I feel like I'm discovering her personality through our interactions."

Do Toddlers Get a Bad Rap?

As you've no doubt noticed by now, toddlers tend to get a bad rap in our society. Instead of celebrating their growing independence and the accompanying stubborn streak, we tend to treat their quest for autonomy as some sort of counter-revolutionary activity. On those particularly frustrating days—the days when you realize you've heard the word "no" a dozen times already and it's not even 7:00 a.m.—it can be helpful to remind yourself that your toddler isn't trying to undermine your authority; he's just trying to assert his own. As Selma H. Fraiberg notes in her book *The Magic Years*, "It's a kind of declaration of independence, but there is no intention to unseat the government."

Like many parents, Janet, a 34-year-old mother of one, feels that toddlers are greatly misunderstood. "Society leads us to believe that toddlers are terrors and that it's a huge burden to be a parent of a toddler," she explains. "In fact, once you understand that a lot of your child's 'bad' behaviour can be explained by developmental issues (she screams and cries while pointing at something because she doesn't have the words to tell you that she wants to touch it; she cries when she can't put her own shoes on because she lacks the coordination to do so and yet she really wants to help out; she cries when you're busy in the kitchen because she can't see what you're doing above the counter), then it becomes a challenge to help your child overcome the developmental obstacles and to channel his or her energies positively. This doesn't always work and there are times when the child is really a handful, but most of the time it's an exciting challenge to be raising your own little human being, particularly as you discover more about your child's personality, his or her likes and dislikes."

Catherine, a 32-year-old mother of four, believes that a lot of parent-toddler conflicts could be avoided if parents made a greater effort to try to understand what life must be like for a toddler. "Imagine what it would be like to be a couple of feet tall and trying to find your place in the world. You're not permitted to touch anything, you can't go where you want, you can't eat what you want, everything is so big, everyone else makes decisions for you, and people don't always notice that you're there—unless you do something bad. It must be terribly confusing, perhaps frightening, and we as parents need to help them through this time so that they can learn to trust themselves and the world around them. Speak to them with respect. Listen to their opinions. Acknowledge their fears and feelings. And finally, love them as they deserve to be loved."

CHAPTER 2

The Incredible Growing Toddler

"I love the fact that parents and kids grow together. You don't suddenly find yourself with a toddler; your baby turns into a toddler and you both move through the stages together."

—LISA, 36, MOTHER OF TWO

Mother Nature was very wise indeed to schedule a little pre-season training before sending you off to the big leagues (a.k.a. toddlerhood). After all, the powerful bond that you've been forging with your child right from day one will serve you well during the exciting and action-packed toddler years.

The toddler years are, after all, a time of amazing firsts for both you and your child—a time to learn and grow together. You'll have the opportunity to look on in wonder as your toddler adds to her repertoire of skills week by week, day by day, sometimes even hour by hour.

And in between the major milestone achievements that the child development books pay so much attention to—the moment when your child utters her first words or takes her first steps—there will be a million and one other mini-milestones to celebrate as your child makes her journey through toddlerhood. The first time she manages to steer the spaghetti fork from the bowl to her mouth. The first time she remembers to pat the cat *gently*. And, of course, the first time she pees in the potty!

In this chapter, we're going to focus on toddler development. We'll start out by talking about how understanding toddler development can make you a better parent and what developmental milestones can—and can't—tell you about your child. (Hint: Walking on your first birthday doesn't necessarily guarantee you a spot in the McGill Medical School class of 2040.) After we've talked about the limitations of developmental milestones in predicting your toddler's future career path, we'll run through a laundry list of the specific developmental milestones that you can expect your toddler to achieve at various points during the next two years—give or take a couple of months, of course. Finally we'll zero in on two of the more noteworthy milestones your child is likely to achieve during the toddler years: learning how to talk and learning how to walk.

How Understanding Toddler Development Can Make You a Better Parent

Your toddler just had a major meltdown in the middle of the grocery store. How you interpret his actions and how you choose to respond to them will tend to hinge on your understanding of child development: how accurately you are able to grasp his intentions and to size up his abilities at this stage of his development.

If, for example, you believe that your toddler is going out of his way to make this shopping trip a misery for you or that he's simply not trying hard enough to rein in his emotions, you're likely to respond with frustration and even anger.

If, on the other hand, you remind yourself that his communication skills are still very much under development—to say nothing of his ability to manage his emotions—you'll be more likely to respond with kindness and empathy. You'll see his kicking and screaming for what it is—an attempt to communicate an overwhelming need such as hunger, tiredness, boredom, or frustration—and you'll accept the fact that he's doing the best that he can with the coping skills he has in place right now (skills that he can work on and build upon over time with help and encouragement from you).

That, in a nutshell, is why it's so important to have a basic understanding of toddler development: it makes it so much easier for you to be the kind of parent you want to be. Not only will you be less likely to take your toddler's actions personally (something that can trigger an immediate overreaction in even an uber-patient parent), you'll be more likely to have realistic expectations of what is possible for him right now, given his stage of development, as opposed to expecting him to behave like a mini-adult.

You see, this is where things tend to get tricky with toddlers. The fact that they're so much bigger and more capable than their younger baby selves can fool us into thinking that they're so much more grown up than they actually are. But just because your toddler looks like a giant in comparison to the tiny infant he used to be doesn't mean that he's all grown up. Or at least not yet. Not by a long shot. His brain is still very much a work in progress—something that goes a long way to helping to explain why he responds the way he does.

This is your child's brain on toddlerhood . . .

Of course, any discussion of toddler development needs to start with an understanding of the toddler brain: how the brain of a toddler is dramatically different from the brain of a child who is even just a few years older—and what this means to you as the parent of that toddler. Here's what you need to know.

A toddler brain is a busy brain. It's going through an intense period of growth and development. Not only is it increasing in size (by age two, a toddler's brain is roughly 75 percent of the size of an adult brain or, to look at it another way, three times as big as it was at birth), it is changing its very architecture at the same time. The toddler years are all about pruning away neural connections that are no longer needed as your toddler leapfrogs into the next stage of his development and replacing them with the types of connections that will allow him to thrive as he moves through childhood and beyond. Neuroscientists tell us that these toddler brain renos are every bit as far-reaching as the much more publicized brain renos of the teen years—something that goes a long way to explaining why toddlers are at least as emotionally volatile as teens.

A toddler brain is a fiercely one-track brain. Toddlers are single-taskers, not multi-taskers. Their brains have not yet developed the ability to juggle two or more competing ideas at the same time. This explains both why they're able to get completely caught up in the moment (and to an extent that would make any mindfulness coach proud!) and why shifting gears can feel like such a big deal to them. Instead of moving fluidly from one task to the next (say building a block tower and getting ready to head upstairs to get ready for bed), your toddler's brain locks on to the activity that is the sole focus of his attention right now. This means that you have to help your toddler to bridge the gap between what he's doing right now (adding another block to that tower) and what you'd like him to be doing in a few minutes' time (brushing his teeth). Your toddler needs to outsource this particular brain function to you until he develops this ability to manage it for himself—something that will happen sometime around the age of three or four.

Where you fit in to the puzzle

All that said, toddler development isn't just about your toddler. It's also very much about you—the role you have to play in supporting his healthy development.

Fortunately, what he needs most also happens to be what comes most naturally to you as his parent: loving, guiding, and encouraging him.

That's because one of the most powerful things you can do to support your toddler's healthy development is to continue to build on the relationship he's been building with you, right from day one. A child whose needs are met consistently by a caring and responsive adult learns to trust that others will take care of him and that his needs will be met consistently. These feelings of safety and security help to lay the groundwork for a strong sense of self and a feeling that he is worthy of love—feelings that give him the courage to explore and interact with his world. And that, after all, is the goal of parenting: to help your child to journey to adulthood, emerging happy and healthy on the other side, ready to connect with others and assume his own unique place in the world.

Wondering what this means in practical terms? Here are some nuts-and-bolts things you can do on a daily basis to support your toddler's healthy development.

- Parent with the big picture in mind—in ways that are in the long-term best interests of your child. Ensure that she feels safe and secure—both within your relationship and in her world. Let her know that you'll be there for her no matter what and that your love and acceptance are unconditional. And work at creating the kind of calm and predictable environment that will allow her to thrive: one that is characterized by both regular routines and clearly conveyed boundaries and expectations.

- Challenge yourself to be really curious about your child. Think about what it would be like to see the world from her point of view—how that might be both incredibly exciting and tremendously frustrating. Not only will this encourage you to be kinder and more empathetic toward your toddler, it will also allow you to develop a deeper understanding of what's at the root of her otherwise mystifying behaviours—something that will allow you to become a wiser and more intuitive parent.

- Be encouraging and supportive when your child is trying to master a new skill. It takes courage to try something new. You can inspire her to keep trying by praising her persistence and, if she seems to be getting nowhere despite her best efforts, helping her to identify which strategies are—and aren't—working for her. "That circle-shaped puzzle piece doesn't seem to want to fit in the square spot. I wonder where else it might fit?"

- Give her time to puzzle things out on her own, but don't be afraid to step in if her frustration level is building to the point where she's likely to experience a meltdown. Allowing her to experience this much frustration won't magically allow her to master a particular task any sooner; if anything, it may make her reluctant to tackle that particular task again.

- Treat failure as an opportunity for growth and learning as opposed to something to avoid or feel ashamed about. Peeing on the floor beside the potty as opposed to in the potty is actually cause for celebration, if you think about it: it means you *almost* made it to the potty in time!

- Allow for repetition. Practice makes perfect, so don't let it drive you slightly bonkers if your toddler wants to build and knock down the same block tower over and over again. She wants to ensure that she's mastered this task before she moves on to something even trickier.

- Provide your toddler with toys and learning materials that can be used in any number of ways. Your child's problem-solving and creative thinking abilities get a much more vigorous workout when she's the one in charge of making her own fun. You don't want to limit that learning by narrowly imposing some toy manufacturer's idea of what constitutes one-size-fits-none fun on your free-thinking toddler.

- Have age-appropriate expectations of your toddler. You can be realistic about what your toddler is capable of right now while also anticipating what she will be capable of achieving soon— and helping her to master the necessary skills to bridge that gap.

- Take time to celebrate each of your toddler's achievements. Don't be so busy sprinting toward the next major milestone that you fail to savour the mini-achievements along the way. You'll find it easier to do this if you pause to recognize childhood for what it is—an important life stage that's worth celebrating in its own right as opposed to merely a stepping stone to adulthood.

- And, speaking of achievements, don't forget to pause to give yourself credit for all the learning and growing you're doing, too. Your toddler isn't the only one going through a major metamorphosis. Parenthood is transforming you at the same time.

• Finally, don't be afraid to reach out for support from your parenting village. After all, if it takes a village to raise a child, it takes a village to support that child's parent(s). So join forces with other parents who share your commitment to raising kind and healthy human beings. The better you are able to support one another, the lighter everyone's load.

Milestones Revisited: Why It's Not a Good Idea to Compare Toddlers

Forget about keeping up with the Joneses when it comes to superficial things like how big a house you live in or what kind of car you drive. If you want to indulge in the ultimate game of one-upmanship, try comparing kids instead!

As you've no doubt noticed by now, parents tend to get very competitive when comparing the achievements of their offspring, constantly looking for evidence that their child is genius material. As Judith, a 33-year-old mother of one, notes ruefully: "Each and every child in the daycare that I direct is 'gifted'—at least according to their parents!"

So what drives parents to compare every detail about their toddlers' development, timing the achievement of the most bragworthy milestones right down to the minutes and seconds? According to Lori, a 31-year-old mother of five, this urge to compare stems from a desire to reassure yourself that your child is progressing on schedule: "It's very tempting to compare one child to another—either to another one of your children or to a friend's child, which can be upsetting for one or both parents. Even though logically we know that all children develop at different rates, it's worrisome when your child isn't doing all the same things as the neighbour's child who's the same age. Parents always want to know if their children are progressing 'normally.'"

Understandable or not, sometimes the endless comparisons can be a little hard to stomach—particularly if you know someone who seems determined to keep proving how much smarter her toddler is than yours. "A friend of mine is constantly telling me how gifted her son is at absolutely everything," complains Kelly, a 31-year-old mother of two. "I resent the implication that my children aren't as special as her child is. It's starting to cause problems in our friendship."

Of course, comparisons aren't always a bad thing. Sometimes they can alert you to the fact that your child may be lagging behind in a particular area of development. Brandy discovered that her older child was experiencing some developmental delays only when her second child began to surpass him in language abilities, social skills, and so on. "It was only then that I knew there was a problem," the 24-year-old mother of two explains.

Still, there are times when comparisons can do more harm than good—a lesson that Kelli, a 32-year-old mother of one, learned the hard way. "I spent most of my daughter's first year of life fretting about the fact that she didn't seem to be developing as quickly as other children her age. She sat, crawled, and walked much later than all my friends' children and she was also a bit smaller. Suddenly, she turned one and is now off the chart for height and weight, running around with ease, and talking up a storm. I spent too much time worrying about what she wasn't doing and not relishing all the wonderful and fascinating things she was doing."

> "We knew Sean would be the last baby, so I think I was content to let him be a baby longer rather than wanting him to grow up and hit all the developmental milestones."
>
> —SUSAN, 37, MOTHER OF TWO

The tyranny of timelines

What parents like Kelli can temporarily lose sight of is the fact that no two children follow the exact same timeline in growth and development. The fact that your child is lagging a little behind is not necessarily cause for concern. As Dorothy Corkille Briggs notes in her book *Your Child's Self-Esteem*, "Every child has an inner timetable for growth—a pattern unique to him. . . . Growth is not steady, forward, upward progression. It is instead a switchback trail; three steps forward, two back, one around the bushes, and a few simply standing, before another forward leap." While it can be helpful to look at timelines summarizing the point by which your toddler can be expected to have achieved particular developmental milestones (see Table 2.1), it's important to keep in mind that what you're looking at is a rough sketch rather than a rigid blueprint for development. So take heart: the fact that your toddler isn't progressing at quite the same rate as the other kids at daycare when it comes to mastering the potty doesn't necessarily mean that she's sentenced to a lifetime of being an "also ran." It simply means she has other things on her mind than perfecting her toileting techniques!

That's not to say that charts outlining the key developmental milestones for the toddler years are entirely without merit. If they were, I would hardly have chosen to include such a detailed one in this book. (See Table 2.1.) What these charts can do is give you an indication of the rough order and the approximate age at which toddlers tend to master particular skills and an approximate idea of when these milestones are generally achieved by a "typical" toddler (although who that mythical toddler is, I have no idea). Here's the thing: toddler development is a wonderfully messy thing. It doesn't proceed at a predictable rate and there's a massive amount of spillover, with each area of toddler development affecting each and every other area. That's what makes it so fascinating *and* so frustrating—both for you and your toddler.

"My twins were slow to walk, slow to talk—just basically behind when I compared them with their two older siblings. I should never have compared them. That was my first mistake. And having family members constantly asking if they were doing this or that yet drove me nuts! Finally, I decided to do a little research and found that, in many cases, twins develop at a different rate than singletons. Once I knew that for sure, I was able to reassure concerned family members that there wasn't anything to worry about."

—CATHERINE, 32, MOTHER OF FOUR

Developmental Milestones of the Toddler Years

The toddler years are a very exciting time to be a parent. Every time you turn around, your toddler has mastered something new. See the table on the following page for an overview of what you can expect from your incredible growing toddler during the momentous months ahead.

When There May Be Cause for Concern

It's a rare child who manages to achieve each and every developmental milestone right on target. While there's generally little cause for concern if your toddler is a little bit late achieving the odd milestone, you should let her doctor know if she's consistently lagging behind or if she's significantly late in achieving any of the key developmental milestones. While most toddlers make minor deviations from the developmental timeline, if a toddler is consistently missing milestones it could be an indication that her development is lagging behind that of her age mates for some reason. According to Statistics Canada, developmental delays occur in approximately 17 percent of boys and 11 percent of girls under the age of three, so it's important to be alert to the warning signs of a developmental delay. Here's what to look for.

Your toddler is 13 months of age and she . . .
- still doesn't have the ability to grasp objects or transfer objects from one hand to the other;
- still can't sit on her own;
- can't pull herself to a standing position;
- isn't creeping or crawling;
- doesn't differentiate between people she knows well and complete strangers;
- doesn't pay any attention to gestures;
- is unable to follow simple directions;
- is totally uninterested in social games;
- has yet to start making any vowel or consonant sounds;

continued on page 30

2.1 Developmental Milestones: Your 12- to 18-Month-Old

Physical and motor development	Cognitive and language development	Social and emotional development
Your toddler's on the move! He's either taken (or is about to take) his momentous first steps. His wide-legged gait makes it very clear why children this age are known as toddlers! From a functional perspective, this way of walking makes a lot of sense: it lowers your toddler's centre of gravity and helps to improve his stability. You'll also notice that these first efforts at walking require a tremendous amount of concentration: your toddler is constantly checking where his feet are in relation to objects around him.	Your toddler is learning new words every day. He pays careful attention to the words you say and does his best to parrot them. He's likely to be uttering his first recognizable words soon, if he hasn't already. Most children utter their first word sometime around their first birthday—between 10 to 14 months of age, on average.	Your toddler may appear to be endlessly capable and fiercely independent, but he still relies heavily on his connection to you. In fact, knowing that he can count on you to offer comfort and reassurance is what allows him to be brave enough to explore the rest of his world. Your ability to understand who your child is (which means both appreciating his strengths and identifying the areas where he needs a little extra support) and to respond to his needs in a timely and sensitive way will continue to encourage his healthy development.
Your toddler is counting on you to keep him safe because his ability to propel himself around the room vastly exceeds his ability to anticipate danger. You can help to keep him safe (or, at least, safer: a few tumbles are both inevitable and a crucial part of learning how to get around on two legs!) by creating a safe environment that's designed to maximize his opportunities for movement and exploration and by providing adequate supervision (because it's pretty tough to completely toddler-proof your child's entire world).	Because he understands more words than he can actually use, he also relies on gestures (pointing at a snack he'd like to eat) and body language (wriggling in protest, as you try to change his diaper) to communicate his thoughts and feelings. It's important to let him know that you understand what he's trying to communicate. The gap between what he wants to say and what he's capable of saying is a source of considerable frustration to him.

Your toddler is able to understand the meaning of simple, one-step instructions, like "Go get your shoes." You can help him to grasp the meaning of what you're saying by using gestures (pointing at his shoes) and then confirming that | Your toddler is tuned into other people's emotions, but, at this point in his development, he continues to assume that everyone else is thinking the same thoughts and feeling the same feelings as he is. This is because he has not yet developed the ability to see the world from another person's point of view. At this stage in his development, it's all about him!

And speaking of emotions, your toddler's emotions can be dramatic and volatile. He |

continued

2.1   Developmental Milestones: Your 12- to 18-Month-Old (continued)

Your toddler's in explorer mode. He learns by doing, which explains why he takes such a hands-on approach to discovery. He loves to push and pull objects, nest them inside one another, and bang them together to make noise. Every new discovery fuels his curiosity and his confidence, spurring him to want to learn even more.

Your toddler is capable of stacking blocks and working with very simple frame-style puzzles (the kind where a piece with a handle fits into a wooden or plastic frame of the same shape). He's also becoming a pro at nesting objects inside one another. His self-feeding skills are improving and he enjoys helping you to turn the pages in his books.

Your toddler may be beginning to show a preference for one hand over the other, but he still uses both hands quite freely.

Your toddler can now use his index finger and thumb to pick up small objects like peas from the tray of his high chair. What he's demonstrating is the much-lauded pincer grip!

he's understood your message (exclaiming, "Yes, you're getting your shoes!" when he crawls or toddles off to get them).

Your toddler enjoys functional play (play that imitates the types of things he sees you doing, like using your cell phone or pushing a vacuum cleaner around the house). He also enjoys cause-and-effect play—for example, discovering what happens when he plays with a jack-in-the-box.

Your toddler is also becoming capable of imaginative play (sometimes called "pretend play"). This represents a major cognitive breakthrough: it demonstrates that your toddler is now able to understand symbols and abstract ideas. The world of play is no longer limited to concrete objects that represent just one thing. A bowl can be a bowl—or a hat!

Your toddler is learning how to classify objects. He's just beginning to be able to group toys by colour or shape.

may be laughing one moment and crying the next—or vice versa. He's beginning to develop strategies for calming himself, but he's still going to be relying on you for help in achieving calm for some time yet. And when he wants your help, he wants it right now. A toddler's needs are immediate, intense, and personal!

2.1 Developmental Milestones: Your 18- to 24-Month-Old

Physical and motor development	Cognitive and language development	Social and emotional development
Your toddler seems to be in perpetual motion. He's driven to explore his world and to master increasingly complex physical manoeuvres. A simple trip to the playground becomes an opportunity to explore his physical capabilities: how it feels to walk on different types of terrain or to zoom down a slide.	Your toddler is able to follow more complicated instructions than he was just a few months ago. He can now carry out a two- or even three-step set of instructions: e.g., "Put away the puzzle and go get a book."	Your toddler is becoming increasingly self-aware. In fact, he's now able to recognize himself when he looks in the mirror. But with his growing self-awareness (his understanding that he's his own person—someone separate and distinct from you) comes an increased ability to experience emotions like jealousy. You can help him to make sense of complex and puzzling emotions by talking to him about what emotions are and how they work.
Your toddler has developed a fascination with climbing—something that can mean anything from making his way up a couple of stairs to trying to stand on the kitchen table.	Your toddler is going through a "word spurt," adding about a word a day to his massively expanding vocabulary. He's also starting to string together short sentences of two or three words. The words your toddler uses tell you a lot about what matters most in his world. He has a particular fondness for words that describe familiar people and objects (*mama, dada, doggie*) and that express his desire to be in control (words like *no* and *mine!*) He tends to use his own name to refer to himself as opposed to relying on the appropriate pronoun.	Your toddler can tell the difference between intentional actions (tossing your drink on the floor) and unintentional actions (accidentally spilling that drink)—an indication that he's developing the ability to read and interpret other people's underlying motivations.
Your toddler is able to squat while playing. He may also be able to walk down the stairs while holding the railing and he may have enough coordination to kick a ball or to throw and catch that ball from a standing position.	Your toddler's attention span is increasing and his recall memory is improving. He'll amaze you with his ability to point to the various parts of his body as you name them. ("Where's your nose? Where's your elbow?")	Your toddler may exhibit a sudden attachment to a transitional object like a blanket or a teddy bear. Research has shown that 60 percent of toddlers form such an attachment.
	Your toddler still isn't fully capable of thinking through the consequences of his actions (in fact, it will be a couple more decades before that ability is fully developed in his brain), so he's still counting on you to keep him safe. That means alerting him to potential dangers and helping him to put the brakes on his impulses. (He has not yet developed the ability to put on the brakes for himself.)	

2.1 Developmental Milestones: Your 24- to 36-Month-Old

Physical and motor development	Cognitive and language development	Social and emotional development
Your toddler uses a more mature heel-to-toe walking motion rather than the waddling gait of a younger toddler. He can jump a small distance off the ground and, with practice, may even be able to jump over small objects.	By the time your toddler celebrates his second birthday, his vocabulary will have expanded to roughly 200 to 250 words. He's using more words than ever before, but he still sounds very much like a toddler. His sentences are often quirky and adorable. (Hey, verb tenses, plurals, and subject-verb agreement are tough concepts for a toddler to master!)	Your toddler can identify himself in a family photo. Just a few months earlier, he would have pointed to himself and said, "Baby."
Your toddler continues to delight in active play—and for good reason. Active play allows him to discover what his body *is* capable of and to revel in his new-found abilities.	Your toddler loves language games that play around with sound and rhythm. He loves imitating sounds that he hears in his environment (for example, a police siren or the sound of a dog barking).	Your toddler is becoming increasingly aware of other people's expectations of him. This can lead to feelings of pride when he meets those expectations as well as feelings of shame (when he feels like he's fallen short). He'll need your help making sense of these emotions and figuring out what to do with these feelings.
Your toddler's fine motor skills are more fully developed. He can move objects from one hand to another, and colour with crayons, and manipulate increasingly small and intricate objects, like puzzle pieces.	Your toddler is beginning to understand words that convey the concept of quantity (*some, more, gone*) and spatial relationship (*up, down, behind, under, over*).	Your toddler's language abilities may be growing by leaps and bounds, but he still struggles to find the words to express his emotions. So resist the temptation to tell him to "Use his words" when he's in the middle of a full-fledged meltdown. He simply isn't capable of that yet.
	Your toddler is starting to use words to describe his own inner state as well as what he's observing in the world around him. A two-year-old's vocabulary is peppered with words like *see, want, look*, and *taste*, but, by the time he reaches age three, he will have added words that reflect his understanding of more abstract concepts: words like *think, know*, and *remember*.	Your toddler is learning how to interact with other children, but his social skills
	Your toddler frequently talks out loud to himself, delivering a play-by-play description of what he's thinking or feeling. This is	

because he has not yet learned how to distinguish between the two key functions of language: narrating our inner experience and allowing us to communicate with one another. It will be a few more years before he figures out that he can think certain things without having to say them out loud—another momentous cognitive breakthrough.

Your toddler is beginning to understand that conversations don't have to be narrowly limited to what's happening in the here and now: they can also draw upon past experiences or anticipate the future. Your toddler is also beginning to understand that conversations can be based on shared knowledge: what I know as well as what you know.

Your toddler still hasn't grasped the concept of what it means to tell the truth. When he tells a lie, it's typically the result of forgetfulness, an active imagination, or just plain wishful thinking (he wishes he hadn't spilled the chocolate milk on the carpet, so he tries to convince you—and himself—that it didn't happen).

are very much a work in progress, so don't expect miracles when it comes to sharing or cooperation. (See Chapter 4 for advice on helping him to develop his newly emerging friendship skills.)

- doesn't imitate sounds;
- doesn't blink when fast-moving objects approach her eye.

Your toddler is 18 months of age and she . . .
- still isn't showing any interest in people or toys and doesn't seem to understand the functions of common household objects (e.g., telephone, toothbrush, spoon);
- is unable to stand without assistance;
- is not walking yet;
- doesn't appear to recognize any underlying patterns in your family's day-to-day routines;
- doesn't appear to understand anything you say;
- has fewer than 15 words in her spoken vocabulary;
- isn't making any attempts to imitate your actions or your words;
- doesn't demonstrate any sort of attachment to you;
- doesn't exhibit a variety of emotions, including anger, delight, and fear.

Your toddler is 24 months of age and she . . .
- does not yet recognize herself in the mirror;
- doesn't show any interest in pictures or familiar objects;
- has not yet developed a mature heel-toe walking pattern (e.g., she tiptoes rather than walks);
- is not able to feed herself;
- is not able to take off her own clothes, shoes, and socks;
- is not yet using two-word sentences;
- doesn't understand how to classify or group objects;
- doesn't engage in any imitative play;
- doesn't demonstrate any sense of achievement in her accomplishments.

Your preschooler is 36 months of age and she . . .
- drools a lot or has very unclear speech;
- isn't speaking well enough for people to be able to understand her;

- is not yet using three- to four-word sentences;
- is not yet asking questions;
- is unable to understand and follow simple commands and directions;
- is unable to say her own name;
- doesn't seem to enjoy playing near other children;
- doesn't engage in any sort of "pretend" play;
- is unable to focus on an activity that she enjoys for even 5–10 minutes;
- is unable to build a tower using more than four blocks;
- has difficulty manipulating small objects;
- is unable to draw a circle;
- falls often or has a great deal of difficulty with stairs;
- is unable to jump up and down without falling;
- is unable to balance on one foot;
- still needs help dressing herself;
- has extreme difficulty being away from you.

Not every child who struggles in one of these areas is going to be diagnosed with a developmental delay, but it's a good idea to flag any of these issues sooner rather than later, so that your child's development can be monitored a little more closely until it becomes clearer what is (or isn't) going on.

In some cases, the reason for the delay may be apparent. If your child was born prematurely, for example, or has been diagnosed with a developmental delay, your doctor will encourage you to think in terms of her developmental age rather than her chronological age. "I think that when you have preemies, you're even more acutely aware of milestones," says Jennie, a 32-year-old mother of two. "We were always working to help the boys meet their milestones." And if your child was born with a serious medical condition, you may have to take that into account as well. "Our second child had a serious heart defect, which made it impossible to compare her to her older sister," explains Karen, a 33-year-old mother of three. "She didn't reach 10 pounds until her first birthday. So we learned how to accept each child as she was and to celebrate her achievements individually."

Regardless of when your toddler achieves a particular developmental milestone—whether it's sooner rather than later, or vice versa—you can expect to experience tremendous pride and joy. Jennie, 32, reflects on what it's been like to watch her twin with cerebral palsy master the walking-related milestones that came much easier and sooner to his more able-bodied twin: "We thought Matthew's first steps were miraculous, and they were, but Andrew's first steps are a wonder to behold. He has yet to take unassisted steps, but in the past 12 months he's gone from being a child who may never take a step to a child who's capable of moving his legs forward, bearing weight on them, and who is very, very close to taking a step." Jennie feels particularly joyful when she recalls what it was like to watch Andrew start using his walker: "The smile on his face when he realized that he was mobile for the first time and face-to-face with the other kids was worth all the frustration and struggle to get him to that point."

If your child is diagnosed with some sort of developmental delay, you'll want to find out as much as you can about the challenges that he is facing and to connect with other parents whose children are facing similar challenges. Information and support are crucial.

Here are some other important points to keep in mind if your toddler is diagnosed with a developmental delay:

- **Deal with your feelings head-on.** Some parents experience a tremendous amount of guilt and sadness when their child is diagnosed with a developmental delay, wondering if they are somehow responsible for their child's difficulties. It's important to remind yourself that your child's delay is not your fault.
- **Focus on what makes your toddler similar to other children the same age rather than on what makes him different.** Instead of zeroing in on what sets him apart, stop to consider all the things he has in common with other children the same age.
- **Be prepared to modify activities to make them more relevant and useful to your child.** You may wish to choose slightly different types of play materials or to introduce shorter, more frequent

opportunities for play to take advantage of your child's interests, abilities, and attention span.

- **Accept the fact that the toddler years may be extra frustrating for your child.** Your toddler may be cognitively ready to master a particular task, but may lack the physical skills required to carry it off—something that can lead to tremendous frustration for him and for you.

- **Celebrate your child's achievements large and small,** and be patient and persistent even if your child's progress is frustratingly slow.

- **Stay grounded in the here and now rather than worrying about the future.** Your child may surprise you with his progress over time.

one step at a time	Sometimes development in one area slows down when a toddler is busy mastering other types of skills. In other words, if your toddler is absorbed in learning the mechanics of walking, she may not be much of a conversationalist right now!

On the Move

After months of dress rehearsals, it's finally curtain time! Your toddler is ready to take those momentous first steps. Better make sure you've got your smartphone handy: this is one of those moments you'll want to capture for posterity. "When I saw Victoria walk for the first time, I felt unbelievable pride," recalls Laura, a 33-year-old mother of one. "You would have thought she'd won a gold medal!"

Baby steps

Of course, there is a lot of behind-the-scenes work to be done before your toddler is ready to start walking.

- **She needs to grow out of her "baby body" and into the body of a toddler.** A newborn baby's head is huge in relation to the rest of her body, which puts her centre of gravity smack dab in the middle of her chest. And then there's the fact that her nervous system has not yet matured to the point where it can orchestrate all the complex movements involved in walking. That's why most children don't learn to walk until after their first birthday: it takes that long for them to acquire the necessary "equipment" to become fully mobile. And while we're talking body types, here's a bit of trivia to share the next time you're comparing notes with other parents: babies with bigger heads tend to start walking later than their smaller-head peers (no, it's not because these supposedly smarter babies are busy hanging out at the library); and babies with leaner body types tend to become mobile before their chubbier counterparts.

- **She needs to build up the strength in her legs**—something she accomplished during all those months of kicking her feet, putting weight on her legs, and cruising around the furniture.

- **She needs to be able to balance herself on one foot for brief periods of time**—the basic skill involved in walking.

"Brendan waited until he was almost 17 months to walk on his own. He'd been cruising around furniture with barely a finger holding on since around 12 months, but I guess he chose not to take the big step until he was ready. He's always been cautious about things, so maybe he simply didn't feel confident enough to try walking on his own."

—JULIE, 30, MOTHER OF ONE

- **She needs to have the confidence to start walking.** If you've tried your hand at any adventure sports, you'll know that there's a bit of a leap of faith involved in hang-gliding or white-water rafting for the very first time. Well, if you think about it, walking is the ultimate adventure sport from a toddler's perspective: despite the fact that you're feeling kind of shaky standing in one spot on two feet, you somehow have to find the confidence to lift one leg and—yikes!—try to take that first step. It's hardly surprising, therefore, that risk-taking tots tend to master the art of walking months earlier than their more cautious counterparts. (Who knew there was such a thing as an X-treme toddler!)

And even after your toddler finally takes the plunge by attempting to take those shaky first steps, she'll still be honing her walking skills for another two years. The first order of business? Losing that lurching zombie-like walk! Over time, she'll learn how to keep her feet a little closer together and to point her toes straight ahead rather than outward while she walks. She'll also learn how to get to a standing position by bending one knee and pulling herself up. Initially, her key method of "launching" herself will be to spread her hands on the floor, straighten her arms, lift her bottom in the air, and use her hands to push herself into a standing position. It may not be the most graceful manoeuvre, but it tends to be highly effective. Note: See Table 2.2 for a breakdown of the key walking-related milestones that most toddlers achieve between one and three years of age.

2.2 Look Who's Walking!

Here's a summary of the key walking-related milestones for the toddler years. Studies have shown that 90 percent of toddlers will be able to . . .

- walk while holding onto a parent's hand or by "cruising" along a piece of furniture such as a couch by age 12.7 months;
- stand alone briefly by age 13 months;
- stand alone well by age 13.9 months;
- walk alone well by age 14.3 months;
- begin to run by age 18 months;
- walk up steps by age 22 months;
- run with ease by age 24 months;
- stand on tiptoe by age 24 months;
- step backwards by age 24 months;
- jump by age 30 months;
- kick a ball forward by age 30 months;
- climb a low ladder by age 30 months;
- lean forward without losing balance by age 30 months;
- pedal a tricycle by age 30 months;
- hop by age 36 months;
- climb stairs using alternating feet by age 36 months.

Walking the walk

Wondering what's behind that classic toddler waddle? Here's the scoop from a physiological standpoint. When toddlers are first learning how to walk, they find it difficult to keep their balance.

That's why they like to walk with their feet wide apart, their toes pointed either out or in, and their arms spread out to either side. It provides them with a little added stability.

While most toddlers quickly outgrow the pigeon-toed (toes pointed inward) stance, some children are born with a twist in the foot or the leg that causes them to favour sitting positions that may perpetuate the problem (e.g., sitting on their feet or in a "W" position). If this is the case with your child, you'll want to encourage her to use other sitting positions (because sitting in this position puts extra strain on her hips and knees and limits her ease and range of movement) and you'll want to talk with her doctor about whether any additional treatment is likely to be required. Note: High muscle tone (which is characterized by limbs that feel rigid or inflexible) can also lead to sitting in a "W" position. In this case, physical or occupational therapy would be recommended to stretch affected muscles and strengthen opposing muscles.

By the way, there's no need to worry about your toddler's flat feet. It takes until around age six for a child to develop a full arch. And here's another noteworthy statistic: according to the Canadian Paediatric Society, 97 percent of children under age 18 months have flat feet—mostly because they have a fat pad on the underside of their feet. (I know: they should refer to this condition as "fat feet" rather than "flat feet"!) In most cases, flat feet are only a temporary phenomenon. By age 10, only 4 percent of children will still have flat feet.

There are some foot-related oddities, however, that can be cause for concern. If your toddler prefers to walk on tiptoes rather than on flat feet, you'll want to point this out to her doctor because this could be an indication of a neurological or muscular problem. And if your child is still bow-legged (i.e., there's a noticeable gap between the knees when she walks) at the age of three, you'll want to get an opinion on this as well because it could be a sign of vitamin D deficiency or some other medical problem.

Don't rush to squeeze your toddler's feet into a pair of shoes. According to the Canadian Paediatric Society, there's growing evidence that wearing shoes in early childhood interferes with the development of a normal longitudinal arch. Your toddler needs to graduate to shoes only when she starts walking around on surfaces that could injure her feet. At that point, you'll want to take her to the shoe store to invest in a brand-new pair of shoes. (While hand-me-down clothing is great, it's best not to rely on hand-me-down shoes.)

When you're shopping for shoes, you'll want to look for a pair that features square rather than pointy toes, that is flexible enough to allow for full movement of the foot, and that provides just the right amount of traction (enough to keep her from slipping, but not so much as to cause her to trip).

You'll also want to make sure that the shoes you buy fit your toddler's feet properly. That means checking to ensure that . . .

- There's enough room for her toes to wiggle (there should be about 1.5 centimetres of wiggle room at the front of the toe when she's standing up);
- The shoe is wide enough to fit comfortably (there should be a bit of space on either side of her foot);
- The heel won't slip and cause blisters (make sure you can fit your pinky finger in between the back of your child's shoe and her heel).

Here's a bit of additional from-the-trenches advice on how to test-drive shoes in the shoe store. Have your toddler walk around in a new pair of shoes for a minute or two. Then remove them and yank your child's socks off, looking for any red pressure marks on her feet. That should provide you with a pretty good indication of whether or not the shoes are pinching her feet.

Growing pains

Of course, walking is more than just a physical challenge for your toddler; it can be emotionally challenging as well. She may need time to come to terms with her new-found walking abilities. On the one hand, she may have an almost insatiable desire to explore the world around her now that she's mobile; on the other hand, she may miss being carried around by you and may signal her ongoing need for closeness by becoming extra-clingy. She may decide to treat your lap as "home base," periodically returning for a reassuring cuddle as she repeatedly orbits around the room!

And now that she's mastered the art of walking, she may be motivated to set more challenging goals for herself. (Forget walking! She wants to hop, skip, and jump, too!) While this is great in principle—after all, every parent wants a motivated kid—sometimes it doesn't play out quite so neatly in real life. Your toddler is likely to experience a great deal of frustration when she discovers that she can't accomplish everything she sets out to do—or at least not right away. To make matters worse, her frustration level will also be fuelled by the large number of tumbles she's likely to experience during her early days as a biped: a wrinkle in the carpet or a slight incline in the floor may be all it takes to cause her to trip and fall. You can help to minimize the number of tumbles by taking steps to make her environment safer, but it's impossible to prevent every single fall: you can expect your toddler to sport a goose egg or two and numerous other bumps and bruises while she's learning how to coordinate the mechanics of movement. And, of course, if there's a Murphy's Law that applies to toddlerhood, it goes something like this: if there's only one item in your room that could injure your toddler, she'll be magnetically drawn to it just as it starts to fall—and the size of the resulting goose egg will be inversely proportional to the number of hours until your doctor's office reopens.

This stage can be emotionally challenging for you, too, of course: not only do you have to contend with your toddler's seesawing emotions, but you may also be experiencing an emotional tug-of-war yourself. While you may be bursting with pride at your toddler's achievements on the walking front, you may also feel downright weepy about her babyhood winding to a close. Catherine, a 32-year-old mother of four, remembers feeling thrilled but also a little wistful when her toddlers started walking: "Those baby steps were the first steps they took toward independence."

And, if you dare to admit it to yourself, you may also be hit with a totally irrational fear: the kind of fear that creeps up on you in the middle of the night when you're at your most vulnerable. This crazy but oh-so-common worry? That you're on the verge of becoming obsolete! After all, your toddler is growing more and more capable by the day. Surely it won't be much longer until she no longer needs you at all!

Fortunately, I can offer you a truckload of reassurance on this front. It'll be years before your child's burgeoning abilities do you out of a job. While your toddler will inevitably need less and less hands-on help as the months march on, she's still nowhere near ready to ask to borrow the car keys—unless, of course, she wants to chew on them or use them to play in her toy car! So don't be afraid to allow yourself to relax and enjoy this exciting stage of your child's life: your toddler will still be your "baby" for a very long time.

Talk, Talk, Talk

Learning to talk is the other key developmental achievement of the toddler years. After months of wondering what your child has been thinking about, you finally get a window on her world!

Say anything . . .

It can be difficult to predict in advance when your toddler is going to utter her first words, but researchers have identified some factors that influence when a child is likely to start talking.

The number of languages spoken at home: Children who are born in families in which more than one language is spoken may be slower to talk than children who grow up hearing only one language (although this continues to be the subject of considerable debate). Still, there's no need for concern that growing up in a language-rich environment will prevent your child from learning how to speak English: studies have shown that bilingual and multilingual children eventually catch up with their peers.

Gender: Girls tend to speak and form phrases earlier than boys, and they're more likely to use words that express emotion. They're also quicker to use language as a problem-solving tool during play. (Little boys, on the other hand, are more likely to try to work through the same problem with action.) The good news? These gender differences in language tend to become less pronounced over time. Of course, it's hardly surprising that toddler girls tend to do better in the language department than toddler boys. Studies have shown that mothers tend to use more open-ended questions and longer, more complex sentences when they're speaking with two-year-old girls as opposed to two-year-old boys. They vary their speech patterns in other significant ways as well: studies have shown that mothers are likely to use "motherese" (the exaggerated speech patterns that mothers around the world use with their infants) when communicating with girls this age, but that their conversations with boys the same age are likely to be more matter-of-fact, focusing on whatever the boy happens to be doing at the time. With more and more parents embracing more gender-neutral parenting practices, perhaps these differences will start to wane.

Genetics: Children tend to follow in their parents' footsteps in language acquisition. If you were an earlier talker, your child may be, too. So dig out your old baby book to find out whether you were talking up a storm at a very early age or were more the strong, silent type!

Birth order: This shouldn't be a surprise to anyone who grew up with siblings: birth order is another important factor in language acquisition. First-born children are more likely to have larger vocabularies during the second year of life than children with older brothers and sisters, and are more likely to reach the 50-word vocabulary milestone (the point at which toddlers typically begin to use two-word sentences, incidentally) a little sooner. It's not difficult to figure out why this is the case. While baby number one has the limelight all to herself, younger children don't have quite the same opportunity to enjoy their parents' undivided attention, something that can slow their rate of speech development.

All is not lost for second and subsequent children, however: studies have shown that they make better conversationalists than first-borns. Because they've had more experience with multi-person conversations, they learn at an earlier age how to tell when it's their turn to speak and when it's their turn to listen.

Whether or not the child is a twin or other multiple: Twins and other multiples sometimes spend so much time communicating with one another that they can be quite literally in their own world. Consequently, they may be less tuned into the world of adults, which can make it a bit more challenging for them to master the fine points of communicating with someone other than their fellow multiples.

Your child's overall development: Toddlers with underlying medical conditions can also be slower in learning how to talk. Children who have been born prematurely, for example, tend to achieve particular speech milestones around the time that would be expected for their adjusted age (or "corrected age") rather than their chronological age.

How to help your toddler learn to talk

Of course, all other things being equal, a child who is given opportunities to work on her budding communication skills will acquire language at a much more rapid rate than a child who doesn't receive the same amount of hands-on support and encouragement. Here's what you can do to help the process along:

Recognize the importance of having really tuned-in, one-on-one conversations with your toddler. The only way she is going to be able to learn about the give-and-take of conversation (to say nothing of the meaning of all those words that pop out of your mouth) is by having the opportunity to engage in deep conversation with you. A deep conversation involves being completely tuned into what the other person is saying—by paying attention to all of their communication channels: the words they are saying, the gestures they are using, and the other non-verbal cues such as facial expression and tone of voice that help to signal their meaning. No one expects you to have this kind of in-depth conversation with your toddler each and every time you go to communicate. You're not going to be able to maintain sustained eye contact with her when you're driving through heavy traffic. But it's important to recognize the difference between having a focused conversation and having the more superficial conversation that tends to happen on the fly, when we're distracted by other people and/or technology—and to commit to having these focused conversations with your toddler as often as possible. And, speaking of technology, you might want to tuck your smartphone out of sight when you're having this kind of focused conversation with your toddler: research has shown that the mere presence of a smartphone interferes with the quality of conversation, even when that smartphone isn't in use.

Don't just talk "at" your toddler. Give her the opportunity to talk to you, too. It's easy to remember to do this once your toddler starts uttering words (or sounds that at least remotely resemble words). It can be a bit tougher to do this when your toddler is responding with gestures and other body language. But it's just as important to give her the opportunity to keep up her side of the conversation—and to respond to what she's saying in a way that lets her know that she's been understood. Saying something as simple as, "You see that bird!" when she's pointing at a bird provides the validation she's seeking ("Hey, Mom understands me!") while giving her the words she needs when she needs them. That's the recipe for super-charged language learning!

Don't expect a screen to be a substitute for a parent, particularly when it comes to language acquisition. While you might think that an educational show on TV or a language app on your iPad would have the advantage when it comes to helping your child to learn how to talk, no technology can rival the impact of a responsive and tuned-in parent.

Talk at a language level that's just above your toddler's current level. That way, you can build upon her existing vocabulary by exposing her to related words. Don't feel as though you've got to sit there and read the dictionary to her, however. This language exposure will happen naturally if you simply make a point of talking to her about what she's seeing and doing over the course of her day. And take advantage of the opportunity to expand on her single-word utterances. If she says "ball," expand her thought for her; for example, say, "Play ball?" You'll be helping her to build her vocabulary by providing her with action words (you've teamed up her noun with your verb!) and, at the same time, you'll be making her feel heard and understood (which is pretty much the best feeling in the world).

When you ask your toddler a question, try to phrase it in such a way that it requires more than a yes or no answer. After all, shaking her head "yes" or "no" doesn't provide for the most exciting of conversational possibilities! Instead of asking her whether she'd like an apple, ask whether she'd like an apple or a banana. She'll get the chance to practice saying "apple" or "banana" as well as the satisfaction of deciding which type of fruit she'd like to eat. (And, as you'll discover in Chapter 3, toddlers love nothing more than feeling as if they're the ones in charge!) Of course, it's unrealistic to expect your child to utter a crystal-clear "apple" or "banana" the first time around: she'll likely mumble something and then point to the piece of fruit she wants. That's okay. What's important is that she's trying to communicate.

Resist the temptation to correct your toddler if she makes an error in her speech. Instead, simply use the word in a sentence and repeat it back to her in a natural way. There's no need to point out that she's made a speech error or to ask her to attempt to say the word correctly. Speech errors are extremely common in young children. You don't want to insist on perfection each time your toddler opens her mouth!

Try not to hit the panic button if you happen to hear her parroting a colourful word you really wish she hadn't heard. If you can take a relatively low-key approach, she'll be less likely to remember and repeat it (which means she'll be less likely to want to trot out that high-impact word the next time her grandparents are visiting). If she appears to latch on to a particular word with great glee, your best bet is to try to replace the problem word with an even more appealing (but much more G-rated) alternative. Try declaring, "Oh, flip it!" (or similar) in her presence, using your best opera diva voice and accompanying it with equally dramatic gestures. With any luck, she'll switch to that.

Don't be alarmed if you catch your toddler talking to herself. She's simply honing her language skills. Whether she's talking to a favourite toy or giving an impromptu monologue directed at no one in particular, what she's doing is perfectly normal and will only help to improve the quality of her speech.

Make sound play a part of your toddler's day. Make up simple sound patterns (e.g., beep, beep, beep) and encourage your child to imitate you. Then wait for her to come up with a sound pattern and mimic her, too. Or make sounds as you play with toys or listen to the sounds that you hear as you take a walk around the neighbourhood. (You can turn this into a bit of a game if you use your smartphone to make a recording of the neighbour's dog barking, someone's car alarm going off, and so on. Then you can go home, play back your recording, and encourage your toddler to remember what made the different sounds.)

Look for other opportunities to play with language, too. Teach your child nursery rhymes and then, once she's familiar with them, pause so that she can fill in the blanks. And teach your child some fingerplays (simple poems accompanied by hand movements: think "The Itsy Bitsy Spider" or "Twinkle, Twinkle, Little Star"). She'll enjoy pairing the words with the actions.

Worried about a speech and language delay?

You're certainly in good company. Approximately 5 to 10 percent of children are diagnosed with some sort of speech and language delay.

Fortunately, most speech problems can be resolved if they are caught early on. That's why it's important to know what to look for and when. (See Table 2.3.)

2.3   **Warning Signs of a Speech and Language Delay**

You should at least consider the possibility that your toddler may have a speech and language delay if the following applies.

She's two years of age and she . . .

- doesn't seem to be making much progress from month to month;
- doesn't react normally or consistently to sounds;
- uses mostly vowels as opposed to a mix of vowels and consonants;
- uses one catch-all sound or syllable to refer to large numbers of objects (e.g., "duh" or "duh-duh");
- is sticking to single-word utterances rather than two- to three-word phrases;
- doesn't use common words like "bye-bye" or seem to enjoy basic speech-and-language games like peekaboo;
- doesn't integrate new words into everyday speech (e.g., she uses a word once but then seems to forget that the word exists);
- doesn't point to common objects in books when you ask her to identify them;
- gives up easily if she's not able to communicate a message to you.

She's three years of age and she . . .

- is unintelligible to others;
- has a very limited vocabulary;
- can't produce words or phrases spontaneously (i.e., she can only repeat back what you're saying);
- can't follow simple directions;
- has a highly nasal sound to her voice or some other unusual voice quality.

That said, you don't want to become overly anxious too soon. After all, there's considerable variation when it comes to language acquisition. While a "typical" toddler can be expected to utter her first word around the time of her first birthday, a child who achieves that milestone at any point between 10 and 24 months is still considered to be within the normal range (although your child's doctor *is* likely to recommend a thorough assessment if your child hasn't uttered her first word by age 18 months). And, as for having crystal-clear speech every moment of every day, that's a bit much to ask of any toddler: studies have shown that a typical three-year-old is intelligible just 75 percent of the time.

What's more, you don't want to assume your toddler has a speech problem just because she happens to stutter from time to time. Stuttering is very common in toddlers—so common, in fact, that most speech-language professionals recommend that parents wait until after a child's third birthday before becoming overly concerned. Most children go through a stuttering phase at some point. It's most likely to be a problem if a child is tired, excited, or upset. That said, if the stuttering lasts for longer than three to six months or continues past age three, you may want to have your child's speech checked.

Stuttering occurs in 5 percent of children and is four times as common in boys as girls.

And if there is a problem?

If your toddler shows signs of having a speech and language delay, her doctor may want to send her for a hearing check. This is because hearing problems are responsible for a significant number of speech delays. Your child may have been born with some sort of hearing problem or there may be lingering fluid from a middle ear infection—something that can interfere with your toddler's ability to hear. If fluid in the ear turns out to be the problem for your child, tubes in the ears and/or a dose of antibiotics to clear up the infection may be recommended. (Note: You'll find detailed information about ear infections in Chapter 8.)

Your child's doctor will also want to evaluate her motor skills to see if an inability to coordinate the muscles in the mouth and the throat is at the root of her problem. Speech involves the coordination of more than 100 different muscles in the vocal tract. If a motor skills problem is diagnosed, speech therapy will likely be recommended.

Your child's doctor will also attempt to determine whether some underlying medical condition may be responsible for her difficulties. Cerebral palsy and other neuromuscular disorders, severe head injuries, strokes, viral diseases, intellectual challenges, and physical impairments such as cleft lip or palate are all known to contribute to speech difficulties. In many cases, however, the cause of a speech and language delay is unknown.

mouth muscles

Some toddlers have difficulty speaking because their mouth muscles are underdeveloped. Your doctor may suspect that this is the cause of your child's speech problems if she prefers soft food that requires little chewing, lets food fall from her mouth when she's eating, drools a lot, breathes through her mouth, and is extremely difficult to understand. While you're waiting for formal speech therapy to begin (and due to the shortage of speech-language pathologists in many parts of Canada, that wait can be considerable), you may want to try the following exercises to help develop your toddler's mouth muscles.

- **Give your toddler opportunities to practice blowing:** Bubble-blowing is a perennial favourite with toddlers, particularly if you put a few drops of food colouring in the bubble-blowing solution. Blowing a feather across the kitchen table or blowing on a harmonica or a whistle are other great ways of getting your toddler to give her mouth muscles a workout.
- **Sucking straws:** Encourage your child to put her lips near the top of the straw and purse her lips as much as possible. Other variations that work the same muscles? Sucking on a strand of cooked spaghetti.
- **Humming:** Humming can also help to develop muscle strength, so put on some hum-worthy tunes and start humming along with your toddler.

CHAPTER 3

Who's the Boss?

"If we expect toddlers to misbehave, they will live up to that expectation. Terrible twos? Not in my house. Yes, toddlers become wilful and stubborn and have tantrums, but children of all ages have moments like that. Some adults have moments like that, in fact! But with toddlers, it's generally pretty easy to figure out what the problem is and how to cope with it."

—ANITA, 38, MOTHER OF FOUR

We all need a friend like Anita—an experienced mom who's willing to take us aside on the eve of toddlerhood and whisper reassuringly, "You're going to be just fine!"

You see, while raising a toddler may not exactly be a cakewalk, it's nowhere near as dreadful as the doomsayers would have you believe (you know, those helpful folks who make it sound as though it's nothing short of a miracle if you manage to make it through to your child's third birthday with your sanity relatively intact). How refreshing it would be to have someone like Anita to turn to when you needed help putting things in perspective. You could text her whenever you need to be reminded that your toddler will eventually make peace with green vegetables, start using the potty, and stop having meltdowns whenever she has to wear something on her feet. (Hey, a little bit of hope can take you a long way.)

As you've no doubt gathered by now, this chapter is all about discipline—what discipline actually means (spoiler alert: it's about teaching, not punishing) and how positive discipline supports healthy child development. We're going to talk about why toddlers are, well, *toddlers*—fiercely independent-minded little beings who are also emotionally volatile, which means they're temperamentally predisposed to have major meltdowns over things that may not even show up on your radar screen. (When was the last time you burst into tears because your cookie broke when you bit into it?) Then we're going to consider how you and your toddler fit into the discipline equation by considering both her temperament and your parenting style. Next, we'll zero in on positive discipline strategies that work well for parents and toddlers alike and how to apply these ideas to three truly legendary (and extraordinarily common) toddler behaviours. Then we'll talk about working through parenting conflicts with your toddler's other parent (because that's the kind of thing you need to know in order to parent in the real world if you're sharing the task of raising a child with another human being). Finally, we'll wrap up the chapter by talking about what to do when you blow it—when you fail to live up to your own ideas about what it means to be a good parent. After all, it's not a matter of *if* you'll make a misstep when it comes to parenting: it's a matter of *when*. That's one of the many humbling realities of parenting!

What Discipline Really Means—and Why This Matters

What come to mind when you think about the word "discipline"? If you're like most of us, odds are you conjure up images of an army recruit learning discipline through an utterly punishing boot camp experience. That's because, in our culture, we've come to associate the word "discipline" with "punishment." Is it any wonder that so many parents dread the idea of disciplining (in this case punishing) their kids?

If you find yourself experiencing a sense of dread whenever you think about disciplining your toddler, it could be because you've fallen into the all-too-common trap of assuming that discipline implies punishment when, in fact, it is actually about teaching your child in a way that allows him to learn and grow. (The English word "discipline" is derived from the Latin word *disciplina,* which means to teach or to learn.) "Toddlers are looking to you to be their guide," explains Lisa, a 36-year-old mother of two. "You're helping them to become responsible people who nonetheless remain curious and excited about the world around them."

Making this simple mind shift can be a total game changer for you as a parent. Instead of seeing discipline as a burdensome task that risks damaging your relationship with your child, you start to see it as something positive and exciting: a shared journey of discovery. Because that, in a nutshell, is what discipline is all about. You have the unique privilege of serving as your child's guide, helping him to make sense of who he is, how his mind works, and how he fits into the world. What this means in practical terms is that you're interpreting and guiding his behaviour and helping him to develop the skills he needs to thrive as a human being.

That's not to say that this is always straightforward and easy. On many days, it's not.

"Discipline is difficult because no one likes to be the heavy," explains Annie, a 44-year-old mother of one. "It's also demanding. It takes a lot of energy—often when there isn't much to spare."

And then there's the fact that parents are subjected to so much unwanted advice and unwelcome judgment when it comes to discipline.

"I wish we didn't have to do so much of our disciplining outside the home," says Sharon, a 29-year-old mother of three. "Children seem to always test our rules in new environments, which means strangers look on and judge."

The key to feeling less judged by strangers and less frustrated with your toddler is to think of discipline as a dance between you and your toddler—a joint activity with a shared goal that also ideally involves some give-and-take from both partners. What powers the dance is, of course, the relationship between you and your toddler—your deep connection with and commitment to one another. Who cares what some insignificant bystander has to say about the inevitable stumbles and missteps? What matters is the dance, not the observer . . .

Your Toddler's Declaration of Independence

Do you find yourself feeling like the job description of parent is being radically rewritten as you head into the toddler years? It's not your imagination. Things have shifted. You're now being asked to share power with an increasingly independent-minded human being. And when you're knee-deep in the parenting trenches (e.g., you're dealing with your toddler's tenth shriek of protest of the day and it's not even 8:00 a.m.), it can be easy to lose sight of the fact that your toddler's declaration of independence is actually something to be celebrated. The very same behaviours that you find most frustrating to deal with—her strong will and powerful need to test any and all limits, for example— are proof positive that your toddler is developing a strong sense of who she is and where she fits into the world.

You see, here's the thing: toddlers don't mean to be tyrants. Really, they don't. They just happen to be embroiled in a developmental stage that requires them to repeatedly demonstrate their independence from you. (This early declaration of independence is, of course, a dry run for the more pronounced version you can expect your child to make during the teen years.)

You'll find it easier to accept—and perhaps you'll even start to embrace—your toddler's growing independence if you shift your focus from how much she's pulling away from you to how much she continues to rely on you (and will continue to do so for many years to come). Here are just a few examples of the many ways that you continue to be indispensable to your toddler—what she needs from you and why.

- **She needs help making sense of her emotions**—emotions that can feel too big and too scary to handle on her own. Giving her the words to label the feelings she's experiencing and encouraging her to be curious about her emotions will help her to figure out what these feelings mean and how best to respond to them. And, as she begins to make sense of her own emotions, she'll start to figure out how to make sense of other people's emotions (as opposed to simply assuming that everyone else is experiencing the exact same emotions as she is—the deliciously self-centred worldview of the toddler!).

- **She needs help putting the brakes on in situations that could put her at risk.** A toddler brain is a live-for-the-moment kind of brain. Your toddler has not yet developed the ability to mull over the future consequences of her actions. Her decision-making abilities are very much rooted in the here and now. So while you may be able to foresee the potentially disastrous implications of dashing into the street to retrieve a ball, she hasn't developed that ability yet. Bottom line? She's counting on you to keep her safe.

- **She needs to be able to count on the security of your love even while she's busy exploring her world.** Yes, your toddler wants it both ways: she wants to feel fiercely independent and deeply connected to you at the same time. In fact, it's the security that she derives from her connection with you that gives her the courage to venture out and try new things. She knows you've got her back, should she run into trouble, and that your love for her is unconditional. She can fly free, like a kite, because she knows you're hanging on to the string for dear life. She's both incredibly free and reassuringly anchored to you.

- **She needs you to respect her desire to make choices**—even when those choices can feel transient or even arbitrary to you. (The very same kid who gobbled down an entire bowl of blueberries yesterday won't so much as touch a single blueberry today.) These kinds of choices are pretty big-stakes decisions for a toddler who is trying to figure out who she is—something she does, in part, by discovering and declaring what she likes and doesn't like. And if this sometimes feels like a bit of a power struggle to you, that's definitely for good reason: she's testing the limits of her power and trying to figure out what this means in terms of her relationship with you—whether she can assert her right to love or hate blueberries without having to worry about jeopardizing her relationship with an even bigger love in her life—you!

So there you have it: a quick rundown of just a few of the many ways that your toddler will continue to need you even while she's increasingly asserting her independence from you. She both needs you and needs to feel separate from you—an emotional tug-of-war that's taking place both inside her own head and in her day-to-day dealings with you. Ahh, toddlerhood . . .

The Parenting Equation

One of your key responsibilities as a parent is to help your child develop an inner compass that will guide her through life, helping her to make the best possible decisions along the way. While you'll serve as her compass during the early years, your ultimate goal is to do yourself out of a job. Parenting is, after all, one of the few occupations in this world where having your position declared surplus is actually a good thing!

> "The hardest thing about raising a toddler is knowing when something is a discipline issue and when it's a learning issue: like when she feeds the dog food from her dinner plate, when she tries to climb the stairs, when she screams for attention, when she grabs another child's toy."
>
> —DEBBIE, 33, MOTHER OF ONE

Of course, when you're putting in long days—and nights—raising a young child, it may feel as though that day will never come—that you're doomed to spend the rest of your life reminding your child to brush her teeth with toothpaste, to wash her hands with soap, and to colour on paper, not walls. The job can be thankless and exhausting at times, which is why it's important to remember that most children do manage to grow up to be reasonably well-functioning human beings—not perfect, but functional! In other words, you can get there from here.

But what do you need to know about raising a happy, healthy child (and future adult) as you head out on this long and convoluted journey? It's a question that's befuddled countless generations of parents. Parenting may be the most important job on the planet, but it doesn't necessarily come naturally or easily to any of us.

The challenge, of course, stems from the fact that there are two variables in the parenting equation: those variables being you and your toddler. Some parents feel confident about setting limits for their child and seem to have been blessed with an intuitive sense of how to do so in a loving and effective way. Others struggle with the whole concept of discipline right from day one. Likewise, some toddlers are naturally compliant and easy to discipline while other toddlers demand mental gymnastics from their parents. So before we get down to the real nitty-gritty of discipline—which techniques tend to be most effective with children of this age group and which ones are not—let's take a detailed look at the two key variables in the discipline equation: your parenting style and your toddler's temperament.

Your parenting style

While no two parents are exactly alike, parenting experts have identified three basic parenting styles: authoritarian, permissive, and authoritative. (Actually, they've identified a fourth style, too—neglectful—but I'm not going to get into that here. I mean, you've already demonstrated your commitment to parenting by virtue of the fact that you're reading this book!) Anyway, here's the scoop on the other three styles.

Authoritarian: As the name implies, authoritarian parents tend to be big on control. Their motto? "I'm the one in charge." They expect immediate obedience from their children and have a strict, unwavering code of conduct that offers little—if any—opportunity for their offspring to question their edicts. And, what's more, they're prepared to enforce their rules by resorting to harsh discipline measures. Children learn to obey authoritarian parents not because they believe their parents' rules are fair or reasonable, but rather because they fear the consequences of not obeying. Sure, authoritative parents manage to achieve compliance in the moment—but it's a rather short-sighted victory. Because the children of authoritative parents have less opportunity to learn how to control their own behaviour, they end up being less disciplined, less independent, and less confident than children raised by less controlling parents. And because the focus of this particular discipline style is on stamping out the bad rather than celebrating the good, children raised in this sort of environment may grow up believing that there's something wrong with them, which can put them at risk of developing an array of mental health problems. In other words, this ain't exactly the recipe for raising happy, well-adjusted children!

Permissive: Permissive parents can be found at the opposite end of the discipline spectrum. Their motto? "Anything goes." They allow practically any behaviour so long as their child isn't in any immediate danger. Consequently, they don't have a lot of rules for their children, and what rules they *do* have tend to be enforced on a rather haphazard basis (e.g., whenever a parent can be bothered). Kids raised by permissive parents lack structure and are deprived of the opportunity to learn how society expects them to behave. They tend to be impulsive, self-indulgent, aggressive, and highly inconsiderate because their parents have always given in to their needs. And since they have yet to master any self-control or self-discipline, they're held hostage by what they think they want in the moment, doing anything and everything on a whim simply because they've got the urge. What they're missing is that all-important inner compass that helps them to guide their behaviour in a more purposeful way—a way that takes into account other people's needs as well as their own.

Authoritative: Most parenting experts agree that an authoritative parenting style works best for parents and kids. The motto that these types of parents choose to adopt? "We're in this together." They set clear limits and have high expectations of their children's behaviour, but—unlike authoritarian parents—they encourage two-way communication and tend to be a bit more flexible in applying the rules. They're known for being fair, consistent, and willing to discuss problems and work through solutions with their kids—a parenting approach that can reap tremendous dividends for the entire family. Authoritative parents tend to be rewarded with well-adjusted, self-confident children who respect themselves and others around them and who demonstrate good self-control. These children tend to be more achievement-oriented than those raised by other types of parents, and as an added perk they tend to be less rebellious during their teen years. (Reason enough to buy into this particular parenting style, don't you think?)

Your toddler's personality type

Of course you're not the only ingredient in that complex equation known as parenting: you also have to factor in your child's temperament—a trait that's at least partially wired into your child before birth and that morphs into his personality as "nature" meets "nurture." (According to psychologists, the split between inborn and acquired personality traits is about 50/50, so you still have a role to play in influencing the type of person your child ultimately becomes. Since you have little control over the "nature" factors, you'll want to do what you can to take advantage of the "nurture" side of the equation, coming up with parenting strategies that will bring out the best—as opposed to the worst—in your child.)

While every psychologist or medical doctor who's ever written a parenting book seems to have come up with a slightly different laundry list of terms to describe children's temperaments, linguistic nuances aside, they pretty much boil down to the same three types that psychologists Alexander Thomas and Stella Chess described way back in the 1950s:

- The challenging or spirited child (a child who doesn't adapt well to new situations and who tends to have a negative attitude much of the time);
- The slow-to-warm-up or shy child (a child who is very cautious and shy when faced with a new situation and who is slow to warm up to new people);
- The easy child (a child who is upbeat, adaptable, and mild to moderate in intensity of response).

Now that you've had an entire year to get to know your child, you should have a pretty good idea of which type of temperament she was born with—whether she's a happy-go-lucky kid who pretty much goes with the flow or a kid who passionately protests even the most minuscule variation to her usual routine or one who shies away from new people or situations. There's no "right" or "wrong" temperament, by the way—just as there's no such thing as a "good" or "bad" baby or toddler. Parenting is all about bringing out the best in kids—playing to their strengths and helping them to work on the areas in which they struggle.

The "spirited" toddler: While disciplining "easy" children tends to be relatively, well, *easy* (you set limits and, over time, your child learns to respect those limits—or at least that's the theory), "difficult" children require extra calmness, patience, consistency, structure, and understanding from their parents.

If you happen to have been blessed with one of those higher-than-average intensity kids, try not to hit the panic button. You're not necessarily doomed to have a difficult run as a parent simply because you have a supposedly "difficult" child! Creative parents quickly learn how to find ways to use their knowledge of their child's temperament to their advantage.

Judith, a 33-year-old mother of one, is the first to admit that her daughter, Meagan, is a high-intensity kind of kid—one that requires a lot of patience and consistent parenting—but she doesn't consider parenting Meagan to be an insurmountable challenge: "We lovingly refer to Meagan as the ultimate drama queen. Everything she does has some sort of dramatic quality to it, including temper tantrums."

The "shy" toddler: Some toddlers are highly cautious—even fearful—in new situations. They're the toddlers who can be found clinging to their mother's legs on the first day of nursery school or hiding behind the couch whenever someone new has been invited over for dinner.

If you're a natural-born extrovert (someone who's never shied away from a new situation in her life!), you'll want to let your toddler know that you "get" her—that you understand how she's feeling and that you're not angry at her for being shy or scared. Although it can be incredibly frustrating to sign your toddler up for a parent-and-tot gym class only to have her spend the entire session crying and begging to go home, she can't help the way she feels, so it's important to be kind and empathetic. At the same time, it's important to continue to encourage your child's attempts at socialization. Continue to expose her to social situations even if she isn't willing to do anything more than tentatively observe the other children from the sidelines. Eventually, she'll become more comfortable with the idea of socializing with other children. It may simply require a whole lot of patience and support on your part.

The "easy" toddler: Think you're going to get off scot-free in the discipline department just because you were blessed with an "easy" toddler? You're dreaming in technicolour. All toddlers require discipline, easygoing or not!

Your key challenge in managing the behaviour of an easygoing toddler may be in finding a discipline method that sticks. Some toddlers with this sort of happy-go-lucky temperament may have trouble clueing into the fact that they're being disciplined! Of course, there's an upside to this situation, as Anita, a 38-year-old mother of four, explains: "My kids are generally 'make lemonade' kinds of kids. Nothing fazes them. They are determinedly cheerful and optimistic and that makes them hard to discipline sometimes, but, on the other hand, I know that these very same characteristics will serve them well throughout their lives."

"The twins are able to get into more trouble than my singletons ever did. One day, I used two wooden boxes to block the doorway out of the living room so that I could fold laundry without the twins disappearing. Claire was trying to climb over the boxes, but couldn't, so Saige got down on all fours so that her sister could use her as a step. Then Saige got up and gave Claire the last boost on her bottom to get her on top of the box and over the other side!"

—KERRI, 36, MOTHER OF SIX

Creative Discipline

Think disciplining a toddler sounds like total drudgery? Think again! Despite what you may have been told, disciplining a child is not about reinforcing the same old rules the same old way day after day.

While consistency is important—after all, you can't expect your child to learn what's expected of him if those expectations change from day to day—disciplining a toddler can actually be a highly creative exercise: the ultimate opportunity to hone your ability to think under pressure!

Rather than allowing yourself to fall into a rut—which tends to reduce the effectiveness of your discipline techniques anyway—constantly challenge yourself to come up with ever-more effective strategies for achieving your parenting goals.

Here are some important points to keep in mind as you start developing your own one-of-a-kind approach to guiding your toddler's behaviour.

- **Calm yourself first.** Then calm your child. When you manage to remain calm in the midst of a toddler's most intense meltdown, you help to calm him, too. (If, on the other hand, you respond with frustration and anger, he's likely to become even more upset.) If you find yourself feeling particularly frustrated by your toddler's behaviour (because, hey, it happens!), focus on your big-picture parenting goals by playing (and replaying) a calming mantra in your head—something like, "Be kind."
- **Make the relationship the priority.** Instead of trying to "make" your child behave (something that implies coercion rather than cooperation), focus on maintaining your connection to your child.
- **Allow your knowledge of your child to guide you as you try to figure out how to deal with the parenting challenge du jour.** Don't feel compelled to follow any "one size fits all" parenting advice delivered by experts who've never had the opportunity to get to know you or your child. Trust your intuition.
- **Ensure that your expectations of your toddler are age appropriate.** Expecting your toddler to behave like a mini-adult (or even

just a much bigger kid) is an exercise in frustration for her and for you.

- **Assume the best of intentions on the part of your toddler until proven otherwise!** When she does something that you really wish she hadn't (like using her crayons to decorate her newly painted bedroom wall), challenge yourself to be curious about what might have motivated this particular behaviour. Perhaps she was just trying to build upon your efforts with the paintbrush by contributing a decorative flourish of her own! So remind yourself to try to see things from her perspective and to try to make sense of her actions on that basis. You'll find it easier to be patient and empathetic.

- **Challenge yourself to see your toddler's behaviour for what it is: a method of communication.** A toddler who is having a complete and utter meltdown isn't trying to misbehave; she's simply telling you that she's doing the best that she can with the skills and abilities she has right now—and that she needs your help to do even better. Instead of trying to quelch an unwelcome behaviour, shift your focus to trying to meet her underlying need or needs instead. Odds are at least part of what she's seeking is a feeling of connection with you—a connection that can help her to calm her own out-of-control emotions.

- **Look for the opportunity to help your child learn.** As I noted back at the beginning of this chapter, discipline is about teaching—about helping your child learn how to function as a happy, healthy human being. And the best way to do that is by providing your child with specific yet supportive feedback and then giving her the chance to try again. Of course, when you're dealing with a toddler, you should expect to repeat this lesson again and again until it eventually sticks. The part of your child's brain that allows her to store and retrieve instructions is still under development. So if you have to repeat the same instructions a dozen times a day, understand that it's not that she's deliberately being inattentive; she's simply working with the cognitive abilities that she has right now—abilities that will continue to evolve over time.

the power of words

Wondering why adults have difficulty remembering events that occurred before age three or four? Researchers in New Zealand think this phenomenon occurs because very young children lack the language skills required to fully process information and later retrieve it. This, combined with the fact that the planning and organizing parts of the brain are still very much under development, may help to explain why toddlers have such a difficult time remembering instructions.

- **Understand that setting limits is an act of kindness toward your child.** You're setting her up for success. Of course, don't expect her to thank you for setting these limits—or at least not yet. After all, it's your toddler's job to test these limits—and test them she will! Doing so helps her to feel safe and secure. Instead of feeling like her world is spinning out of control (how it feels when there aren't any limits), she is reassured by the fact that she's being offered freedom within limits (like the guardrails that are there to keep your car on the road).

"There have been times when I've fallen into discipline ruts where what I've been doing has ceased to work, but I haven't recognized that I need to rethink my reactions to certain behaviours to come up with a new way of handling the situation."

—KELLY, 31, MOTHER OF THREE

- **Keep in mind that actions speak louder than words.** While nobody's expecting you to be perfect, it doesn't hurt to try to model the types of behaviours you want your child to learn. You are your child's most powerful role model, after all. And, yes, it's both a tremendous privilege *and* a rather daunting responsibility . . .

- **Choose your battles.** It's not necessary—or even advisable—to lock horns with a toddler each and every time she tries to assert her will. "Who really cares if she's wearing a dress with rubber boots?" asks Janie, a 33-year-old mother of one. "If it makes her happy, why not? Chances are that next time you offer her the dress and the same pair of boots, she'll pick the dress shoes!"

- **Make sure you have your child's attention before you start trying to guide her behaviour.** That means getting down to her level and ensuring that she's making eye contact and listening to what you have to say. It's not the least bit effective (and it's actually pretty disrespectful) to simply start barking orders from the other side of the room.

- **Say what you mean and mean what you say.** Don't phrase commands as questions unless you're willing to give your child a choice. The moment you ask your toddler, "Are you ready to go to bed?" you leave the door open for her to say no! Even a simple "okay" tacked on at the end of a sentence can be a problem: e.g., "It's bedtime now, okay?"

- **Practice active listening when you're communicating with your toddler.** Help her to put her thoughts and feelings into words, e.g., "You're really hungry" or "You'd like a snack right now." Not only will doing so help to bring down her level of frustration and, with any luck, avoid a major meltdown, but it will also encourage her to play an active role in solving whatever problem is frustrating her at the time. (A solution that she plays a part in creating will be 1000 percent more acceptable to her than one that you come up with and impose.)

- **Help your toddler to feel heard and understood.** One of the most powerful things you can do to calm another human being is to validate that person's emotions—to let that person know that their feelings makes sense. So if your toddler cries out in the night when she's awoken by the sudden boom of a clap of thunder, validate her emotions while you're offering reassurance: "The thunderstorm scared you. I know how that feels. No one likes being woken up in the middle of the night by a loud and sudden boom!"

- **Help your toddler to learn the words that describe her emotions and commit to building her "emotional vocabulary" over time.** The bigger her emotional vocabulary, the easier she'll find it to recognize and manage her own emotions. And, as her perspective-taking skills begin to kick in, look for opportunities to help her learn how to decode emotions in other people—how to form hypotheses about what they may be thinking and feeling and to consider how she might choose to respond. You don't have to hold off on having these discussions until she's able to actually use the language of emotion herself or until she's fully able to figure out that other people have thoughts and feelings different from her own. Your toddler is capable of learning the concept of "frustration" or "excited" long before she's capable of uttering the word herself or reliably spotting this emotion in other people. That's good news for you and your toddler.

- **Stick to positive discipline techniques as much as possible** (the kind of discipline techniques that we've been talking about so far in this chapter and that I go into in further detail in the discipline techniques section below). While it may be tempting to resort to quick-fix techniques like threatened abandonment (threatening to leave your child behind in the grocery store if she won't do what you want right now—a strategy that exploits your child's deep-rooted attachment to you to use it as a weapon to coerce her), bribery (attempting to manipulate her behaviour by heaping on excess praise or offering tangible rewards like stickers or candy—a strategy that encourages her to rely on external rewards as opposed to paying attention to her own internal compass), or time outs (banishing her to her room or a "naughty chair" in the corner when what she really needs in order to tame her too-big emotions is a moment of connection with you), these techniques are painful to your child and risk causing damage to the parent-child relationship if they become your discipline norm.

Bottom line? Not all toddler discipline methods are created equal. Some not only fail to make a challenging situation between you and your toddler better, they can actually make a bad situation even worse.

Wondering what all this means in practical terms—how you can apply the overriding principles of positive discipline to the day-to-day challenges of raising a toddler? That's what this next section of the chapter is all about: tried-and-true nuts-and-bolts techniques for guiding your toddler's behaviour in a way that is helpful, not harmful.

"I think offering rewards changes the focus of behaviour from something that's internal to something that's fairly random and external. It makes it hard for children to interpret their own behaviour and makes them look to others—particularly adults—to do the interpreting."

—LISA, 36, MOTHER OF TWO

Five Discipline Techniques That Work for You *and* Your Toddler

When you're shopping around for a method of discipline that will work well for you and your toddler, you'll want to zero in on one that . . .

- is suited to your toddler's developmental stage and temperament;
- leaves your toddler feeling good about herself;
- leaves you feeling good about yourself as a parent and that supports your big-picture parenting goals;
- is effective at teaching your toddler appropriate behaviour;
- helps to build upon the bond between you and your toddler.

You'll probably find that you'll use different types of discipline techniques in different types of situations, and that you'll have to go back to the drawing board every now and again to come up with something entirely new. (Toddlers evolve over time, so it only makes sense for your discipline methods to evolve, too.) Fortunately, there are plenty of terrific discipline techniques to choose from. Here are five that tend to work particularly well with toddlers:

1. **Prevent problems from occurring in the first place.** An ounce of prevention is worth a pound of cure—actually, 10 to 15 kilograms of cure, when you're dealing with a toddler. Since this is the easiest method of disciplining a toddler—not having to discipline at all!—I decided to put it at the top of the list. You'll find that you can greatly reduce the number of opportunities for conflict if you take steps to anticipate and avoid problems—for example, helping your toddler to understand what's expected of her by putting predictable routines in place, keeping objects that your toddler is not allowed to touch out of reach, and running errands only at those times of the day when she's likely to be at her best (when she's well rested and well fed). While it's unrealistic to expect to be able to head off every possible problem, you'll be amazed at just how many you can avoid by using this technique on a regular basis.

2. **Find creative alternatives to saying no.** Toddlers tend to dig in their heels if they hear the word "no" all the time, so you'll want to find alternatives to overusing that particular word. Here are a few examples of how you can avoid saying no.
   - **If your toddler starts throwing food,** instead of saying "No throwing food," gently remind her that "Food is for eating."
   - **If your toddler wants to get down from the high chair before you've had a chance to clean her up,** don't tell her, "No, you can't get down." Tell her, "First wipe your hands. Then get down."
   - **Use high-impact words like "stop," "hot," or "dirty," instead of "no."** They'll get your message across more clearly and will eliminate the need to say no. (And, in the case of the

word "stop," you'll actually be giving her something to do—
as opposed to merely telling her what *not* to do, something
that's much harder for a toddler to grasp.)

- **Give your child a gentle reminder about a rule when she enters
  a situation that could lead to trouble:** "Remember that beds
  are for sleeping in." If that reminder doesn't get the desired
  response, you may decide to progress to a gentle reprimand:
  "Please stop jumping on the bed. You could fall and bang your
  head. If you don't stop, you'll have to get off the bed."

3. **Offer a substitute.** This is another great way to sidestep a battle
   of wills. You simply defuse a situation by giving her permission
   to do something other than what she's asking to do. Here are a
   few examples.

   - **If your toddler wants to scribble on the front of the fridge,** give
     her permission to do something similar instead—for example,
     she can draw on a piece of paper that's stuck to the fridge, play
     with a set of fridge magnets, or draw a picture of a refrigerator
     and colour it whatever colour she'd like.
   - **If your toddler wants to touch a breakable object like a china
     figurine,** give her permission to look at it but not touch it. Or,
     if you're feeling particularly brave, agree to let her touch it
     while you hold on to it for dear life.
   - **If your toddler wants to pour her milk on her cereal her-
     self,** put her milk in a small measuring cup. That way, if it
     happens to get spilled you'll be faced with a small splash of
     milk to mop up as opposed to a giant puddle.
   - **If your toddler wants to jump on her bed, give her permission
     to jump on the floor instead.** Or offer freedom with limits.
     Let her know that it's okay to play with a ball in the house as
     long as she remembers to roll it, not throw it.

4. **Give your toddler the opportunity to make choices.** As you've
   no doubt gathered by now, toddlers *love* to be the ones running

the show. So why not tap into your toddler's powerful need to be in charge by empowering her to make decisions for herself whenever possible? If, for example, she's refusing to brush her teeth at night, you can give her a choice: she can brush her teeth either before or after her bedtime story. The key to making this technique work for and not against you is to offer only those choices you can live with, to limit the number of choices (more than two tends to be paralyzing, not empowering, to toddlers), and to give your toddler a limited amount of time to make her choice. If she refuses to make a choice within this period of time, you'll have to help her make her decision. For example, if she refuses to choose between the red cup and the blue cup, you'll have to give her an additional choice: "Do you want to decide or do you want me to decide?" If she still refuses to make a decision, then simply say, "I see you want me to decide," and hand her one cup or the other.

"Disciplining your kids does not mean having total control over your child. Kids need to feel they're able to make decisions. At first it may be which colour crayon to use or what type of cereal they want for breakfast. Later they may want to choose their own clothing. Often parents fall into the trap that says they're the ones who are always right."

—CATHERINE, 32, MOTHER OF FOUR

5. **Offer a distraction.** Countless tantrums have been averted on the part of both toddlers and parents as a result of a well-timed distraction. It can sometimes feel like the closest thing you're likely to find to a discipline magic wand. But because it *is* so powerful, you'll want to use it in moderation. Your toddler needs to have the opportunity to wrestle with difficult emotions and powerful impulses if she's going to develop the ability to manage them on her own. While distraction can save the day when you really need to shift your toddler's focus right now—when she's

determined to do something dangerous, for example—you don't want to get in the habit of constantly swooping in to distract her. Doing so robs her of the opportunity to learn and grow—the exact opposite of what you're trying to do as a parent.

Toddler Discipline Challenges: The Big Three

Ask a group of parents to describe their toddlers' most challenging behaviours and odds are they'll start talking about one or more of "the big three": biting, temper tantrums, and difficulty managing transitions. Not only are these three behaviours surprisingly common, they're also extremely frustrating to deal with as a parent, which explains why they make for perennial playgroup fodder. Fortunately, there are ways to handle each of these situations—and in a way that's a win-win for you and your toddler. Here's what you need to know.

Biting

Problem: Your toddler chomps down on the nearest chunk of exposed flesh when she becomes really frustrated with a person or a toy.

How to handle it:
Learn to watch for "pre-biting" behaviours. If your toddler is prone to biting and you see that her frustration level is starting to build, be prepared to intervene immediately to prevent the other person from being hurt.

- **If your toddler manages to bite another child before you can jump in,** show your toddler the bite mark she left and talk about why this is not okay. Say, "That hurts. Joey is crying. Your teeth are for eating, not biting." Don't bite your child back to "teach" her that biting hurts. You'll merely confuse and upset her: "Hey, if biting is bad, why did Mom just bite me?"
- **Try to figure out what triggered the outburst and then focus on meeting the underlying need.** Biting tends to occur when a child is too upset to express her feelings in other ways or lacks the

language skills to do so. Giving her the words to express what she's feeling can help her to deal with the situation in ways that don't involve using her teeth! Note: a book like *Teeth Are Not for Biting* by Elizabeth Verdick may be helpful in teaching your toddler about positive alternatives to biting. And providing your toddler with a teething toy or other non-toxic item designed to be put in the mouth can help her to redirect the urge to chomp down on her brother's arm. (Tell her, "Bite this!" and hand her the item if you sense that a bite is imminent.)

Temper tantrums

Problem: Your toddler flings herself on the ground, kicking and screaming. Her entire body is telegraphing the message, "I can't handle this!"

How to handle it:

- **Be alert to the warning signs of a pending emotional storm.** Being tuned in to what's going on with your toddler will allow you to prevent tiny problems from escalating into something much bigger and more difficult to handle. "The toddler lives in a state of frequent frustration," explains Jo-Anne, a 43-year-old mother of seven. "Learning to jump in before frustration sets in seems to be the key. I sit down and say, 'Hmmm . . . let's see what we can do here' before they fall apart with frustration. I think letting children become too frustrated before intervening creates a sense of incompetence."

- **Let your knowledge of your toddler guide you in deciding what to do.** Some toddlers respond best to physical comfort—a reassuring hug from a loving parent. Others will flip out even more if you attempt to hug or hold them mid-tantrum. In this case, your best bet might be to simply focus on being a calming presence (something that's admittedly easier said than done some days). Note: you'll want to move your toddler to a safer spot if there's any chance she could injure herself while she's throwing her tantrum.

toddlers and breath-holding

It can be scary to watch your toddler hold her breath until she faints or turns blue. As frightening as these breath-holding episodes may be to witness, your toddler's body will "reset" itself as soon as she loses consciousness. She'll start breathing again and recover quickly and completely from her breath-holding episode.

Breath-holding episodes occur in 0.1 percent to 4.6 percent of healthy children. They are most common in boys between the ages of 13 and 18 months and girls between the ages of 19 and 24 months. Most children will outgrow these episodes by age 37 to 42 months.

Ask yourself, "What does my toddler need from me right now?" and then focus on meeting that need. At the same time, ask yourself, "What am I thinking and feeling? What do I, as this child's parent, need right now?" Then try to find a way to meet your own needs, too!

- **Calm yourself and then calm your child.** Calm begets calm. Take a deep, calming breath and repeat a calming phrase that will help you to stay focused on your big-picture parenting goals—perhaps something like, "Be kind."

- **Communicate clearly and concisely with your child.** Use short phrases like, "You need to . . ." She won't be able to process lengthy explanations or instructions while her emotions are raging out of control. So save the so-called teachable moment until later on. When you're ready to have that conversation, talk about what happened and state your expectation with regard to her behaviour—what you think she might want to do differently next time.

- **Give your child a reassuring hug.** She needs to know that your relationship with her is still on track and that your love for her is unconditional—even when she's behaving in ways you may not like or completely understand.

- **Don't be embarrassed if your child throws a tantrum in public.** Any adult who has raised a child of his or her own has likely been in your shoes on at least one occasion; and any adult who hasn't served his or her time in the parenting trenches hasn't earned the right to judge!

toddlers and headbanging

Approximately one in five toddlers engages in headbanging—an activity that is soothing to some children but highly alarming to their parents. Some toddlers engage in headbanging because they find it helps to relax and comfort them. Others do it because they find that it helps them to cope with the pain associated with teething or an ear infection. And still others engage in headbanging when they're having temper tantrums. (It becomes their way of making it painfully obvious to others around them that they're just plain not happy!)

Headbanging is four times as common in boys as in girls and typically lasts from age six months until a child is approximately two to four years of age. The best way to deal with headbanging behaviour is to either attempt to substitute other soothing routines and comforting techniques or ignore the behaviour entirely.

Try not to worry that your child will end up with a severe head injury as a result of all that headbanging; this activity is what the experts refer to as a "self-regulating behaviour." In other words, if it hurts too much, your child will stop doing it.

And here's another reassuring bit of information: brain scans of individuals who were headbangers as children don't show evidence of any abnormalities, so there's no proof that this admittedly disturbing habit will affect your child's long-term development.

Managing transitions

Problem: Your toddler hates switching gears, whether it means finishing breakfast and then heading out the door in the morning or making the shift from playtime to naptime. She'd much rather stick with what she's doing in the here and now . . .

How to handle it:

- **Understand that there's a reason why your toddler struggles with transitions.** It's not that she's trying to be difficult: she simply hasn't developed the brain architecture and coping skills necessary to make these kinds of transitions on her own. One of the key skills she's still trying to develop is called cognitive flexibility (the ability to shift attention, plan next steps, and do things in a particular order, like remembering to put her socks on before her shoes). The good news is that life gives her plenty of opportunities to work at developing these skills; and the more she works at them, the closer she'll get to mastering them.

- **Understand the important role that you have to play in helping your toddler to navigate transitions.** Until she develops the skill-set needed to map out a path between what she's doing right now and what you need her to be doing a couple of minutes from now, she'll need you to do that for her. Basically, she's outsourced this function of her brain to you!

- **Keep things simple.** Guide her step by step as opposed to expecting her to act on multi-step instructions. And be prepared to repeat these instructions each time you need her to make this particular transition (as opposed to expecting her to remember the identical set of instructions you delivered yesterday and the day before—an expectation that simply isn't realistic for her right now).

- **Set your toddler up for success.** Recognize the different types of challenges that are posed by different parts of your child's day and come up with creative ways to respond to them. For example, mealtime requires sitting still for prolonged periods of time, so you might want to consider giving your child the opportunity to release some of her excess energy before you expect her to settle into her chair and eat. Likewise, you can help her to anticipate what's happening next by creating predictable routines (it's bedtime right after storytime) and by relying on environmental cues (switching from high-energy to low-energy activities as you ease into bedtime, playing quiet music and dimming the lights).

- **Be patient with yourself and your toddler.** Walking a toddler through the same set of steps over and over again can feel like a lot of work—but so is dealing with a toddler in the midst of a full-fledged meltdown. You'll find it easier to cope with this not-so-fun (and sometimes painfully tedious) aspect of parenting if you make a point of reminding yourself that it won't be like this forever. With repetition (lots and lots of repetition), your toddler will master this particular routine and, as her brain continues to mature, she'll take things one step further by figuring out how to map similar transitions on her own. In the meantime, accept that transitions are going to be hard for her—and for you! Then celebrate the fact that this too shall pass. (Really.)

"I think we sometimes prevent toddlers from trying things, not because they shouldn't do them, but because it's easier or faster if we do them."

—LISA, 36, MOTHER OF TWO

The Art of Co-Parenting

Parenting with a partner? While it's unreasonable to expect to agree with your partner on every possible parenting issue—you will, after all, have made thousands of parenting decisions by the time your child grows up and leaves home—it's important to come up with a game plan for managing those differences. Here are some tips on managing the types of day-to-day parenting disagreements that can lead to conflicts in your relationship.

Accept the fact that you're each going to have your own unique parenting style. Not only were you raised in different households, you're entirely different people. Perhaps your partner feels most comfortable taking a boot camp style to parenting, while you prefer a much more laid-back approach—or vice versa. "I sometimes tease my husband about how he gets to be 'the hero' with Joey and Maggie," admits Alyson, a

33-year-old mother of two. "He tends not to discipline them as much as I do. He also has a higher tolerance for unacceptable behaviour than I do. And he's not home with them as much as I am and therefore doesn't want to spend what little time he has with them disciplining them."

Identify those areas where you actually are in agreement. Chances are you and your partner don't go head-to-head on every conceivable parenting-related issue. And if you do, that's more of an indication of problems in your relationship than of differences in your parenting philosophies. It can be reassuring to discover that you and your partner are on the same wavelength when it comes to big-picture parenting issues and that your disagreements tend to centre on relatively minor points, like how to handle your two-year-old daughter's recent conversion to nudism. And as for those areas where you don't see eye to eye? It's important to come to some sort of agreement about how to handle these particular parenting challenges so that your parenting is reasonably in synch.

Play to one another's strengths. Sometimes it makes sense to divide up the parenting responsibilities so that you each handle the same sorts of responsibilities from day to day: for example, you might be the one to get your child washed and dressed in the morning, while your partner might be in charge of overseeing the bedtime routine. Or vice versa. Not only does this help to ensure that you both receive a bit of downtime from the rigours of parenting, but will also create greater consistency in your child's day-to-day routine. Of course, there's also something to be said for shaking things up a little so that your child learns early on that there's more than one way to wash hair or get ready for bed or tackle pretty much any other tasks of daily living. Sure, consistency is great, but flexibility is pretty amazing, too . . .

Give one another the benefit of the doubt. Recognize that every parent blows it from time to time. Don't hold your partner up to superhuman standards of parenting. And compliment him when he handles a situation particularly well. Everyone benefits from a pat on the back every now and again, including parents.

Don't be afraid to call a time out. If you're unhappy with the way your partner is handling a particular situation, wave the proverbial white flag. That way, you can discuss the situation out of earshot of your children and agree to a common solution. "If Lyle disciplines William in a way that I don't completely agree with, I wait until we're alone to discuss it with him," says Candice, a 28-year-old mother of one. Kimberlee agrees with this approach to co-parenting: "My husband is more demanding of our children," explains the 28-year-old mother of two. "He often has a difficult time 'not sweating the small stuff.' We work to limit our battles, and he and I have developed a code word when we're in the midst of a difficult situation. This allows my husband to gracefully withdraw from his position without undermining his participation in the parenting team."

Know when to call in the pros. Seek help from a neutral third party, such as a family therapist, if you're continually butting heads with your partner on all things parenting. Sometimes a single session with a highly skilled facilitator can help you and your partner really cut to the chase on an issue and to map out a mutually agreeable path forward.

Commit to an ongoing program of parental development, and encourage your partner to come along for the ride. If you find a parenting article or video that's particular helpful to you, share it with your partner. Or take a parenting workshop together. Being exposed to new parenting ideas may help to spark conversations about your hopes and dreams for your children, allowing you to find some neutral middle ground when it comes to even the most difficult of childrearing issues.

Find ways to reconnect with your partner on a regular basis. It's hard to feel that you're on the same parenting page if you've lost touch with one another as a couple. "With a baby, we knew there would be time for us to be alone when the baby napped or slept at night," explains Sidney, a 33-year-old mother of one. "With a toddler, there isn't the same amount of time available." And then there's the fact that there's a whole lot more to argue about when you're making parenting decisions about a toddler versus a baby: "No one ever seems to warn you about the strain that toddlers can put on a relationship," says Alyson, a 37-year-old mother of two. "They only talk about the first year being difficult. But I can tell you that my husband and I have definitely had more disagreements during Joey and Maggie's toddler stages than we ever did when they were babies." Not quite sure what to do about the problem? Consider hiring a college student to come to your house or organizing a childcare swap with another family so that you can escape for "date night" on a regular basis. Don't treat this break from parenting as an unnecessary frill. Instead, recognize it for what it is: an essential investment in your relationship that will reap untold dividends in the well-being of your family.

Be alert to the signs of parent burnout—in yourself as well as your partner. If exhaustion is becoming the norm, you feel like you're parenting on autopilot as opposed to making conscious and deliberate parenting decisions, or you find yourself becoming increasingly disillusioned and even cynical about parenting (you start to believe that you're a bad parent—that nothing you do makes a difference for your child—and you find yourself feeling increasingly disconnected from your child), you should at least consider the possibility that you're experiencing parent burnout. Hey, it happens—and it happens more often than you might think. Research has shown that as many as one in eight parents may be struggling with parent burnout. If you think you or your partner might be that one in eight, it's important to reach out for help from a doctor, a therapist, or another trusted person. It is possible to turn the situation around, but it's a whole lot easier to do so when you have the right support.

Remind yourself and your partner that this is just a stage (albeit a rather exhausting stage). You won't always have young children underfoot. The childrearing years typically last for just one-quarter to one-third of a person's life. Chances are that in years to come you'll look back on these trying times with the fondest of memories—the miracle of parental amnesia!

Coming to Terms with Being a Less-Than-Perfect Parent

As you can see, parenting a toddler can be a bit of a crazy ride—an experience that will push you to your limits and occasionally beyond. There will be times when you say or do something you regret because, hey, you're only human.

Here's the good news: your toddler doesn't need you to be perfect. He just needs you to keep trying. And, when you fall short of your own expectations (as you inevitably will), you have the opportunity to teach him a powerful lesson about what it takes to keep a relationship on track. That means doing the hard work of relationship repair: accepting responsibility for your actions, apologizing to your toddler, and doing what you can to make amends.

It's not about beating yourself up. It's about learning from your experience and coming up with a game plan for doing better the next time around. Because that's the great thing about parenting: you get so many chances to try again.

Besides, by allowing yourself to be a less-than-perfect parent, you'll be giving your toddler permission to be a less-than-perfect kid. And that's a pretty amazing gift to give to any child.

> "Parents are not perfect. There are going to be times when you overreact and times when things don't work out the way you'd planned. It's at these times that the lesson learned is by the parent rather than the child."
>
> —LORI, 31, MOTHER OF FIVE

CHAPTER 4

Fun and Games

"For a small child there is no division between playing and learning; between the things he or she does 'just for fun' and things that are 'educational.' The child learns while living and any part of living that is enjoyable is also play."

—PENELOPE LEACH, *Your Baby and Child*

Playing and learning are as natural to your child as breathing. They are fuelled by his curiosity and his passion for discovery. And as his repertoire of skills increases, his play possibilities increase exponentially as well. That's exciting for him and for you. And play sparks his development in powerful and far-reaching ways by allowing him to . . .

- learn how to interact with other people (and in ways that take into account his goals as well as their own);
- work on a variety of skills—everything from gross and fine motor skills to language skills, to creative thinking abilities, and problem-solving skills;
- improve his focus and to heighten his powers of concentration by sticking with a particular task for an extended period of time.

Bottom line? If you were to ask your doctor to give your toddler a prescription for a happy and healthy life, she might be tempted to reach for her prescription pad and simply scrawl the word "play."

So play matters—*a lot*. And in this chapter, we're going to talk about where you fit into your toddler's journey of discovery: what your toddler learns through play (both about himself and the wider world), and how you as his parent can support that journey.

Setting the Stage for Play

Feeling pressured to play the role of entertainment director—to program and deliver 24/7 fun for your kid (and to ensure that his fun is jam-packed with opportunities for learning?) You're not alone. There's a huge amount of pressure on parents and kids to make every moment of learning count. The good news? It doesn't have to be this hard.

While it's important to provide your toddler with a stimulating environment, you don't have to go to such extraordinary lengths that you end up developing a full-blown case of parent burnout and your toddler ends up feeling completely stressed out and overwhelmed. (After all, he's not a junior executive. He's still a little kid!)

Contrary to popular belief, it's not necessary to painstakingly program every minute of your toddler's day to maximize the number of learning opportunities—nor is it necessarily helpful (or healthy!). A more sensible approach is to let your toddler take the lead: to simply follow him in his own self-directed journey of discovery and to build upon the natural opportunities for learning that are part and parcel of every child's day.

Wondering what this means in practical terms?

It's about providing your child with just the right amount of challenge and stimulation—enough to keep things interesting, but not so much that he collapses on the floor in a shrieking heap of frustration and overwhelm.

And it's about resisting the temptation to take over his learning—something that robs him of precious opportunities for self-discovery. (Toddlers need opportunities for independent play so that they can begin to figure things out on their own.)

That's not to say that you're destined to spend the toddler years sitting on the sidelines, quietly observing your child at play. That would be a missed opportunity for you and your child. Not only will there be times when you *have to* step in (to help your toddler steer clear of danger, or to help him to manage a task that is too challenging for him to handle on his own right now), there will also be countless times when he invites you to join him in play (because playing on his own is only fun for so long). Your challenge, in this situation, of course, is to join in play in a way that is non-intrusive and non-bossy—that supports his developmental need to call the shots. So instead of barging in and saying, "Hey, buddy. Let's make a block tower with these blocks!" you simply slide in beside him and follow his lead. Maybe he wants to pretend that one of the blocks is a fire truck. Or a baby bird. Or a bar of soap . . . You'll never know what he's thinking if you rush in too quickly. So remind yourself to hit the pause button long enough to allow the magic to unfold.

Here are some additional tips on setting the stage for play for your toddler:

Start out by observing your toddler. Be curious about his underlying intent (a.k.a. "learning goal") as he plays. Ask yourself what he is trying to figure out through his play—and help him to articulate these goals for himself. ("It looks like you're trying to figure out if you can make that toy boat stay under water!")

Tap into your toddler's interests as you plan activities that will allow him to learn new things and develop new skills. But balance this off against your toddler's desire to explore and figure things out on his own—something that boosts his confidence, gives him a better sense of his own abilities, adds to his understanding of the world around him, and fuels his desire to learn even more.

Make a wide variety of play materials available to your child. Ideally the materials should support open-ended play (play materials like building blocks and art supplies that can be used in any number of different ways as opposed to toys that can only be played with in narrowly prescribed ways). That's the focus of the activities you'll find elsewhere in this chapter, so you'll find plenty of ideas and inspiration as you keep reading.

Use your knowledge of your toddler to scaffold (or build upon) his opportunities for learning. If, for example, you notice that your child is having trouble sticking with a particular activity, like putting together the pieces of a puzzle, it could be that the activity is either too frustrating or too easy for him—or it could be that he's been working on that particular puzzle for too long. Give the budding scientist an opportunity to puzzle out some of this stuff on his own, but don't be afraid to step in with information and encouragement if he seems to be hitting the frustration wall. Sometimes it's simply a matter of modifying the materials—for example, wrapping an elastic band around a crayon to make it easier for your toddler to grasp.

Look for other opportunities to support your toddler's learning and to help to bridge the gap between the skills he has right now and the skills he is trying to master next. For example, you might help him to figure out what he needs to pay attention to when he's working on a particular activity ("This peg is round, so we need to find a round hole," "This puzzle piece has a flower on it, so we want to find the other flower pieces in the puzzle"). Or you might talk about ways to stick with a task that he is finding particularly challenging right now (perhaps by taking a break and coming back to that uber-frustrating puzzle another time). It's about being tuned in to your child's interests and abilities—about making yourself available to answer his questions and to troubleshoot any problems he encounters in a non-bossy, non-intrusive way.

Accept that some of a toddler's most powerful learning comes from failure—when things don't quite turn out the way your toddler planned. Help him to seize on the opportunity to learn from the experience as opposed to fixating on and being frustrated by what went wrong. Sure, that much-loved bedtime story is a little soggy after being dropped in the bathtub, but now your toddler knows (or at least he's starting to understand) that it's a good idea to keep books away from water.

Understand that toddlers are experiential learners. They learn by doing and then they try to connect what they've just learned with what they already know. This isn't always (okay, ever!) a neat and predictable process. Expect messes, noise, and emotional highs and lows. That's how learning happens—and what makes the toddler years such a wild yet wonderful ride.

Playing with Other Kids

Your one-year-old hasn't shown any interest in playing with other children. In fact, you've noticed that he'd rather play quietly with his blocks in the corner than join in any group activities. Should you be concerned?

Probably not, say the play experts. It takes time for a child to master the art of playing with other children. So don't assume that your one-year-old is doomed to spend his childhood standing on the edge of the playground, watching while the social butterflies in the toddler crowd romp around together, just because he isn't overly social yet. Chances are, it won't be long before he decides to get in on the fun, too. Table 4.1 highlights some important milestones to watch for as he matures.

In the meantime, you'll want to keep your expectations realistic, particularly when it comes to expectations about sharing toys. A toddler isn't capable of fully grasping the concept of sharing because he's not yet capable of understanding that other people's wants and needs are different than his own. Add to that the fact that toddlers don't have a concept of time and you can see why things can go downhill pretty fast when it comes to sharing. Your toddler wants what he wants when he wants it (right now!) and he can't even conceive of the fact that some other kid could want the same toy that he does. Because, hey, the toddler's worldview is "it's all about me!" Your best bet (while you wait for his brain to develop the ability to take into account other people's perspectives) is to minimize the potential for conflicts over toys. If you're hosting a group of toddlers, plan an activity like blowing bubbles that everyone can enjoy at the same time as opposed to expecting the toddlers to patiently wait to take a turn with a much-loved ride-on toy. Trust me: a much better time will be had by all . . .

---

why sharing can't be forced

"The real meaning of sharing—giving of oneself—comes from inside. Toddlers are naturally self-centered. . . . Toddlers do not learn to share by having grown-ups make them do it. Having to give up a toy makes a toddler feel angry, not loving."

—IRENE VAN DER ZANDE, *1, 2, 3 . . . THE TODDLER YEARS*

The play's the thing

And speaking of hosting groups of toddlers, let's talk playgroups!

Playgroups can be a lot of fun for parents and toddlers: parents get the chance to compare notes on the joys and challenges of raising toddlers, while the little ones get the chance to work on their budding social skills. If you aren't able to find a group in your area to join—or if the playgroup you check out doesn't seem to be quite right for you and your child—then you might want to consider starting your own group instead. Here are a few tips on organizing a playgroup:

- **Decide how large you'd like your group to be,** and start spreading the word to other parents you know who have young children.
- **Choose a location for your group.** You might want to have the group meet in members' homes—rotating from one house to the next—or you might prefer to have your group meet at a community centre or on other neutral turf like a playground (a smart way to avoid tugs-of-war over much-loved toys).
- **Choose your time of day with care.** As you've no doubt discovered by now, toddlers tend to be at their best first thing in the morning, when they're most rested. Having an afternoon playgroup can be risky business because it may mean that some of the toddlers in the group will miss out on a much-needed nap—not exactly the best way to guarantee playgroup success.

Type of Play	What It Means and What You Can Do to Promote It
Younger toddlers (under 18 months of age)	
Onlooker play: observing others at play rather than participating themselves. This type of play is the norm for younger toddlers—and, of course, it's extremely common in older kids, too.	Onlooker play helps your toddler learn how to relate to others and gives him an opportunity to acquire language. He also starts figuring out how others are likely to respond to various types of social behaviours (e.g., smiling versus hitting) and what he can do to get the other children's attention. Allow this learning process to unfold naturally, but be prepared to help your toddler if he seems eager to play with the other children but unsure about what he needs to do to indicate that he wants to join in the fun.
Solitary play: your toddler plays by himself, but is still in close proximity to other children. This type of play can be seen in older children, too, but tends to become less frequent.	Solitary play helps your toddler develop a wide range of skills and learn about the world around him.
Older toddlers (18 months to age three)	
Parallel play: your toddler may appear to be playing with other children his age because they're playing in the same part of the room, but if you look closely you'll see that there's no actual interaction between them. It's the start of learning how to play with others.	Starting at around age 18 months, toddlers begin to demonstrate an increased awareness of other children. And, of course, once these older toddlers start to play with one another, they have to figure out how to share toys (a skill that can be tough for any kid to learn). One study found that 70 percent of two-year-olds playing together experienced at least one conflict during a single 50-minute period of observation. And another study found that 84 percent of conflicts between 21-month-olds involved difficulties sharing toys.

Note: Some psychologists question the existence of parallel play, arguing that toddlers *do* interact with one another; adults just don't understand the nature of those interactions. For example, two toddlers may make eye contact and imitate what each other is doing, even though they aren't actively "playing together."

Preschoolers (ages three to four years)	
Associative play: very loosely organized play, e.g., a group of preschoolers may be sharing a box of blocks, but they're each making their own constructions.	Associative play provides a preschooler with opportunities for socialization and teaches him the dos and don'ts of getting along with others.

Note: Children this age tend to be socially awkward at first. Their way of indicating that they want to play may be to walk up to another child and grab what that child is playing with. If this occurs, recognize that your preschooler simply wants to play with the other child. Try to defuse the situation by telling the other children that your child wants to play too, while suggesting to your preschooler that he find something similar to play with nearby.

- **Decide what to do about snacks.** The simplest approach is to have the host family provide the snack that particular week, taking into account any food allergies within the group. If you're hosting your group at the park or the playground, simply take turns bringing the snack.

- **If you do decide to host the playgroup at your house,** you'll want to squirrel away your toddler's favourite toys before the guests start filing in. That way, your toddler won't be stuck in the position of being asked to share his most prized possessions (a.k.a. his toys). You might also want to encourage the other children attending the playgroup to bring along a toy to share (ideally a duplicate of a toy that some of the toddlers in the group have found particularly difficult to share in the past). That way, the "host toddler" (a.k.a. your kid) won't be the only one whose toys are being shared around.

---

the "mine" field

Here's a reassuring fact to tuck away in your brain for the next time your toddler starts shrieking "Mine!" According to the child development experts, claiming ownership of an object is a major intellectual breakthrough. To help nudge the process along, give your toddler plenty of opportunities to play with other children. The more practice he gets with sharing, the easier it will become. Catherine, a 32-year-old mother of four, was surprised when her two-year-old twins came up with a sharing system on their own: "If one of them wants something the other is playing with, he makes an effort to find another really interesting toy to offer his brother in the hope of making a successful exchange. Believe it or not, it usually works!"

Ideas Unlimited: Activities That You and Your Toddler Can Enjoy Together

Looking for some ideas for activities that you and your toddler can enjoy together? You'll find plenty of inspiration in this part of the chapter as we zero in on the following types of activities:

- loose parts play
- arts and crafts
- sensory play
- math
- music

- active play
- science
- dramatic play
- excursions and outings
- reading

Loose Parts Play

Loose parts play refers to play that involves materials (for example, sand, water, building blocks, art supplies, and random found objects like buttons) and spaces (for example, natural spaces and adventure playgrounds) that put children rather than adults in charge of play. As Theresa Casey and Juliet Robertson, authors of the *Loose Parts Play Toolkit*, explain: "Loose parts aren't prescriptive and offer limitless possibilities. . . . Static, unchanging play spaces do little for children whereas environments which can be manipulated, where things move and can be moved, open worlds of possibility."

Loose parts play is beneficial to children because it allows them to "invent, construct, evaluate, and modify their own constructions and ideas through play," according to Casey and Robertson. It encourages creative thinking and problem solving; it provides opportunities for physical activity; and it gives kids the opportunity to work on their cooperative play and socialization skills. You can provide your toddler with opportunities to experience loose parts play by starting a collection of random objects and materials that are likely to be highly appealing to a toddler (scraps of fabric, twigs you find on the lawn, and other miscellaneous treasures). Obviously, you'll need to keep safety in mind (items made of toxic materials or that feature sharp objects aren't exactly toddler-friendly choices . . .), but you'll be amazed how many materials that might otherwise find their way to the landfill or the recycling depot can find new purpose via your toddler's imagination.

As you continue to read through this chapter, you'll begin to recognize countless other opportunities to tap into the power of loose parts play. And that brings us to the next topic for discussion—arts and crafts.

Arts and Crafts

Arts and crafts activities provide toddlers with the opportunity to experiment with various types of materials, learn about colours and shapes, experience different textures, figure out how to use tools like scissors and paintbrushes, develop pride in their own creative abilities, express their feelings through art, and work on both their small muscle coordination and their hand–eye coordination skills.

Of course, before your toddler can start reaping all those arts and crafts–related benefits, you'll need to have the necessary supplies on hand (basic tools and supplies as well as found materials—things that would otherwise end up in the trash or the recycling bin). See Table 4.2.

Here are a few important points to keep in mind when you're rounding up art supplies for your toddler:

- **Steer clear of art supplies that contain toxic ingredients.** Even if you're pretty sure your toddler is unlikely to chow down on a crayon or to knock back a bottle of liquid paint, art materials are still likely to get on his hands and consequently into his mouth. Hey, he's a toddler . . .

- **Seek out toddler-sized art supplies to minimize your toddler's frustration.** Slightly chunkier markers, paintbrushes, and pencils will be easier for him to manoeuvre than the skinnier versions of these products that are designed for use by older children. Note: Some parents purchase small paintbrushes from hardware stores rather than the standard long-handled paintbrushes from craft supply stores because shorter-handled brushes tend to be easier for toddlers to manage.

- **While markers tend to produce spectacular results**—your toddler can get an explosion of colour without having to apply the same amount of pressure that a crayon demands—they aren't without their problems. Caps tend to get left off or misplaced entirely, and—even worse—those stray caps can pose a choking hazard. Add to that the fact that toddlers like to suck on markers or colour themselves with them and you can see why using mark-ers demands fairly careful supervision.

4.2   Stocking the Craft Cupboard

Here's a list of the types of art supplies you'll want to have on hand to nurture your bud-ding Picasso's creativity. Note: Some of these materials may pose a choking hazard for younger toddlers, so keep your toddler's developmental stage in mind as you start stock-ing the craft cupboard. You'll also want to zero in on products that are non-toxic and that won't stain your toddler's clothing or skin or anything else you happen to care about.

Basic Tools and Supplies

Chalk (regular and sidewalk)
Crayons
Glitter glue
Glue
Glue sticks
Markers
Masking tape
Paints (tempera, water-colours, and fingerpaints)

Paintbrushes
Paper (white paper, con-struction paper, tissue paper, etc., in all shapes, sizes, and colours)
Pastels
Pencils (regular and coloured)
Playdough or modelling clay

School glue
Scissors
Sponges
Stamps and a washable pad
Stencils
Tape (Scotch tape or mask-ing tape)

Additional Materials to Collect or Purchase

Aluminum foil
Beads (large)
Berry baskets
Boxes
Buttons (large)
Calendars
Cardboard
Catalogues
Cereal boxes
Clothes pegs
Coffee filters
Confetti
Cotton balls
Crayon pieces
Doilies
Egg cartons
Fabric scraps
Feathers
Felt
Flower pots
Flowers, artificial or dried
Foam and wood shapes

Gift-wrap rolls
Gloves
Greeting cards
Hair rollers (check your local thrift store)
Lace
Lacing cord
Leaves, artificial or dried
Magazines and newspapers
Makeup brushes
Milk cartons
Mittens
Muffin papers
Napkins
Paper bags
Paper plates
Paper-towel rolls
Paper towels
Pasta
Pie tins, aluminum
Pine cones
Pipe cleaners

Plastic containers
Plastic cups and bottles
Pom-poms
Popsicle sticks
Postcards
Ribbon
Rice (uncooked)
Rocks
Socks (for puppets)
Spools
Squeeze bottles (for paint)
Stickers
Seashells
Straws
Tissue paper
Toilet-paper rolls
Toothbrushes
Shoeboxes
Wallpaper scraps
Wood scraps
Wool or string
Wrapping paper

- **Make sure that the child-safe scissors you purchase actually work.** (Some child-safe scissors are so safe that they won't cut anything, including paper.) Ideally, you want a pair with a rounded tip, sharp metal blades, and a special little spring that keeps the scissors from closing all the way. (Toddlers get frustrated if scissors jam on the paper. The little spring thing helps to alleviate this particular frustration. If only all toddler problems could be solved this quickly and easily . . .)

- **Rather than purchasing regular "skinny" crayons that tend to snap in two if a toddler applies a lot of pressure, stick to "chunky" crayons that resist breakage.** Or, even better, look for the ultimate in durability: hockey-puck-shaped crayons. (Talk about an all-Canadian art experience!) Note: You'll find a recipe in this chapter for whipping up a batch using muffin tins. And speaking of crayons, some early childhood educators recommend that you peel the wrappers off crayons so that toddlers can use all surfaces of the crayon rather than just the tip. You'll have to be the judge of whether this will work with your toddler. If he has a strong perfectionist streak, he might go to pieces if he catches you messing with the labels on his crayons! Finally, don't throw away your toddler's broken crayons. Shorter pieces help to promote a more mature pincer grasp because they cannot be held in the fist-like palmar grasp that young toddlers tend to use when they're holding on to a long crayon.

- **Glue sticks may be the neatest way to dispense glue, but they can be incredibly frustrating for toddlers to manoeuvre.** Your toddler may find it easier to use liquid glue than to do battle with a glue stick. Simply drizzle a small puddle on to a scrap of paper nestled inside a shallow dish and provide him with Q-tips or cotton balls for spreading it. Voila! Your glue problems are solved.

- **Liquid tempera paints are more convenient to use than their powdered counterparts and have a more appealing texture, but they tend to be a bit pricier.** Fortunately, you can save money on liquid paints by buying them in bulk from craft supply stores. If you don't think your toddler is going to be able to use all that paint, split your order with another family. Note: If your toddler's paint tends to drip because it's too runny, thicken it up with a small amount of flour or cornstarch. (Note: Add flour or cornstarch only to the paint your child is using in this art session. Paint doesn't keep very well once you've added these ingredients.)

• **While you're loading up on paints, pick up an extra package of sponges.** Then cut holes in the sponges to hold your child's paint jars in place when he's working at his easel. Not only do the sponges help to prevent the jars from tipping over, but they also help to catch any stray drips.

• **Toddlers find it easier to paint at an easel than on a flat surface such as a table.** This is because painting at an easel encourages a toddler to extend his wrist and use a full arm movement—something that provides a more stable position for painting. Don't want to invest in an easel? Use masking tape or magnets to stick a sheet of paper to the side of your refrigerator or steel door and let your toddler paint that way instead.

• **Reluctant to fork over a lot of money for that nice glossy finger-painting paper?** Shelf paper and aluminum foil work every bit as well. And you can skip the paper entirely by allowing your toddler to fingerpaint directly on a hard surface such as a mirror, a window, or a sheet of Plexiglas. You can save the picture for posterity by taking a photo or making a print. To make a print, simply place a sheet of paper on top of your toddler's creation and gently rub a rolling pin over it. Voila! You've now got another fingerpainting to add to your collection—or to mail to Grandma.

• **Some people recommend letting toddlers fingerpaint with chocolate pudding, yogurt, whipped cream, and other foods.** Others insist that this is a bad idea because it sends a mixed message to toddlers about playing with their food—proof positive that there's no element of parenting that's entirely without controversy! And something else that's often recommended (but that's not necessarily a great idea for toddlers) is fingerpainting with shaving cream. Not only is there a chance of skin irritation (most shaving creams are positively loaded with chemicals, including powerful colognes), but your toddler could rub some into his eye—which is likely to result in one very unhappy kid.

- **And speaking of getting stuff rubbed into your toddler's eyes, this is a good reason to "just say no" to glitter until he's a little older.** It looks like tremendous fun—and it is, for older kids—but given how easily a bit of glitter can get into a toddler's eye, it's simply not a good choice at this age.

- **Don't lose sight of the fact that you can make some of your own art supplies.** You'll save money, and in many cases the product will end up being superior to anything you can buy in stores. See Table 4.3 for some recipes that work particularly well.

4.3   Homemade Art Supplies

You don't have to be a gifted chef to get great results from these craft recipes. They're pretty much foolproof . . . (I've never found a homemade paste recipe that I like, which is why you won't find one here. I think this is one art supply that should be purchased, not made.)

Basic Cooked Playdough

- 500 mL (2 cups) flour
- 500 mL (2 cups) water
- 250 mL (1 cup) salt
- 60 mL (4 tbsp.) cream of tartar
- 30 mL (2 tbsp.) vegetable oil
- Food colouring

Combine the flour, water, salt, cream of tartar, and oil in a saucepan and cook over medium heat, stirring constantly. When the playdough begins to form a ball, it's cooked. Cool for five minutes and then knead in food colouring. Note: it's fun to add glitter and scents like vanilla to playdough as your toddler gets older, but it's best to hold off on this while he's still young enough to be tempted to eat the playdough.

Fingerpaints

- 1 L (4 cups) of water
- 125 mL (1/2 cup) cornstarch
- 60 mL (1/4 cup) soap flakes
- A few drops of glycerin
- A few drops of food colouring

Gradually add water to cornstarch, stirring constantly. Cook until the mixture is clear and then blend in the soap flakes. Finish by adding a few drops of glycerin and food colouring.

Poster Paints

- 250 mL (1 cup) water
- 60 mL (1/4 cup) flour
- 3 mL (1/2 tsp.) liquid dish detergent
- Dry tempera paint (available at craft supply stores)

Combine the water and flour in a saucepan, heating the mixture over medium heat and stirring constantly for about three minutes. When it starts to thicken, it's time to remove the mixture from the heat. Add the paint and the dish detergent and, if necessary, an additional 30 mL (2 tbsp.) of water.

Goop

- 250 mL (1 cup) cornstarch
- 250 mL (1 cup) water
- Food colouring

Combine ingredients in a bowl and then pour onto a cookie sheet. You can vary the texture by adding more or less water. Your toddler will have fun "fingerpainting" in the goop.

Hockey Puck Crayons

- Broken crayons (paper removed)
- Aluminum foil
- Non-stick cooking spray

Line an old muffin tin with pieces of aluminum foil and coat the foil with non-stick cooking spray. Then fill each muffin cup with broken crayons. (You can either sort the crayons by colour or go for a multicoloured effect.) Place the muffin tin in a warm (not hot!) oven and remove the tin once the crayons have melted. Allow the mixture to cool and harden and then pop each crayon "hockey puck" out and peel the foil off.

Keeping everything organized

Once you accumulate all these bits and pieces, you'll need to figure out what to do with the resulting avalanche of materials. You might find it helpful to set aside a kitchen cupboard for paint bottles, packages of paper, and other large items, and use a fishing tackle box or toolbox to hold smaller items. (The trays are ideal for pencils, crayons, and paintbrushes, while the larger storage area underneath is ideal for feathers, foam chips, and other art supplies.) Cutlery holders can also work well for organizing your toddler's art tools and supplies. The main thing to keep in mind is that the materials need to be easily accessible to your toddler so that he can quickly switch into art mode when a moment of inspiration strikes. That doesn't mean giving him immediate access to the super-messy supplies like paint and glue, but he should be able to get at washable crayons and other similar supplies relatively easily.

Mess patrol

You'll also want to give some thought to how to contain the mess, since even children's art supplies that claim to be washable don't always live up to their name. ("The product labels on the paints and markers may say 'washable,' but that doesn't mean they come out of all fabrics and surfaces," warns Anita, a 39-year-old mother of four.) But you don't want to be a total spoilsport when it comes to messes, of course: As Julie, a 30-year-old mother of one, notes, "Being messy is part of the fun!"

- **Designate a certain area of your home as the craft zone.** After all, it's one thing to mop a bit of paint off your kitchen floor, and quite another to try getting that same blob of red paint off your living room rug.

- **Minimize the amount of cleanup and prevent your child's art supplies from damaging your kitchen table**—throw a plastic tablecloth or shower curtain across the table before your toddler starts doing crafts. A quick wipe-down with a damp sponge is all that's required once your toddler is finished working his magic with paint and glue.

- **Figure out what you need to do to protect your toddler's clothing.** You can use a paint smock, an old raincoat (cut off the sleeves and put it on your child backwards), or an apron-style bib to protect your child's clothing. Of course, if the weather's nice, you may find it easier to simply strip your child down to his diaper.

- **Get in the habit of adding a squirt of liquid soap or liquid laundry detergent to your child's liquid paints to encourage any paint-related stains to wash out more easily in the laundry.** And if your toddler manages to get a blob of paint under his paint smock, rub some soap into the spot right away. Then, when he's finished painting, whisk the paint-splattered garment away and soak it until the paint stain starts to lift.

- **Realize that less can be more when you're dishing out the art supplies.** It's a lot easier to clean up a spill from a small container of *decorating to hide dirt*

You'll be less stressed about craft splatters and other toddler-related stains if your home is decorated to hide dirt. Here are some points to consider the next time you go into reno mode:

- Go with matte rather than glossy finishes on walls, countertops, and floors. High-gloss finishes tend to emphasize spills, scratches, and fingerprints—the last thing you need when you've got a toddler on the loose!
- Paint any exposed woodwork with semi-gloss paint that can be wiped down easily.
- When you're choosing paint colours, zero in on medium-tone rather than dark or light colours, since these shades do a better job of hiding dirt.
- Think durability if you're in the market for wallpaper. Don't settle for anything less than a high-quality washable vinyl or your wallpaper will be damaged in no time.

Toddlers tend to pick at wallpaper seams and have even been known to tear off large chunks of wallpaper. You might even choose to hold off on wallpapering until your toddler comes through the prime wallpaper-removal stage.

Stick with easy-to-clean flooring in the high-traffic areas of your home. If you've got your heart set on carpeting, stick with highly textured berbers. And avoid indented or embossed tile or floor coverings, unfinished wood trim, and carpet in the kitchen or bathroom, all surfaces difficult to keep clean.

paint or glue than a huge, litre-sized bottle! To minimize the disaster potential, put small amounts of glue or paint in small containers or on pie plates. Your toddler can then apply the paint or glue using a cotton ball, a Q-tip, a small paintbrush, a Popsicle stick, or a small piece of sponge held by a clothes peg.

- **Hang wet paintings to dry on a clothesline in your basement or bathtub.** That way, your toddler is less likely to accidentally sit down on a wet, paint-covered masterpiece.

- **If all else fails, check out the stain removal chart in Chapter 7** (for dealing with stains on clothing) and the craft stain removal chart (Table 4.4) for dealing with craft–related stains on various types of household surfaces.

4.4 Craft-Related Stains

A few splatters and spills are inevitable when toddlers are doing crafts. Here are some tips on getting craft-related stains off some common household surfaces:

- Use baking soda and a damp cloth to remove crayon marks or tempera paint from painted walls and wood. If that doesn't do the trick, you can also experiment with baby oil, liquid detergent, silver polish, or toothpaste.
- If you're faced with a really chunky buildup of crayon, try painting a layer of rubber cement over the crayon mark. Once the rubber cement has had a chance to dry, you should be able to peel off most of the crayon.
- Rub a slice of dry bread over your wallpaper to remove pencil marks.
- Use white vinegar to remove ballpoint pen marks from walls and wooden surfaces.
- To remove stickers from walls, saturate the sticker with white vinegar or vegetable oil.
- To hide scratches in wooden furniture, reach for your toddler's crayon box. Then use a crayon of the appropriate shade of brown to "colour in" the scratches.
- To remove crayon marks from carpeting, place a thick stack of paper towels on the stained area and use a warm iron to heat up the wax. The heat should help to draw the crayon up into the paper towels.

Note: The usual stain removal disclaimers apply! Tackle a less noticeable area first and then proceed with caution, using the least powerful stain removal technique first. And when you pull out that iron, be sure to keep the temperature low. The last thing you want to do is to melt or burn a hole in your carpet.

Nurturing your child's creativity

The best way to encourage toddlers' creativity is to provide them with the necessary arts and crafts materials and then back off. "Don't show them how to do it, don't tell them how to do it, and don't label their creations," advises Brandy, a 24–year–old mother of two. "Let them use their imagination instead."

Julie agrees that it's important to take a hands–off approach to art activities. "I think it's crucial for parents to let kids do crafts their own way," the 30–year–old mother of one insists. "If they want to make a puppet with six eyes, that should be okay."

Contrary to what many parents believe, it's not necessary to "teach" your toddler how to do art by helping, correcting, or making suggestions to improve the quality of the final product. A better strategy is to comment on the process ("Wow, you're using a lot of different colours today!") and encourage your toddler to talk about his work ("Tell me about your painting"). And if your toddler comes up with unconventional ways of using his art materials, do what you can to encourage that free thinking. Let him know that you think his idea about painting with pipe cleaners is really cool! Kelly, 31, finds that she and her two toddlers have more fun when they try something a little out of the ordinary—like painting, cutting, and gluing playdough. Ditto for Julie, a 30-year-old mother of one: "We paint with all kinds of things: fingers, sponges, fat brushes, thin brushes, Q-tips, apples cut in half, and potatoes with shapes cut into them," she explains. Kristina, a 32-year-old mother of two, is also a strong believer in encouraging toddlers to "colour outside the lines"—both literally and figuratively. "Fingerpainting on the kitchen linoleum floor is the best!" she insists.

Of course, a willingness to allow your toddler free artistic rein doesn't necessarily guarantee that he'll develop a passion for art. Some toddlers—particularly those of the exceptionally wiggly variety—don't want anything to do with crafts. "I have two noncrafty kids," says Jennie, a 32-year-old mother of two-year-old twins. "I've tried and tried, but they will not sit long enough to attempt a project—even something as simple as fingerpainting. They're just not interested."

If, like Jennie, you have a toddler who turns his nose up at crafts, your best bet is to wait a few weeks or months before trying to whet his interest in art again. You might, for example, try squirting a few different colours of liquid paint into a ziplock bag along with a bit of cooking oil and then showing your toddler how to "fingerpaint" by squishing the paint around. Note: This type of activity is likely to have greater appeal for a particularly active toddler than an art activity that can only be enjoyed while sitting down. And it will encourage toddlers who generally prefer to steer clear of sticky, messy textures to at least venture in the vicinity of the art table.

And, of course, the best way to encourage your toddler's creativity is to let him know just how much you value his art by displaying it in a place of honour in your home. There are countless ways to do this, but here are a few ideas:

- **Hang his artwork on the refrigerator door where it can be admired each time someone is looking for a snack.**
- **Hang his artwork on the inner surface of any exterior steel doors in your home.** (Four strategically placed fridge magnets can do a great job of holding artwork in place so that it doesn't blow away when someone opens the door.)
- **Hang a miniature clothesline along one wall in your child's bedroom so that he can clip his artwork to it.**
- **Buy some inexpensive picture frames or make some frames of your own out of cardboard or other materials.**
- **Laminate your toddler's artwork to make a special set of placemats.** You might even encourage your toddler to make a second set to give to his grandparents or some other relative or friend on the next special occasion.
- **Scan one of your toddler's creations and use the image as the screen saver on your computer or smartphone.**

the science of scribbling

Don't make the mistake of assuming that your toddler's scribbles are nothing more than random doodles. Believe it or not, there's actually some order in that sea of markings. Toddlers start out by drawing a series of horizontal lines, eventually progressing to vertical lines, too. Then they move on to drawing incomplete circles, closed circles, and spider or sun patterns. So there you go: a crash course in the science of scribbling!

Some fun arts and crafts activities to try

Now that you've loaded up on art supplies and given some thought to how you're going to simultaneously contain the mess *and* nurture your child's creativity (no small feat, that), it's time to get down to the real nitty-gritty. Here are a few fun things to try with your toddler:

- **Give your toddler the opportunity to practice some "pre-cutting" activities like filling eye droppers and turkey basters with water or using plastic tongs to lift cotton balls.** The movements used are similar to those involved in manipulating a pair of scissors.

- **When your toddler has mastered the kinds of finger movements required to guide a pair of scissors, show him how to hold papers and scissors properly (by using a "thumbs up" position for each hand).** Then, when your toddler is actually ready to practice his cutting skills, give him lines to practice cutting along. Tip: Draw a thick line on a narrow strip (4 to 5 centimetres in width) of heavy paper using an extra-wide magic marker. Your toddler can practice cutting along the line. Start out with straight lines, progressing to curvy lines as your toddler becomes more skilled at handling the scissors.

- **Help your toddler drizzle some glue on a sheet of construction paper.** He can then sprinkle sand, cornmeal, or birdseed on top of the glue to make a picture.

- **Gather up textured objects like leaves and use them to make rubbings with crayons.** (Place the leaf underneath the sheet of paper and rub the crayon on top of the sheet of paper. You should end up with an imprint of the shape of the leaf.)

- **Trace your toddler's hand and feet on a sheet of paper or let him make handprints and footprints with paint.** (This is a great outdoor activity for a warm summer day.)

- **Attach bubble wrap to a paint roller.** Your toddler will enjoy observing how the bubble wrap affects the design he's able to produce with the paint roller.

- **Give your toddler a bunch of fun alternatives to paintbrushes:** sponges, feathers, old toothbrushes, combs, Q-tips, a potato masher, apple slices cut into shapes, and so on.

- **Make a stamp pad by placing wet paper towels in a small bowl and covering the paper towel with paint.**
- **Give your child the chance to paint the house or the sidewalk with coloured water.** (It won't actually colour anything, but the water will look like paint while it's in the pail.)

left or right?

Your toddler comes pre-wired to favour a particular hand. As her fine motor skills improve and she begins to engage in single-handed activities such as colouring, it'll become increasingly apparent which hand she favours. Tip: If you place utensils in the middle of a dish (as opposed to one side of the dish) and craft supplies such as crayons and markers on top of a piece of paper (and in the middle once again), you'll be encouraging your child to pick up on her natural hand preference as opposed to merely reaching for items with the closest hand.

While the vast majority of children are right-handed, one in 10 boys and one in 12 girls are left-handed and one in 200 children is ambidextrous (equally comfortable using either hand).

If your child ends up favouring her left hand, you'll want to supply her with left-handed scissors and other left-handed tools to make her life easier. And when you teach her how to tie her shoes, you'll want to do so facing her so that she can mimic your movements using the opposite hands.

Whatever you do, don't try to fight her hand preference. Forcing her to use her other hand could lead to hand–eye coordination problems down the road, so this is definitely one of those situations where you'll want to follow your toddler's lead.

- **Roll a cob of corn in a shallow dish containing a thin layer of paint and then roll it along a piece of paper.**
- **Dip a plastic strawberry basket in a shallow dish containing a thin layer of paint and then press it on a sheet of paper.** Hint: a Frisbee or a tin pie plate tends to work particularly well.

- **Place a blob of paint in the centre of a large sheet of paper.** Drive a toy car through the puddle and watch how the wheels leave tracks on the page.

Sensory Play

Sensory play refers to any activity that stimulates your toddler's senses. It includes many of the art activities mentioned above as well as many of the music and movement activities we'll be discussing later in this chapter. What could be more sensory, after all, than squeezing playdough through your fingers, walking through puddles of paint with your feet, or listening to the beating of a drum?

Sensory play provides a fun and relaxing way for your toddler to learn about the world around him. It also gives him a chance to experiment with such basic mathematical concepts as volume and measurement and to encounter gravity and other scientific principles. Add to that the fact that sensory play allows him to improve his fine motor control and hand–eye coordination skills, and you can see that your toddler can learn a great deal through this type of play.

Here are a few of the most popular types of sensory play activities for toddlers.

Water play

It's no wonder toddlers and their parents love water play: water is readily available and it's free! While you might want to round out your child's water play by including funnels, pumps, and other types of water-play accessories (see Table 4.5 for a few ideas), the key ingredient is nothing other than good old-fashioned H_2O.

Your toddler has a prime opportunity for water play every time he hops in the bathtub, but you may wish to provide some additional water-play opportunities by either placing a bin of water and some water-play accessories on the kitchen or bathroom floor or putting a few inches of water in a wading pool, baby bathtub, or oversized plastic bin. (Obviously, you'll want to supervise your child carefully, since children have been known to drown in even a couple of inches of water. That means staying within arm's reach of your toddler whenever she's playing in water and steering clear of distractions like smartphones.) Your toddler will also enjoy watering the grass, using squirt bottles, and pouring water through a water wheel.

Water play is so much fun that it can be easy to lose sight of the benefits it delivers—which are considerable. Water play promotes physical development, builds social skills (and in a way that helps to minimize conflict because toddlers aren't being asked to share the water!), and encourages discovery, creativity, and imaginative play. So you'll want to find quick and easy ways to incorporate water play into your toddler's regular routine, both inside and out of doors.

bubble fun	Here's something fun to try the next time you're helping your toddler blow bubbles. Dip a plastic strawberry box in bubble-blowing solution and hold it in front of a fan. You'll both be delighted by the resulting cascade of bubbles.

4.5   Water-Play Accessories: What to Have on Hand

Bottles
Bowls
Bubble-blowing solution (you can make your own by combining equal parts of liquid dish soap and water)
Buckets
Cups
Eye droppers
Funnels
Ice cube trays
Ladles
Measuring cups
Measuring spoons
Pitchers
Plastic containers (including some with holes punched in the bottom)
Plastic tubing
Salad spinner
Scoops
Shovels
Sponges
Squeeze bottles
Squirt bottle (trigger style)
Strainers
Straws
Styrofoam meat trays
Toy boats
Turkey baster
Watering can
Water piping (available from your local plumbing store)
Water pumps
Water wheel

Playing with bath toys is fun. Cleaning them? Not so much. Here's a way to keep them clean with minimal hassle on your part. Simply store your child's bath toys in a mesh lingerie bag and hang the bag from the tap so that the toys can drip dry between uses. Then, when it comes time to give them a more thorough cleaning, simply tie the bag shut and drop it into your washing machine or dishwasher. (Keep your dishwasher's heat setting on low so that you don't inadvertently end up melting some of your toddler's favourite toys.)

Sand play

Like water play, sand play can be enjoyed both indoors and outdoors. (Good thing, or Canadian kids would end up being a little short-changed in the sensory play department!) All you need is a large plastic container with a lid or sandbox. (If you go the outdoor sandbox route, a lid is a must. Otherwise, your child's sandbox could quickly become the neighbourhood cat's favourite litterbox.)

As for what to put inside your child's sandbox, white play sand is the crème de la crème of sand, known for its fine, almost silky texture. You can find it at your local hardware store or department store.

If you'd like an alternative to sand, you can use rice, cornmeal, oatmeal, or birdseed instead. Just remember to discard it on a regular basis so that it doesn't become a breeding ground for disease and/or attract rodents or bugs! And some parents choose to avoid using food products in the sandbox for the same reason they don't allow their children to fingerpaint with chocolate pudding or yogurt: they think it sends young children mixed messages about food.

Here's some good news if you're on a bit of a budget: a lot of water toys can double as sand toys. (And, of course, a lot of water toys can be made from things you already have around the house—which makes them free or next to free.) You might also want to add a few bells and whistles, however: things like shovels, spoons, coffee scoops, sieves, a flour sifter, some old plastic dishes, small fishnets, shells, twigs, rocks, gardening tools, and some sandbox-sized cars, animals, or people.

Snow play

And now we come to the ultimate Canadian sensory play experience—
playing in the snow! In addition to lugging your child's sand and water
toys out into the backyard, you might want to try some of the following
activities with your toddler.

Winter bubble fun: If your toddler loves blowing bubbles in the summer, he'll have even more fun blowing bubbles when the temperature
goes below zero. It's possible to catch the bubbles on the bubble wand
and watch them freeze.

Ice cube surprise: Place some toys in a milk carton and fill the milk carton with water. Place it outside until it's frozen and then bring it back
inside. Then peel off the carton and place the ice block in a large bowl.
Your toddler will enjoy watching the toys reappear as the ice block melts.

Frozen rainbow: Here's a variation on the previous activity. Instead of
freezing toys in the carton, freeze layer upon layer of water that has
been coloured with food colouring. If you use enough colours, you'll
end up with a rainbow effect. Your toddler will enjoy watching the
rainbow melt before his eyes.

Snow painting: Fill plastic squirt bottles with coloured water. Your toddler will have a great time "painting" the snow.

Other sensory play ideas

The sky is the limit in sensory play opportunities, but here are a few
things you might want to try with your toddler.

Playdough fun: Playing with playdough and other types of modelling materials (including goop) is a terrific form of sensory play. Your
toddler will enjoy using a variety of accessories with his playdough,
including cake-decorating tools (provided the playdough is extra soft),

plastic dishes, a cheese slicer, cookie cutters, a playdough press (you can pick one up at a garage sale or buy one new), an egg slicer, a pizza cutter, plastic knives, Popsicle sticks, a rolling pin (you can make your own using wooden dowelling), and, as we mentioned earlier, a pair of toddler-safe scissors so that he can cut the playdough into pieces.

Cooking: Cooking is the ultimate sensory play experience because it can appeal to all of your child's senses—unless, of course, you make something "yucky" that his taste buds aren't willing to try! Because a toddler's attention span is pretty limited, you'll want to stick to "quick and dirty" recipes like applesauce rather than attempting more involved ones like a soufflé. (Besides, what do you think your odds are of having that soufflé rise just perfectly when you've got a toddler running around your kitchen?!!)

Music

Music is another form of sensory play. It helps your toddler develop his listening skills, promotes the development of auditory memory, stimulates the imagination, and can help him to relax and unwind. So sing with your child. Take your toddler to concerts and other live music events that are geared to very young children. (Concerts for adults are sometimes too long and too loud.) Make some homemade musical instruments. (See Table 4.6 for some basic instructions.) And commit to finding other fun ways to enjoy music with your toddler, like flipping on some tunes with a powerful beat and encouraging your toddler to lead your family "marching band" around the house.

hearing alert

Don't allow your toddler to listen to music with headphones on unless you're monitoring the volume carefully. If he were to crank up the volume too loud, he might end up doing permanent damage to his hearing.

4.6 Homemade Musical Instruments

Type of Instrument	How to Make It
Pots and Pans	Time to organize your own in-house pots-and-pans band! This is the easiest type of homemade instrument—one that doesn't require any work on your part at all. Simply set your toddler loose in the pots-and-pans cupboard. He can bang on your pots with a metal or wooden spoon, bang pot lids together like cymbals, or turn a cookie sheet into a gong.
Shakers	Shakers can be made out of just about anything: containers with lids (e.g., potato chip cans, caramel corn and nut cans, coffee cans, empty dishwasher detergent bottles, or empty pop bottles); plastic Easter eggs that can be taken apart and filled; salt and pepper shakers; tin pie plates; and so on. Simply fill the container with something that will make a really satisfying noise when shaken—marbles, rice, pasta, beans, nuts and bolts, or small rocks, for example, and then glue the lid on tightly.
Washboard	Believe it or not, you can still purchase metal washboards. That's great news because they make terrific musical instruments. All your toddler has to do is rub the washboard with a wooden stick or a metal spoon, and voila—an explosion of sound.
Wooden Blocks	Cut two hand-sized pieces of wood for your toddler to bang together. You can either leave them *au naturel* or attach a small piece of sandpaper to each block so that they make a satisfying swooshing sound. (If you go the sandpaper route, you'll want to supervise their use extra carefully to prevent any skinned knuckles and/or sanded furniture.)
Kazoo	Cover the end of a toilet-paper roll with a piece of tissue paper, holding the tissue paper in place with an elastic band. When your toddler blows against the tissue paper, he'll be rewarded with a kazoo-like sound.
Twanger	What toddler can resist a twanger—a musical instrument that consists of a doorstop attached to a piece of wood? Just one quick word of caution before you set your future pop star loose with his twanger: make sure that the rubber tip at the end of the doorstop is glued on securely to eliminate the risk of choking.

Notes: While it's possible to make your own homemade drums, tambourines, and bells, you'll get better results by purchasing rather than making these items. So invest your creative energies in making some other type of homemade musical instrument.

Steer clear of musical instruments like triangles and cymbals that require more advanced fine motor skills than your toddler is likely to have at this age.

Dramatic Play

As the name implies, dramatic play involves acting out scenes based on real life—like pretending to be you! Dramatic play isn't all fun and games, however. It's also highly educational. It allows toddlers to build their vocabulary, develop both their fine- and large-muscle skills, work on their hand–eye coordination, experiment with people and things, explore and learn to make sense of the world around them, face problems and come up with creative solutions, and express feelings they may not feel comfortable expressing in real life.

Don't assume you have to go broke trying to supply your toddler with all kinds of costumes and props in order to set the stage for dramatic play. A little imagination can take your child a long way. A towel can be magically transformed into a magic carpet or a superhero's cape in the blink of an eye. And, of course, some of the best treasures of all can be found if you dig deep enough into your clothes closet. So dig deep . . .

Of course, you'll want to keep your toddler's safety at the forefront. That means, keeping the strings on costumes short and not allowing your child to wear capes and other dangling types of clothing on playground equipment.

Puppets

Puppets also allow for all kinds of fabulous dramatic play possibilities. You can purchase ready-made hand or finger puppets or—if you're feeling inspired—you and your toddler can make puppets at home. Here are a few ideas to get you started.

Paper bag puppets: Paper bag puppets are, without a doubt, the easiest type of puppet for a toddler to make. You simply decorate a paper lunch bag with crayons or markers, glue on a few construction paper accessories, and voila!—you've got a puppet to play with. The only drawback to paper bag puppets is that they can't withstand a lot of abuse, like being dipped in your toddler's milk or smooshed into a plate of spaghetti, and, what's more, they can rip easily if your toddler is putting a lot of gusto into a puppet performance.

Paper plate puppets: Paper plate puppets are almost as easy to make as paper bag puppets and tend to be a bit more durable. Simply fold a paper plate in half and decorate it. Unfortunately, your toddler may have a bit of difficulty getting your puppet's mouth to open and shut, so you may have to play puppeteer with this type of puppet.

Sock puppets: An old sock can be transformed into a puppet by gluing or sewing on pieces of fabric, felt, wool, vinyl, or paper. (Of course, you'll want to avoid buttons, googly-eyes, and other hard objects for now in case your toddler manages to pull them off and swallow them.) You can either leave the sock loose and floppy so that your toddler can insert his hand all the way to the end of the sock or you can stuff part of the sock with paper or fabric to give the puppet a more stuffed animal-like appearance. Note: if you stuff part of the sock, you'll probably want to mount the puppet on a wooden dowel to make it easier for your toddler to manipulate.

Finger puppets: Cut the fingers off an old pair of gloves and you'll be able to whip up a whole family of finger puppets for your toddler. You can glue on small pieces of fabric, embroider on some eyes using a bit of wool, or draw a face on the puppet using a permanent marker. (Obviously, you'll want to maintain total control over the permanent marker rather than share it with your toddler.)

Papier-mâché puppet faces: Papier-mâché puppets are easier to make than you might think. Simply blow up a balloon and papier-mâché it. (Combine 125 mL [1/2 cup] of all-purpose flour with 500 mL [2 cups] of cold water. Add this mixture to a saucepan containing 500 mL [2 cups] of boiling water. Remove the mixture from the heat, stir in the 3 tbsp of sugar, and allow the mixture to cool. Then dip newspaper strips into the paste, using your thumb and forefinger to squeeze off any extra paste, and apply them to the balloon, leaving a small opening around the knot of the balloon.) Allow the papier-mâché to dry completely (it will take about 12 hours) and then apply another two or three layers. Once those layers have also had a chance to dry, pop the balloon. (Important: Get rid of the popped balloon immediately so that your toddler can't accidentally choke on it.) Then insert a wooden dowel through the opening at the bottom of the balloon and papier-mâché the dowel into place. Once the papier-mâché has dried completely, you and your toddler can paint and decorate the puppet.

Once you've finished making puppets, you may want to make some sort of puppet theatre. The easiest thing to do is to hang a baby gate across the bottom half of a doorframe and cover the gate with a towel. Your toddler can crouch behind the gate and give a puppet show. If you'd like to come up with something more elaborate, you can make a puppet theatre by carving a hole in a large cardboard box or by constructing a puppet theatre out of plywood or particle board.

Excursions and Outings

Starting to develop a case of cabin fever? Why not plan a few outings with your toddler? Not only will the two of you have a lot of fun exploring the neighbourhood, but you'll also be helping your toddler learn about his world. In addition to everyday destinations such as the post office, grocery store, and drugstore, you might want to plan to hit the beach, a nature sanctuary, a children's museum, and/or the train station. If your toddler doesn't get to travel by bus very often, you might want to make that part of the adventure, too.

Active Play

Looking for a reason to make physical activity an important part of your toddler's daily life? Here are a whole bunch. Physical activity builds strength, flexibility, and stamina; reduces the risk of heart disease, diabetes, and obesity; and promotes the development of muscles and bone mass. It also improves the quality of sleep; minimizes aggression, anxiety, and depression; and boosts self-confidence. It can even help to boost creativity and concentration!

Fortunately, there's plenty you can do to encourage your toddler to adopt an active lifestyle. The key is to make active living a part of his daily life from a very early age—which means tapping into his natural love of movement.

- **Flip on some of your favourite tunes and dance with your toddler.** You'll both get a terrific workout and have a lot of fun.
- **Encourage activities and games that give your toddler the chance to work on his balance and coordination skills**—for example, stooping and retrieving toys from the floor while maintaining a standing position, walking while pulling a toy, kicking a ball or rolling it back and forth, and throwing a ball or a beanbag.
- **Play "jack-in-the-box."** Show your toddler how to curl up into a tiny little ball and then spring up like a jack-in-the-box. Not only will he have fun yelling "pop" and trying to surprise you, he'll also be strengthening his legs, improving his balance, and increasing his spatial awareness.
- **Make an indoor obstacle course using pillows, cushions, cardboard boxes, tables, chairs, and other common household objects.** Then, on the next sunny day, put together an outdoor obstacle course instead.
- **Teach your toddler how to play "over and under":** crawl over couches and under tables. Or make a bridge with your body and have him crawl under your body or through your legs. Not only is this great exercise, it's a powerful way to help him to work out the meaning of important spatial concepts.
- **Play "the zoo game."** Pretend to be animals by imitating their movements: be a snake that's slithering across the grass, a kangaroo that loves to hop, or a bird that's flying around the backyard.
- **Attach a large plastic beach ball to an elastic string and hang it from a doorframe.** Since the ball is so lightweight, you won't have to worry about it doing any damage.
- **Play a game of hockey using pool noodles and a beach ball.** You can turn an oversized cardboard box on its side and use that as your goal. (Boy, does this book tell you everything you need to know to raise a Canadian kid or what?!!)

- **Make a beanbag toss game or set up a pint-sized basketball hoop.**
- **Play "kick the can."** It'll give your toddler a bit of kicking practice, and he'll get the satisfaction of listening to the deliciously loud noise a tin can makes as it bounces along the sidewalk.
- **Show your toddler how to do a log roll by sticking his arms above his head and rolling along the grass or down a hill with a gentle slope.** (Remember how much fun you had doing this when you were a kid?)
- **Play a game of "Simon Says."** Your toddler will have fun running and stopping, and will also get a chance to work on his self-regulation skills at the same time as he practices listening to and following directions.
- **Forget fingerpainting; try foot painting instead!** Put a large sheet of mural paper on the sidewalk. Pour non-toxic paint into a large shallow tray. Then have your toddler dance across the page. He'll get some exercise and will end up with a colourful mural to hang on his bedroom wall.
- **"Shadow dance" outside on a sunny day.** Make sure that the sun is behind you and your toddler and then watch how your shadow dances across the grass as you dance.
- **Show your toddler how to make "angels" in the snow by lying on his back and swishing his arms up and down and his feet from side to side.** The motions involved in making a snow angel help to promote good coordination—and provide excellent training for jumping jacks!
- **Remind yourself that toddlers thrive on unstructured play**— running, swimming, climbing, playing in the sandbox, and splashing around in the wading pool—so be sure to provide opportunities for this type of spur-of-the-moment, unscripted fun, too.

One final thought before we wrap up this discussion on toddlers and physical activity. There's a world of difference between telling kids about the benefits of being physically active and showing them that fitness is a priority in your own life. If you're not physically active your-self, your words are likely to lose their impact. You have to be prepared to walk the talk—literally.

Math

Your child may not be ready to learn how to count, but he's already master-ing some key mathematical concepts, like grouping objects and measuring things. Here are some fun ways to build on these important mathematical building blocks.

Grouping and matching objects

- **Have an indoor scavenger hunt.** Give your toddler two different-coloured pails and encourage him to walk around the house col-lecting objects of the same colour (e.g., red things to go into the red pail and yellow things to go in the yellow pail).
- **Encourage your toddler to help you spot objects of various shapes as you walk around the neighbourhood:** square windows, round garbage can lids, triangular hopscotch marks, and so on.
- **When you're folding the laundry, encourage your toddler to help you match up the different colours of socks.** Not only will he be getting important practice with matching objects, he'll be proud that he's able to help with such an important job.
- **When you're unloading groceries, let your toddler help you to separate the items by category:** canned foods versus fresh fruits and vegetables, for example.
- **Collect pebbles or shells at the beach and then sort your treasures according to their texture, shape, or colour.**
- **Play matching games with your child.** Either invest in a card or board game that teaches young children how to match up objects or make your own set of cards.

Measuring games

- **The best place to learn about measuring is in the bathtub,** so make sure your toddler has measuring cups, measuring spoons, and containers of various sizes. (See the material on water play earlier in this chapter.)

- **Show your toddler how to organize toys or blocks so that they range in size from smallest to largest.**
- **Make a cardboard handprint or footprint for your toddler so that he can use it as a tool for measuring common household objects**—a fun alternative to a ruler.

Science

The universe is a living laboratory for your toddler—a fact you've no doubt observed on those days when he seems hell-bent on testing the principles of gravity and every other scientific principle known to human-kind. Here are a few simple ways to encourage your budding Einstein's growing interest in the scientific principles at work in everyday life:

- **Provide him with cause-and-effect toys** (manufactured or homemade) so that he can start learning about the relationships between objects.
- **Give him opportunities to experiment with sound.** He'll be amazed to discover how loud and echoey his voice sounds, for example, if he shouts into a large concrete tunnel. And he'll be intrigued to find out just how different it sounds when you put sand as opposed to rice inside a homemade shaker.
- **Plant a butterfly garden in your backyard so that you'll attract brightly coloured butterflies to your garden all summer long.**
- **Take a trip to the zoo to check out the animals or a walk in a nearby field to look for flowers and bugs.** Or let him stay up really late one night to check out the stars in the sky.
- **Finally, make a point of nurturing your toddler's curiosity by encouraging him to ask questions about the world around him.** If he's not much of a conversationalist yet, help to formulate his questions for him by paying attention to his gestures, theorizing about what he's trying to figure out, and giving him the words to express those ideas.

Reading

One of the greatest gifts a parent can give a child is a love of reading. After all, early exposure to books can help a young child develop an array of skills, including listening, auditory memory, visual memory, and critical thinking.

Here are some other important reasons to read to your toddler:

- **It's fun.** What could be more enjoyable for you or your toddler than snuggling up on the couch to share a favourite book? For years and years I wrapped up the bedtime routine by reading my kids the same story, a book that was rather appropriately called *I Love You, Goodnight*. Nearly three decades later, they still remember vivid details of the story.

- **It provides your toddler with additional exposure to language.** He's in prime language acquisition mode these days, so he'll benefit tremendously from this exposure, particularly if you make a point of engaging in what linguists refer to as "extended discourse" (basically, picking up on the ideas that are being expressed in the book and using them as a launching pad for a conversation with your child about how those ideas relate to his own life).

- **It helps to improve your toddler's attention span.** His interest in the story will encourage him to sit still, focus on the book, and tune out the rest of the world—skills that will serve him well throughout his academic life.

- **It teaches him how reading works**—the fact that a squiggle on a page can stand for something in the real world and that there's a way to learn how to crack the code called reading.

- **It teaches him how books work.** He'll learn the mechanics of reading—in our culture, we read books from front to back and we read the text from left to right—and he'll also discover to his amazement that the same words leap off the page each time the book is opened, regardless of who is reading the story.

- **It helps him to understand how stories work:** the fact that there's a beginning, a middle, and an end.

- **It helps him develop his imagination by giving him lots of things to think about long after the book has been put back on the shelf.** Just think of how often you end up reflecting back on something you read: that happens with toddlers, too.

What you can do to encourage your toddler's love affair with books

Looking for ways to encourage a lifelong love of reading? Here's what the experts recommend:

- **Demonstrate your own love of books.** Let your toddler catch you reading on a regular basis. And seize every opportunity to demonstrate how reading fits into your life. "I make a point of pointing out words that we see when we're in the car, such as the word 'stop' on a stop sign," says Brandy, a 24-year-old mother of two. Rita, a 37-year-old mother of two, has chosen to take a similar approach: "If I'm baking, I show Timothy how I read the recipe. I also show him labels on foods and words on TV. I think if he sees how reading is involved in everything we do on a daily basis, he'll realize how important reading is."

- **Make storytime part of your child's daily routine.** Don't reserve books just for bedtime. Read to your child at other times of the day, like when he's sitting in his high chair, when he's having his bath, or when you're standing in line at the grocery store. It's a powerful way to teach your toddler that reading can happen anywhere, anytime.

- **Rotate your toddler's books so that there's always something new and exciting to read.** A book that's just reappeared after a month-long sabbatical in the basement will feel like a new book to him.

- **Find creative ways to make the book you're reading come alive for your child.** Rather than droning on in a monotone, vary the volume and pitch of your voice to keep your toddler interested.

- **Play listening games.** Change a character's name to see if your child will notice, or pause at various points in the story to ask your toddler questions about the book.

- **Give your toddler a chance to "read" the book back to you (to tell you the story in his own words).** It's great practice for him in understanding how books and stories work and can be a lot of fun for you, too. And don't get upset if your toddler has his heart set on hearing the very same story night after night. Toddlers learn through repetition. Eventually, he'll move on to another book.

- **Don't force your toddler to listen to the entire book if he loses interest halfway.** You want reading to continue to be a positive experience for him—not an exercise in torture! If your toddler has a hard time staying still long enough for you to read him an entire book, try reading to him while he's sitting in the tub. Just make sure that any book you bring to the bathroom won't be any worse for wear if it ends up getting hit with a wave of water: the book is likely to get as much of a bath as your toddler. (See the section that follows with more tips on choosing toddler-friendly books.)

- **Finally, don't feel pressured to load up on educational toys and apps designed to promote language learning.** You're your child's best language acquisition app! It's the give-and-take between parent and child that sparks language learning.

Choosing toddler-friendly books

Here are some important points to keep in mind when you're shopping for books for your toddler:

- **Choose books with sturdy, tear-resistant pages**—and look for ones that are washable and/or wipeable, too.

- **Keep it simple.** Look for picture books featuring bright, eye-catching illustrations, little text, and one major idea per page.

- **Stay relevant.** Toddlers prefer books that accurately reflect their own life experiences, so you'll want to choose books with relatable stories and clear and realistic illustrations or photos that your child will recognize (as opposed to abstract, cartoon-style illustrations).

- **Have fun with language.** Look for books that feature repetitive language or refrains, so that your child can master them and chime in. And take advantage of your toddler's love of rhymes. (Researchers at Oxford University have discovered that children who are exposed to rhymes the most often are quicker to grasp the idea that words are made up of individual sounds—a key building block for reading.)

homegrown words

Don't assume that every book you give your toddler has to be a book you've purchased in a bookstore, picked up at a garage sale, or borrowed from the library. Homemade books, including photo albums, make a wonderful addition to any toddler's library. Here's how to make one out of a ziplock bag.

• Trim some pieces of cardboard or boxboard so that they'll fit snugly inside a series of ziplock bags. (Ideally, you'll want eight or more bags.)

• Decorate the cardboard or boxboard with photos from magazines, copies of family photos, and other eye-catching images that you think your toddler might enjoy.

• Tape the ends of the bags together to form a book. (If you don't intend to make any further revisions to the book, you can tape together the ends of the bags that are open. But if you do intend to update the contents from time to time, you'll want to tape the sealed ends of the bags together instead.)

Note: Choose extra-sturdy ziplock bags (as opposed to one made from flimsier plastics) and supervise your child when he is reading his ziplock-bag book.

Inside the Toy Box:
Your Best Toy Buys for the Toddler Years

Feeling overwhelmed by the sheer number of choices you face each time you set foot in a toy superstore? You're certainly in good company. Many parents find it difficult to choose among the growing number of products competing for their toy-buying dollars. The challenge, of course, is to learn how to sidestep all the gimmicky gizmos that promise to be a source of endless delight to your toddler. (That delight inevitably wears thin around the time the toy packaging hits the recycling bin.) Here are some tips on choosing toys that will entertain and stimulate your toddler—without going broke in the process:

> **garage sale SOS**
>
> Wondering how to clean up the toys that you've purchased second-hand? While good old-fashioned soap and water will get rid of most of the grime, here are some trade secrets from other parents on doing battle with squeaks, stains, and stickers.
>
> - Use petroleum jelly to lubricate moving parts and eliminate squeaks in toys like tricycles.
> - Use nail polish remover to get rid of marker and pen marks on hard plastic toys like balls.
> - Use rubbing alcohol to get rid of glue residue left behind by labels and stickers.

- **Choose toys that are age appropriate (see Table 4.7).** Toys designed for younger children will bore your toddler, while toys designed for older children will cause him massive frustration. That said, be sure to take manufacturers' claims about the age range for a particular toy with a grain of salt. Some of these toy claims appear to have been made by people who've never so much as laid eyes on a toddler!
- **Zero in on toys that are durable and easy to clean.** Otherwise, you'll be making constant trips to the dump and the toy store to get rid of and replace broken toys.
- **Look for toys that are versatile and that can grow with your toddler, like a bucket full of brightly coloured wooden blocks.** The beauty of toys like blocks is that they can be played with in many different ways and there's no "right" or "wrong" way to play with them.
- **Look for toys that will stimulate your toddler's imagination and give him the opportunity to master new skills.**

- **Don't go overboard.** It's not necessary (or advisable) to spend a small fortune on toys for your child. Your child can learn a great deal by playing with ordinary household items such as pots and pans, funnels, basic art supplies, and so on. You can also stretch your toy budget considerably by hitting garage sales or consignment stores (see Chapter 9 for some important safety tips on purchasing items secondhand), joining a toy library, or pooling toy dollars with other families (that way, you can share the costs of big-ticket items like large plastic climbers and play kitchens and then simply rotate these toys from house to house to house).

4.7 Terrific Toys for Toddlers

Arts and crafts supplies	Pegboards (large pegs only)
Balls	Picture dominoes
Blocks	Plastic beads (large, snap-together style)
Board games (cooperative)	Pull toys
Books (including audio books)	Push toys
Building toys	Puzzles (choose two- to four-piece insert
Card games	puzzles for younger toddlers)
Construction toys	Ride-on toys (wide wheelbase for added
Dramatic play materials	stability)
Dump and fill toys	Sand and water toys
Lacing cards (for older toddlers only)	Shape sorters
Magnetic letters and shapes (toddler-sized)	Soft dolls and puppets
Musical instruments	Stacking toys
Nesting cups and blocks	Tents and playhouses
Nylon tunnels for crawling through	Toy telephones

Toy storage smarts

Toy boxes may look attractive and may help to hide the mess momentarily, but they're not your best bet for toy storage. They pose a hazard to toddlers, since toy boxes with heavy lids can bonk heads or crush fingers, while poorly ventilated toy boxes have been known to cause suffocation deaths. As well, the toys tend to get all mixed together, leaving your child with the rather daunting task of having to go digging through the entire toy box in order to find all the pieces of the puzzle he wants to do.

(And, of course, he'll manage to empty the toy box in the process.) Here are some parent-proven alternatives:

- **Keep your child's toys in easy reach**—ideally on low, sturdy shelving units in his bedroom or your family room. That way, he can get them out when he's ready to play and he can start to assume responsibility for putting them away when he's finished with them.

- **Store your child's multi-piece toys in see-through storage containers with lids.** (If you use a non-see-through container, you'll want to cut out a picture of the toy from a catalogue or the original packaging or take a snapshot of the toy so that your toddler will know what's inside the plastic container.) Stackable plastic bins, plastic laundry baskets, plastic dish bins, tote bags, and mesh bags also work well. Hint: To ensure that the plastic containers stack properly, buy a large quantity of the same size and brand at the same time.

- **Use the area under your toddler's crib or bed for storing less frequently used toys.** (If you've still got space left under the bed, use it to stash away some of his too-big clothing, too.)

- **Use clear shipping tape to reinforce the corners of new games and puzzles that come in cardboard boxes.** The boxes will stand up a lot better. When the inevitable happens, however, and the box finally gives up the ghost, simply transfer the puzzle pieces into a ziplock bag. If you're lucky, you'll be able to salvage the picture of the puzzle from the lid of the box. If it's too late for that, simply take a picture of the puzzle the next time your child completes it and then tuck that photo inside the bag along with the puzzle pieces.

- **Get some of your child's least favourite stuffed animals off the floor by dropping them in a hammock,** storing them in shoe racks in the bottom of his closet, or clipping them to a clothesline attached to the ceiling of his bedroom. Obviously, you'll want to keep his absolute favourites within easy cuddling distance.

- **Don't feel you need to keep each and every toy within easy reach at any given time.** It's better to rotate your toddler's toys on a regular basis so that there's always something "new" and exciting for him to play with. If you notice that your toddler seems to have grown bored with a particular toy, pack it away for a few weeks. Chances are he'll be delighted to see it again a few weeks or months from now. If he still seems bored with it at that point, consider setting it aside to give away, swap, or sell. He's clearly outgrown this particular toy.

Toddlers and Screen Time

The Canadian Paediatric Society (CPS) made headlines recently when it recommended a complete ban on screen time for children under the age of two. Its rationale? Spending time in front of a screen is habit-forming and it can interfere with healthy development in toddlers: everything from brain development to language acquisition to being physically active. Add to that the fact that toddlers aren't able to transfer what they learn from the two-dimensional world of screens to the three-dimensional world in which they live and you can see that the disadvantages of screen use very much outweigh the pros.

One of the challenges you will face in guiding your child through the toddler years will be deciding what to do about screen time—your toddler's as well as your own.

Let's tackle your toddler's screen time first because, frankly, that's the easy part. When screen time is introduced (starting at age two), it should be capped at no more than an hour a day because too much screen time means "lost opportunities for teaching and learning," according to the CPS. You should make a point of maintaining screen-free times—ideally during family meals (to encourage healthy interaction) and before bedtime (to avoid the melatonin-suppressing effects of screens and the resulting sleep-related fallout). And you should aim to be active and engaged with your child when he's using screens as opposed to taking a hands-off approach. You'll also want to pay close attention to what kind of content he's consuming—to ensure that it's educational, interactive, and age appropriate.

Of course, it's not just smartphones, tablets, and laptops that are cause for concern. Spending too much time in front of the television can cause problems, too. "High exposure to background TV has been found to negatively affect language use and acquisition, attention, cognitive development and executive function in children under 5 years old. It also reduces the amount and quality of parent-child interaction and distracts from play," notes the CPS. And here's something else you need to know about toddlers and TV: your toddler doesn't have to be actively watching a program to be harmed by the effects of TV. Background noise from a television set can interfere with a toddler's ability to learn.

Here's the thing: young toddlers have a critical need for interaction with parents and other adults in order to foster healthy brain development—something that they're less likely to receive when they (or their parents!) are busy staring at a screen. So one of the most powerful things you can do to support your child's healthy development is to model the healthy use of screens. That means making conscious and deliberate choices about when you want to access your smartphone (as opposed to constantly diving in and out of social media all day long). It also means keeping your smartphone out of sight when you're playing with your child (both to eliminate the temptation to hop on to Facebook and because the mere presence of a smartphone detracts from the quality of human interactions—*even when the smartphone isn't in use*).

It's a lot to think about, I know—and, as a member of the first generation of parents charged with the challenge of raising kids in an era of mobile (and seemingly ubiquitous) screens, you're very much in guinea pig mode. The good news is that you have what it takes to make technology work for—not against—your family. It's all about being mindful about what is and isn't working and on staying focused on what matters most of all: the relationship between you and your child.

CHAPTER 5

What's for Dinner?

"To a child, there is nothing paradoxical in saying: 'I don't like it—I never tried it!'"

—BEE WILSON, *First Bite: Learning How to Eat*

Until you've lived through it, you cannot possibly comprehend the frustration of having each and every meal you so lovingly prepare given the thumbs down by a two-foottall food critic—the same person, I might add, who's been known to eat lint-covered Cheerios from inside the couch! While some toddlers are enthusiastic eaters who eagerly devour anything and everything that's placed in front of them, these happy-go-lucky tots tend to be the exception rather than the rule. In this chapter, we're mainly going to be focusing on the other type of toddler—the not-so-silent majority who are only too happy to give a thumbs down to any new food that dares to show up on the dinner table. We'll start out by talking about the key developmental reasons that explain why feeding a toddler can be such a challenge. Then we'll tackle the fundamentals of toddler nutrition. (The key take-away message? It's not what goes into a toddler's mouth at any single meal that matters; it's what makes it in on a day-to-day or week-to-week basis that counts.) Finally, we'll wrap up the chapter by considering some important health and safety issues (choking, food-borne illness, and food allergies and food intolerances) and by tackling the logistics of dining out with a toddler.

Why Feeding a Toddler Can Be Such a Challenge

Wondering why your toddler has suddenly become such a discriminating diner? There are a number of developmental factors at play.

- **Your toddler's appetite is on the wane.** Because your toddler is no longer growing at the same rapid rate that she was when she was a baby, she no longer needs the same amount of food. While she managed to double or even triple her birthweight during her first year of life, she will gain only a kilogram or two per year during each of the two toddler years. Because she doesn't need as much food to sustain her current rate of growth, it makes sense that she's not as hungry. You're also likely to notice that her appetite varies considerably from one day to the next—that there are days when she barely picks at her food and days when she happily devours almost everything in sight. So rather than obsessing about what goes into her mouth on any given day, try to focus on what she eats from day to day—or maybe even from week to week.

- **Your toddler knows what she wants—and when and how she wants it.** As you've no doubt gathered by now, toddlers are creatures of habit—and their love of the familiar carries over into the world of food. Your toddler may insist on having the same food served the same way on the same plate day after day. You'll quickly discover just how much ritual matters to your toddler if you dare to break any of her non-negotiable culinary "rules"—for example, by allowing her peas to touch her potatoes. Of course, this doesn't mean that your toddler will necessarily hold herself to the same rigid standards of consistency; heck, she reserves the right to change her food preferences every day!

- **Your toddler is able to communicate her food preferences much more clearly than she could when she was younger.** Your toddler no longer has to rely on making disgusted-looking faces or pushing her food out with her tongue to let you know that she's not a fan of the veggie du jour; now she's able to communicate her displeasure with words. While it can be helpful to know exactly where she stands on particular issues, there may be days when you wish she didn't say "Yuck!" quite so emphatically or often.

- **Your toddler is still a rookie when it comes to feeding herself.** It takes time to learn how to coordinate the muscles involved in chewing and swallowing and to figure out how to pick up food with her spoon and then navigate that spoon to her mouth. (Hey, remember how awkward you felt the first time you tried to use a pair of chopsticks?) She may also be highly distracted by the taste, texture, sight, and smell of her food—something that gives a whole new meaning to the concept of leisurely dining!

> "I think if you want your child to enjoy food and not be too picky, you have to allow them to get dirty. Kids are washable, after all."
>
> —MELANIE, 38, MOTHER OF EIGHT

- **Your toddler may be fiercely independent about feeding herself—even if she still lacks the necessary skills.** "My daughter went through a frustrating stage around 12 months of age when she would not let me feed her with a spoon," recalls Christina, a 26-year-old mother of three. "She would only eat foods that she could feed herself—very frustrating because she wasn't able to feed herself baby cereal or yogurt. We had to serve her finger foods and let her feed herself. I ended up offering her cheese, cooked chicken cut into cubes, bread, baked or mashed potatoes, cooked pasta, and any vegetable that could be boiled and then chopped into small pieces." Note: see Table 5.1 for some additional details on how your child's self-feeding skills will evolve during the toddler years.

Bottom line? Your toddler isn't going out of her way to make mealtimes more challenging. She's just busy being a toddler.

---

toddler food quirks

Don't be surprised if your toddler refuses to have anything to do with a broken cookie or bruised banana. The appearance of these foods conflicts with her ideas about what a cracker or banana is supposed to look like. The solution? "Give her a whole cookie and a piece of banana without a bruise," advises Anita, a 38-year-old mother of four. "It's cheaper than therapy!"

No More Food Fights!

You've no doubt heard all sorts of rumours about those infamous parent-toddler face-offs over food. They are, after all, the stuff of which mealtime legends are made: a frustrated parent and an irate toddler glaring at each other over an untouched serving of casserole.

But contrary to popular belief, feeding a toddler doesn't have to be this way—not if you're clear about who does what at the dinner table. It's your job to decide what type of food to serve and when to serve it, and it's your toddler's job to decide whether she wants to eat and, if so, how much she wants to eat. If you stick to these basic rules of engagement, you'll find mealtimes a whole lot less stressful.

That's not to say that your in-house food critic will magically expand her repertoire of foods overnight or that she'll start applauding the moment you place her dinner plate in front of her (not that you would want to turn eating into some kind of high-stakes performance). But if you're like most parents, you'll gradually learn how to work around her many food-related idiosyncrasies—something that will help to dramatically reduce the number of battles over broccoli and Brussels sprouts.

So what does this mean in practical terms?

You want to keep the big picture in mind.

5.1   **Feeding Milestones for Toddlers**

Your 12- to 18-Month-Old . . .

• is fascinated by what other people are eating and may take great delight in trying to feed *you*;

• eats a variety of nutritious foods;

• delights in making her own food choices;

• isn't quite as hungry as she was when she was a baby;

• enjoys eating food with her hands (although she is starting to figure out how to use a spoon);

• has switched to drinking from a sippy cup;

• is capable of telling you when she's had enough to eat and when she wants more.

Your 18- to 24-Month-Old . . .

• enjoys eating food with her hands, but is becoming more skilled at using a spoon and possibly a fork, too;

• enjoys experimenting with different food textures;

• has increasingly distinct food preferences (she likes what she likes and she hates the rest);

• is easily distracted while she's eating.

Your Two- to Three-Year-Old . . .

• delights in feeding herself;

• is becoming more skilled at guiding the spoon to her mouth, but still tends to make a bit of a mess;

• has clear rules and rituals when it comes to foods (e.g., certain types of foods aren't allowed to touch one another);

• may tend to become fixated on one or two favourite foods over an extended period of time—something that's known as a food jag;

• is less prone to choking, although choking is still a major cause for concern;

• tends to dawdle while she's eating.

Your goal is to help your toddler to learn to eat in a way that will help to support her long-term health and happiness. That means ensuring that she grows up being able to recognize and respond to internal cues signalling hunger and fullness as opposed to being swayed by external cues, like the time on the clock or the presence of a mouth-watering plate of cookies or the desire to please (or rebel against) a parent. It also means ensuring that she remains open to trying new foods—something that will help her to acquire a taste for a wide variety (as opposed to a limited repertoire) of foods. It's about talking, teaching, and—above all—role-modelling these kinds of healthy eating behaviours.

One of the most powerful things you can do to encourage the development of these kinds of healthy habits is to make family mealtimes a priority. That's not to say that you need to sit down to dine as a family at every single meal (or even every single day), but it does mean that you want to do so as often as you can. Here's why. For starters, sit-down meals tend to feature both a wider variety of foods and foods that are more nutrient-rich than meals that are eaten on the run. They also provide opportunities for young children to learn important lessons about food and eating. Of course, in order for this learning to occur in a way that works for (and not against) our children, we need to model healthy food choices (gravitating toward fresh as opposed to processed foods) and healthy eating behaviours (ditching the screens when it's time to sit down for a meal and aiming for a relaxed and conflict-free mealtime).

You'll find it easier to keep mealtimes reasonably stress-free if you challenge yourself to take a toddler's eye view of the challenge that is mealtime. That means recognizing the following toddler facts of life . . .

Transitions are tough for toddlers. It's hard to make the switch from playing with your favourite toy to sitting at the dinner table. You can help your toddler to make the switch by allowing for plenty of transition time—giving your toddler the time she needs to wind down from playtime before it's time for dinner, for example, and cueing her to the fact that dinnertime is fast approaching by sticking to some sort of predictable pre-dinnertime routine. Verbal warnings can also be helpful. You can do a countdown, telling your toddler that "It's five minutes until dinnertime" and then "It's two minutes until dinnertime" and then, finally, "It's dinnertime." Although toddlers don't have any concept of time, they quickly learn that the third warning means that it's time for dinner. If you want to do the countdown in a more concrete way, simply tell your toddler, "One more puzzle" before dinner. (Obviously, you'll want to choose an activity with a concrete beginning and end. Otherwise, dinner could be on hold indefinitely while you wait for your toddler to "finish playing" with her toys!)

Toddlers want to eat when they want to eat—and this is a good thing. Get in the habit of feeding your toddler when she's hungry. This will encourage her to tap into her body's natural hunger signals. If she happens to get hungry an hour before dinner is ready, give her a healthy snack and don't fret if she doesn't finish all of her dinner. Note: If you find that your toddler doesn't have much appetite at dinnertime, it may be because she's still full from her afternoon snack. If this continues to be a problem, you might want to try cutting back on the size of the snack in the future or offering it to your toddler a little earlier in the afternoon.

Toddlers don't need as much food as adults. It's unrealistic to expect a toddler to devour adult-sized portions and, if you present her with too much food, she may be so overwhelmed by the amount of food on her plate that she loses her appetite entirely. So think smaller servings: instead of offering her a full piece of toast, start out with a quarter- or a half-piece instead. (She can always ask for more if she's still hungry.) Trust your toddler to eat the right amount of food. She's the best judge of how much food she needs. You'll probably notice that your toddler eats more at some meals than others, and that she may pick at her food one day and then eat everything in sight the next. She's simply adjusting her food intake to match her day-to-day energy needs—a skill that (sadly) many adults have lost along the way.

Toddlers love it when you give them options. Some parents find that toddlers respond particularly well to "buffet-style" meals where they can pick and choose from an assortment of foods on the dinner table. ("My toddlers seem to prefer the simplest meals—meals where they can identify what they're eating and choose what they want," notes Kerri, a

36-year-old mother of six.) You don't have to hire a short-order cook to pull this off, by the way: simply offer your toddler small servings of the various foods you're having for dinner that night. Who cares if she goes a little overboard with a particular food on a particular night as long as everything you're offering her is a suitable choice? As Bee Wilson notes in *First Bite: How We Learn to Eat*, "When your only food preferences are good ones, preferences become unimportant." And even if that food preference seems to stick around for a while (in which case you're dealing with a "food jag"—a temporary fixation with a particular food), try to keep your cool about it. Food jags tend to be relatively short-lived, so it shouldn't be long before she ditches her "orange foods only" diet in favour of a diet featuring a wider variety of food choices.

A toddler's reaction to unfamiliar foods is both developmentally and evolutionarily appropriate. First of all, toddlers are creatures of habit. They gravitate toward the familiar. A food that she's eaten and enjoyed in the past is going to beat a mystery food (even an incredibly delicious mystery food) hands down, simply by virtue of the fact that she's never had any direct experience with that food. And, secondly, being cautious in your food choices makes a lot of sense from an evolutionary standpoint. A small amount of something poisonous might not kill you, but an entire meal of it might. It's therefore much more prudent to nibble at a new food tentatively and wait to see if you keel over (or, better yet, watch your parents eat that same food on multiple occasions before you deign to let it touch your own lips) than it is to down an entire dinner plateful with great gusto. You can work around this temporary wariness (it tends to be less of a problem by the time a child is six or seven) by giving your toddler the opportunity to experiment with new foods at times outside of mealtimes and by letting her touch, smell, lick, and possibly even taste minuscule quantities of the food (as opposed to trying to offer her huge servings right away). You can also increase the likelihood of her wanting to try new foods by giving her the opportunity to see other children (ideally children who are just a little older than she is) eagerly devouring foods that she continues to be skeptical about. Finally, recognize that it can take multiple exposures (sometimes as many as 10 to 20 exposures) to a new food before a toddler actually decides she likes it. So don't assume she hates a particular food: it could be that she simply doesn't like it *yet*.

Toddlers don't understand the concept of "good foods" versus "bad foods." And you want to keep it that way! While you might be tempted to bribe your toddler to eat her vegetables by promising her an exciting dessert, you'll not only be teaching her to value dessert over vegetables, you'll actually be encouraging her to steer clear of veggies. After all, if you have to go to great lengths to convince her to try a sprig of broccoli, there's got to be something wrong with that broccoli—right? This is one of the reasons that dietitians are now encouraging all of us to steer clear of the good foods, bad foods trap—because it really can do a number on our heads over the long-term.

Toddlers are leisurely diners. It takes them a while to pick up their spoons and get down to the business of eating. So remember to allow adequate time for your toddler to eat. That way, she won't have to feel rushed. Besides, there's a lot to be said for focusing on the social aspects of mealtime. Instead of treating meals as a task to be plowed through in record time, recognize them as an opportunity to slow down and connect with other family members—something that enhances both relationships *and* the enjoyment of food.

Serving Toddler-Friendly Meals and Snacks

The amount of food that toddlers need varies tremendously from toddler to toddler. Some are surprisingly hearty eaters, while others eat like birds. Your toddler's age, body size, activity level, growth rate, and mood will determine how much food she actually needs and wants on any given day. Your job is to ensure that she's provided with a variety of foods daily, and her job is to decide what does—and doesn't—make it in her mouth. As long as a toddler is full of energy, continuing to grow at a healthy rate, and eating a variety of healthy foods, you can feel confident that her food intake is adequate—that she's getting enough fuel and nutrients. After all, variety is the spice of life *and* the recipe for a healthy toddler.

When you're planning your toddler's meals and snacks, you'll want to ensure that you're offering her foods from each of the four food groups. See Table 5.1 for some parent-proven advice on serving up toddler-friendly options.

kitchen science

Your toddler isn't trying to drive you crazy by dumping her spaghetti on the floor. She just wants to see if the same laws of physics that apply to toys also apply to food. (And, if truth be told, she's also eager to find out if you'll react the same way when she dumps her spaghetti as you do when she dumps her blocks on the floor!)

The best way to deal with this common—and messy—situation is to play it cool. Calmly remind her that food belongs in the bowl, not on the floor. And if you get the sense that your toddler is performing for an audience—for example, her older brother who finds it gut-splittingly funny to see the spaghetti flung all over the floor—you might want to convey the message to your older child that he who laughs hardest gets to mop up the floor.

Of course, physics experiments involving food don't tend to happen until a toddler gets restless and bored, so you'll also want to learn to spot the warning signs that she's finished eating and ready to give anything in grabbing distance the old heave-ho. At this point, you'll simply want to remove her food and lift her down from her high chair or booster seat.

One other quick tip: It's easier to dump food that's on a plate than food that's on a high chair tray, so you might want to try packing away her dinner plate for now. Just be sure to keep your toddler's high chair tray meticulously clean to prevent it from becoming a breeding ground for bacteria.

Finally, here's something else to think about as you try to trouble-shoot this problem: Is your toddler actually hungry when she arrives at the table? If your child doesn't seem to be particularly hungry at meal-time, you may want to keep tabs on the amount of milk she's drinking and the number of snacks she's consuming over the course of the day.

Fruits and Vegetables   *Four servings per day*

A serving is . . .

- 250 mL (1 cup) leafy raw vegetables or salad
- 1 piece of fruit
- 125 mL (1/2 cup) fresh, frozen or canned vegetable or fruit or 100% juice

Why your toddler needs foods from this food group

Vegetables and fruits are a good source of fibre and an excellent source of vitamin C as well as hundreds of disease-fighting compounds called phytochemicals. Vegetables are also an excellent source of vitamin A, folate, and iron.

Tips on making toddler-wise choices

- Vary your toddler's fruits and veggies. Look for opportunities to encourage your toddler to acquire a taste for dark green and orange veggies because they tend to be particularly nutrient-rich.
- Give veggies star billing. Serve them ahead of other foods so that they become the sole focus of your child's attention. Researchers have discovered that kids eat four times as many vegetables when vegetables are served on their own as opposed to being teamed up with other foods.
- Don't be surprised if your toddler prefers raw veggies to cooked ones. Most vegetables acquire a stronger, more bitter taste when they're cooked—something that turns toddlers (and some adults!) off.
- When you're choosing canned fruits, look for products that are canned in 100% fruit juice or water rather than syrup.
- Limit your toddler's consumption of juice—or avoid it entirely, if you can. (See "The truth about juice" elsewhere in this chapter.)

Grain Products   *Three servings per day*

A serving is . . .

- 1 slice (35 g) bread or 1/2 bagel (45 g)
- 125 mL (1/2 cup) cooked rice, pasta, or couscous
- 1/2 pita (35 g) or 1/2 tortilla (35 g)
- 30 g cold cereal or 175 mL (3/4 cup) hot cereal

Why your toddler needs foods from this food group

Grain products are critical for converting food to energy and for maintaining a healthy nervous system. They're also an excellent source of B vitamins, minerals (especially iron), and fibre (if whole-grain products are served).

Tips on making toddler-wise choices

- Continue to serve your toddler iron-fortified cereals for as long as she'll eat them. Infant cereals are an important source of iron for young toddlers. Tip: You can increase the amount of iron that is absorbed from infant cereal by serving it with foods that are high in vitamin C. You might, for example, want to get in the habit of topping off your child's bowl of cereal with a few sliced strawberries or offering her a glass of orange juice on the side.

continued

- Aim to have 50% of your toddler's grain intake made up of whole grains (brown rice, bulgur, graham flour, oatmeal, whole-grain corn, whole oats, whole rye, whole wheat, wild rice).

Milk and Alternatives   *Two servings per day*

A serving is . . .
- 250 mL (1 cup) milk or fortified soy beverage
- 175 g (3/4 cup) yogurt
- 50 g (1 1/2 oz.) cheese

Why your toddler needs foods from this food group

Milk products are an excellent source of protein, calcium (the mineral responsible for keeping bones healthy and strong), and vitamins D, A, and B12.

Tips on making toddler-wise choices

- Toddlers under the age of two should drink only homogenized milk products (as opposed to lower-fat varieties). (While you eventually want to help your child to acquire a taste for lower-fat foods, a child under the age of two needs access to higher-fat foods to support her growth and development.)
- There's no need to seek out "toddler formula" for your toddler unless you are specifically advised to do so by your child's health care provider.
- If your toddler is lactose intolerant, you will need to look for lactose-reduced milk. If your toddler can't drink milk because of a milk protein allergy, you may need to supplement her diet with calcium and vitamin D. Note:not all dairy-free milk substitutes are fortified with supplemental calcium and vitamin D.
- Avoid serving your toddler more than 625 mL of milk per day. Excess milk consumption is linked to iron deficiency and anemia. It also discourages a toddler from eating other foods.

Meat and Alternatives   *One serving per day*

A serving is . . .
- 75 g (2.5 oz.)/125 mL (1/2 cup) cooked fish, shellfish, poultry or lean meat
- 175 mL (3/4 cup) cooked beans
- 2 eggs
- 30 mL (2 tbsp.) peanut butter

Why your toddler needs foods from this food group

Meat and alternatives are an important source of proteins and B vitamins and minerals (particularly iron). Protein helps to build and repair body tissues, including muscle, bone, and blood, and to manufacture the antibodies needed to fight infection.

Tips on making toddler-wise choices

- All foods made from meat, poultry, fish, dry beans or peas, eggs, nuts, and seeds are considered to be part of this food group.
- Some toddlers reject meat initially because they don't like the chewy texture. In this case, stick to softer meats and alternatives instead: lean ground beef, meatballs, boneless fish, eggs, tofu, baked beans or other legumes, and peanut butter. And, of course, you can also make a piece of meat more tender and moist by stewing

it or cooking it slowly in a covered dish so that it's able to retain its natural juices.

- Get in the habit of trimming visible fat from meats before cooking and removing skin from poultry before you serve it to your child. And if you serve luncheon meats to your child, stick with lower-sodium, lower-fat varieties. And try to find alternatives to frying and deep-frying meat, fish, and poultry, like barbecuing or grilling instead.
- Certain types of fish (mainly the larger predatory fish that survive in the water the longest) are not safe for young children because they contain larger qualities of environmental toxins.

Notes:

- **The number of food servings that a toddler requires varies from toddler to toddler and from day to day.** Younger toddlers don't need as much food as older toddlers. One-year-olds may not even be able to manage to eat the minimum number of servings recommended for each food group. A more active toddler, or a toddler with a higher metabolism and a larger build, will need more food than the mythological "average" toddler. And growth spurts can make any toddler's eating habits unpredictable.

- **Not sure about serving sizes?** A quarter cup is roughly an egg-sized portion of food; a half cup is roughly an ice cream scoop-sized portion of food; and one cup is roughly a baseball-sized portion of food.

- **Aim to serve your child fresh unprocessed foods as often as possible.** You want her to develop a taste for foods in their purest, most natural forms.

- **When your toddler is thirsty in between meals and snacks, offer water.** Drinking water keeps your child hydrated, helps to prevent constipation, and regulates your toddler's energy level (stamina). It doesn't need to be bottled water unless there's a specific concern with your municipal water supply or if you're unsure about the quality of the water from your well.

- **Vitamin and mineral supplements are rarely necessary if a child is eating a variety of foods, is growing well, and is in good health.** If you do decide to give your child a pediatric vitamin supplement, make sure that you keep the vitamin jar well out of her reach. Ingesting large quantities of vitamins can be harmful to a toddler.

Snack attack

Because toddlers have small stomachs and relatively high energy needs, most need to eat every two to three hours. Consequently, you'll probably want to schedule snacks for midway between breakfast and lunch, midway between lunch and dinner, and at bedtime.

Snacks served to toddlers should be "mini-meals" that are packed with important nutrients. While the sky is the limit when it comes to drumming up ideas for toddler-friendly snacks, it never hurts to have a few ideas on hand for those days when your creativity is running on empty. Here are a few toddler favourites:

- Whole-grain crackers and cheese
- Muffins (low sugar, high fibre, with fruit or grated vegetables blended in)
- Fresh fruit salad (apple, banana, cantaloupe, pear, watermelon, for example)
- Fresh veggie salad (shredded carrots, chopped lettuce, chopped cucumber, for example)
- Vegetable plate (with yogurt dip)
- Plain yogurt flavoured with fruit puree or mashed fruit
- Eggs (hard-boiled and cut into wedges)
- Hummus or bean dip on a wedge of pita or a mini-pita
- Tortilla with bean dip and sliced or diced green peppers
- Rice cakes with melted cheese
- Fruit and yogurt smoothie
- Cottage cheese with fruit
- Tofu with peaches
- Sandwich fingers with fruit or veggie tidbits
- Oatmeal cookies and apple slices
- Homemade granola bars with lots of fruit and fibre
- Ready-to-eat cereal (low-sugar, whole-grain varieties)

- Tiny portions of anything else you might serve at mealtime, including breakfast

Of course, there's an art to making snacks work for (and not against) your toddler. What you don't want to do is treat snacks as a licence to graze incessantly—or to chow down on foods that wouldn't make the cut at mealtime. You want your toddler to learn that we eat and then we move on and do something else (as opposed to munching away all day). She'll find it easier to understand this if you get in the habit of serving her snacks in her high chair or booster seat and if you resist the temptation to offer food whenever she's bored, unhappy, or restless. You also want her to think of snacks as little more than sized-down portions of the very same types of foods that show up at the table at mealtime (as compared to a standalone category of "treat foods" that are low in nutrients; laced with sugar, salt, and fat; and only paraded out at snack time).

In other words, your goal is to lay down the groundwork for a lifetime of healthy eating by teaching your toddler how to be a savvy snacker right from day one.

The truth about juice

Contrary to popular belief, juice is not a necessity in a toddler's diet. It's definitely a frill—and a frill that you may want to hold off on introducing to your toddler's diet for as long as possible. While fruit juices are an excellent source of vitamin C and may also provide a variety of other important nutrients including folate, potassium, vitamin A, and calcium, they shouldn't become a mainstay of your toddler's diet. Here's why:

- **Fruit juices can take the edge off your toddler's appetite at meal- time and make it less likely that she'll consume a variety of other types of foods.**
- **Unlike the fruit that it was originally derived from,** fruit juice doesn't contain fibre, so she's less likely to feel full after drinking (as opposed to eating) a serving of fruit.

- **Too much fruit juice can interfere with the absorption of nutrients and add empty calories to your child's diet.** It can also trigger toddler's diarrhea—a condition that is caused by excessive quantities of sorbitol and fructose in the digestive tract—and make diarrhea triggered by garden-variety gastrointestinal infections a whole lot worse. Note: prune, apple, pear, peach, and cherry juice tend to be particularly high in sorbitol—a non-digestible type of sugar—which is why they tend to have an especially powerful laxative effect.

If you decide to include juice in your toddler's diet, you'll want to . . .
- limit the number of servings of juice to one or fewer per day ("I allow juice only at breakfast," says Stephanie, a 29-year-old mother of one. "I've always had that as a rule for my daughter so that she won't have the chance to develop a juice habit.");
- offer your child unsweetened juice as opposed to fruit "drinks," "punches," or "cocktails"—beverages that tend to contain large quantities of sugar, but little in the way of real juice;
- avoid unpasteurized apple cider and fruit juices—a potential source of deadly E. coli bacteria;
- dilute your child's juice with water (e.g., one part juice to two or three parts water) to reduce its sweetness and reduce your toddler's overall juice intake. Note: you'll still need to keep tabs on the number of servings. Diluted juice still contains juice, after all . . .

You'll also want to resist the temptation to use a sippy cup or bottle of juice as a pacifier to soothe your toddler. This is an unhealthy habit to get into for both dietary and dental reasons. You don't want her to get into the habit of turning to food to soothe herself whenever she's feeling anxious or bored. And having her teeth constantly bathed in juice (or any beverage other than plain water) can cause tooth decay.

Equipment 101

Wondering what feeding-related paraphernalia is essential and what's a complete waste of money? Here's what you need to know.

High chairs and booster seats: Chances are you've been using a high chair (either a free-standing high chair or a high chair that either straps to the seat of a kitchen chair or hangs off the kitchen table) to feed your baby since she started indulging in the messier types of solid foods. While you'll probably get a few more months out of that high chair, you can expect your toddler to make the switch to a booster seat some-time between age one-and-a-half and two. When you're shopping for a booster seat, look for a model that's easy to clean and that features a secure strapping system to keep the booster seat in place. Note: if your child is sitting in a booster seat, make sure that there is somewhere for her feet to rest—either on the chair itself or on a stool that you've pro-vided for this purpose.

Bibs: When you're shopping for a bib, think functionality, not fashion. Yes, those frilly little white bibs are adorable, but they don't provide much in the way of protection when a really serious stain comes calling. In those types of situations, you're far better off going with the heavy-duty artillery: a hard plastic bib with a scoop in the bottom. "I found that these were the best type of bib," says Lise, a 35-year-old mother of two. "They really cut down on the mess and you can wash them in the sink along with your dishes." Other moms swear by children's paint smocks (not only are they waterproof, but they also cover a lot of square inches of toddler!) or T-shirt style bibs made out of stretchable fabric (they're easy to get over your toddler's head). Avoid plastic bibs with pockets, says Lori, a 31-year-old mother of five: "Food gets down inside the pocket and it can be a real pain to get out." Ditto for bibs with strings. The strings get gummy and stained, and they tend to get tangled up in your toddler's hair. Velcro and snap fasteners are a much better bet for toddlers.

Toddler-sized cutlery sets: Toddler-sized cutlery sets can be very use-ful provided that you don't expect much from the fork. Toddler-sized forks—plastic forks in particular—tend to have ultra-dull prongs that render them completely useless. So you'll probably be further ahead if you simply purchase a couple of toddler-sized spoons and give the forks a pass until your toddler is ready to move on to regular cutlery. If you want to introduce all three pieces of cutlery right from day one, however, you'll want to purchase spoons with short handles, blunt tips, and rounded bowls; forks with short handles and short, blunt tines; and knives that are small with rounded tips.

Bowls: Look for toddler-sized dishes made of non-breakable materials. Plates with curved sides and small cups with broad bases generally work best. While bowls with suction cups on the bottom have been on the market since the beginning of time, I've yet to encounter a parent who thinks they're actually worth purchasing. "Those suction bowls don't stick to anything—and I tried about five different brands," insists Cindy, a 27-year-old mother of two. Jennifer, a 33-year-old mother of one, agrees: "Suction-cup bowls that stick on the high chair tray are a complete waste of money. Sarah would pull at them until they came loose, sending their contents flying across the room."

> "People are amazed that I don't 'teach' my children how to use utensils. I provide them with a fork and a spoon, and they learn how to use them by watching the rest of us and imitating us. I'll occasionally tell them 'other way' if they have the spoon upside down and can't figure out why the food keeps falling down on the tray, but most of the time I just give them their fork and spoon and let them go to it."
>
> —KERRI, 36, MOTHER OF SIX

Cups: Not everyone is a fan of sippy cups. Some speech-language therapists blame them for promoting tongue thrust and improper oral positioning, both of which can contribute to speech and feeding difficulties. (Children with developmental delays are particularly at risk.) They recommend instead that you consider transitioning your child to a regular cup (you'll need to hold on to it) or a cup with a straw (ditto, unless you are able to track down a sippy cup that features a built-in straw).

If you do decide to go with a sippy cup (and frankly most parents will at least some of the time), you'll want to choose one that is easy for both you and your toddler to manage (for example, a cup that features a screw-on or snap-on lid design that is easy for you to get on and off, but isn't for your toddler, and one that allows the right amount of liquid to flow—neither too much nor too little). The best way to figure out if you've found "the right cup" for a particular toddler is to give her the chance to test-drive it. (Your child should not be biting on the spout, and her lips should be firmly closed around the spout so that no liquid leaks out of the corners of her mouth while she's trying to drink.) Note: Even after you've zeroed in on the world's most wonderful sippy cup, you'll want to make a point of continuing to offer your child drinks from a regular cup, so that she can work on mastering this all-important skill, too. Drinking from a regular cup will gradually become your child's norm, with the sippy cup only popping up for use on days when you're dining out or otherwise on the move.

from bottle to cup

While there's no great rush to wean your baby from the breast, most doctors recommend that bottle-fed babies make the switch to a cup around their first birthday (while breastfeeding may, of course, continue well beyond that time). Toddlers who drink from bottles can develop an overdependence on liquids (which may discourage them from acquiring a taste for a wide variety of foods, which, in turn, limits their access to the full range of nutrients contained in those foods) and, if they're in the habit of sipping from a bottle all day long, they may also develop tooth decay (unless, of course, the bottle only contains water). To help your toddler make the switch from a bottle to a cup, start by introducing a two-handled sippy cup (ideally one with a weighted bottom that will tend to right itself if she accidentally knocks it over). Then make it a rule that she has to sit in the high chair or booster seat rather than wander around and play while she's drinking from a bottle. This (plus offering her the choice of water in a bottle versus milk in a cup) will help to reduce the bottle's appeal. (Ideally, you want the bottle to disappear completely by the time your child is 15 months of age.)

Food Safety Issues

It's important to pay attention to three important food safety issues while you're raising a toddler: choking, food-borne illness, and food allergies and intolerances.

Choking

Choking is one of the leading causes of death among children under five years of age. It can happen if toddlers are eating too quickly; not chewing their food properly; laughing, crying, or running around with food in their mouths; or eating chunks of food that are too large for them to handle.

Toddlers are at particular risk of choking because they have sharp teeth at the front of the mouth that allow them to bite off chunks of food, but do not yet have all the back teeth that are responsible for the grinding and crushing of food.

Here are some important tips on preventing a choking tragedy:

- **Supervise your toddler closely while she's eating.** If she starts to choke, you'll want to be able to react quickly. (Note: you'll find some step-by-step instructions on coping with a choking emergency in Chapter 9.)
- **Assess your toddler's chewing and swallowing abilities and make food choices on that basis.** Some children are more prone to choking than others.
- **Steer clear of foods that are known to pose a choking hazard for toddlers:** gum, hard candy, nuts and seeds, popcorn, and raisins. And offer wieners only if they've been sliced lengthwise in quarters, grapes if they've been sliced in half lengthwise, and hard fruits and vegetables (for example, baby carrots) if they've been grated or chopped into small pieces.
- **When you're serving peanut butter to a toddler, make sure that you spread it thinly.** Otherwise, the food may become stuck in her throat when she tries to swallow.
- **Don't allow your toddler to eat with single-use disposable plastic forks.** It's too easy for her to bite off and swallow the prongs.

(Note: durable plastic utensils that are designed to be used by toddlers don't pose the same risk.)

- **Insist that your toddler sit in an upright position while she's eating.** Don't allow her to eat anything while she's laughing, crying, running around, or lying down.
- **Don't feed your toddler while she's in the car.** Sudden starts and stops can cause a child to choke, and if your toddler starts choking while you're on a busy highway, you may not be able to pull over quickly enough to deal with it.
- **Know what to do in the event of a choking emergency.** Sign up for a first-aid course that includes training in cardiopulmonary resuscitation (CPR).

Food-borne illness

Food-borne illness (a.k.a. food poisoning) can result in stomach pain, diarrhea, or vomiting, and in rare cases, can lead to serious or even life-threatening complications like kidney failure, blood infection, and even paralysis. Because toddlers are more susceptible to food-borne illnesses than older children, you'll want to take extra care when you're preparing your toddler's foods. Here are some important points to keep in mind:

- Wash your hands thoroughly in hot, soapy water both before and after handling food.
- Steer clear of unpasteurized milk and fruit juices. The risk of food poisoning is greater with these types of products because they haven't been through the germ-killing pasteurization process.
- Rinse fruits and vegetables thoroughly under tap water before serving them to your toddler.
- Refrigerate or freeze meat and poultry after purchase. And when it's time to thaw meat or poultry, thaw it in the refrigerator rather than at room temperature.
- Ensure that raw meat and poultry is kept away from other foods and that all surfaces that come into contact with raw meat and poultry are decontaminated after use.

- Cook meat and poultry thoroughly. Ground meat and rolled roasts should be cooked until the meat is brown and the juices are clear, and poultry should be cooked until there is no pink left near the bone. Hot dogs and luncheon meats should be heated thoroughly. Avoid serving sushi and other raw fish to a toddler.
- Serve cooked foods promptly and make sure that any leftovers are placed in the refrigerator as soon as possible. And when you reheat leftovers, ensure that foods are reheated all the way through.
- Finally, don't allow your toddler to eat products that contain raw eggs (e.g., uncooked cookie dough). And make sure that she steers clear of other foods that are at risk of being contaminated with harmful bacteria: raw milk and raw milk cheeses (such as queso fresco); soft cheeses (such as feta, Brie, Camembert, Roquefort); bean sprouts; and alfalfa sprouts.

Food allergies and intolerances

While people tend to use the terms "food allergy" and "food intolerance" interchangeably, they actually refer to two entirely different types of reactions to food. Here's what you need to know about each.

The term "food allergy" is used to describe an immune system reaction (an allergic reaction) that is triggered by eating a particular food or food additive. Symptoms of anaphylactic shock (a life-threatening emergency) that are likely to appear immediately after ingesting a particular food include hives, swelling, vomiting, and difficulty breathing. Eczema may be a sign of a less severe food allergy (although most children with eczema don't, in fact, have food allergies).

If your toddler is diagnosed with a food allergy, you'll need to take steps to avoid the offending food. This may be relatively easy when you're cooking meals from scratch at home, but it can be a lot more challenging when you're buying packaged foods or eating out. You'll probably want to ask your doctor or public health nutritionist for a list of ingredients that could cause problems for your toddler: for example, not every product that contains wheat identifies it as such in the list of ingredients, with wheat sometimes being identified as gluten.

It is important to have food allergies diagnosed accurately so that appropriate nutrition and allergy management plans can be created for your child. This is particularly important for a child with multiple allergies. Children who are at risk of anaphylaxis should carry an epinephrine kit so that they can receive injections immediately, in the event of a reaction, which should be treated as a life-threatening emergency.

Children under the age of five are more susceptible to food allergies than older children. This is because their digestive systems are not yet mature. Common trigger foods include cow's milk, nuts, eggs, peanut butter, fish, and shellfish. While children tend to outgrow allergies to certain foods, including milk, wheat, and egg, other allergies—including nut and fish allergies—tend to be permanent.

So that's the lowdown on food allergies. Now let's talk about food intolerances. A food intolerance is an adverse reaction to food that does not involve the immune system. If your toddler experiences such symptoms as bloating, loose stools, and gas after eating a particular food, she may have a food intolerance—difficulty tolerating a particular food or food additive like artificial flavour or colour. Because it's easy to mistake some of the symptoms of a food intolerance with those of a food allergy, it's important to have food intolerances properly diagnosed in order to rule out the possibility of a food allergy.

Lactose intolerance is a common example of a food intolerance (although one that tends to be more of a problem for older children and adults). A person with lactose intolerance lacks an enzyme needed to digest milk sugar. When she eats milk products, symptoms such as gas, bloating, and abdominal pain may occur. It's not unusual for a toddler to develop a temporary case of lactose intolerance following a bout of stomach flu or diarrhea. This is because, in the aftermath of such an illness, lactase (the food enzyme that aids in the digestion of lactose) may be in short supply. You can generally reintroduce lactose once your child begins to feel a little better.

pica eater . . .

Some toddlers develop a strange craving for non-edible substances such as dirt, paint, string, cloth, or hair. This condition—which is known as pica—is most common in children between the ages of 18 months and two years. Contrary to what nutritionists used to believe, it's not triggered by any clearly identifiable nutritional deficiency.

Pica generally only lasts for a couple months, but until your toddler outgrows it, you'll have to monitor her closely to make sure she's not dining on driveway dirt or other potentially harmful substances. If the pica persists, seek medical advice. Pica may be an indication of an underlying neurodevelopmental issue.

Whining and Dining

Dining out with a toddler doesn't have to be a recipe for disaster—not if you know how to avoid some of the most common pitfalls. Here's some from-the-trenches advice from parents who have taken their toddlers to restaurants and lived to tell.

- **Choose the restaurant with care.** You'll have plenty of time to hit the five-star restaurants after your kids are grown. For now, stick to spots that are 100 percent kid-friendly. According to Tanya, a 30-year-old mother of two, that means a restaurant with high chairs, booster seats, a good kids' menu, crayons and colouring books, and plenty of background noise! ("Noise is good because it's not so noticeable if your toddler ends up making a lot of noise," she explains.) A special menu for kids is helpful, since there's no point spending $20 on an entrée for your toddler if he's likely to manage to eat only a mouthful or two. (Hint: If the restaurant you've chosen doesn't have a kids' menu, see if there's a suitable side dish or appetizer that could serve as your toddler's dinner— or if the restaurant is willing to serve your toddler a half-portion. Or plan to share a few bites of your own dinner rather than ordering a separate dinner for your toddler.)

- **Call ahead.** If you have a large family or a toddler with a very limited attention span, call the restaurant ahead of time to see if they'll start preparing your order before you arrive, suggests Kerri, a 36-year-old mother of six. There's nothing worse than having your toddler run out of patience before your food has even hit the table.

- **Plan to hit the restaurant early.** Not only will you beat the crowds, you'll also ensure that your toddler's dinner arrives before her blood sugar has a chance to hit rock bottom, triggering a major meltdown. "Plan to get to the restaurant at least half an hour before your toddler's regular mealtime, just in case it's busy and you have to wait," suggests Sue, a 35-year-old mother of three.

- **Ask for a booth in a less crowded part of the restaurant so that you'll have more room for your toddler and her paraphernalia and won't feel quite as self-conscious about disturbing other diners.** It's hard to enjoy your meal if every childless patron in the restaurant is glaring at your toddler.

- **Let your server know that you're operating on "kid time."** You may not have the luxury of waiting 20 minutes to place your order or for your bill to arrive! Anita, a 38-year-old mother of four, makes a point of asking for the bill as soon as she and her family have ordered. "That way, we can leave the restaurant quickly if we have to."

- **When you order your toddler's dinner, hand the waitress your toddler's sippy cup and ask that the kitchen staff pour the drink directly into her cup.** It'll save you the inevitable mess associated with trying to transfer liquids from cup to cup at the dinner table.

- **Be sure to tote along everything you could possibly need:** a bib for your child (disposable restaurant bibs are almost always useless); baby wipes and/or a slightly soapy wet washcloth that you've sealed in a ziplock bag (dry napkins won't do much when it comes time to clean up a spaghetti-smeared toddler); a fully stocked diaper bag (make sure you've got at least one spare outfit); a sippy cup (a more toddler-friendly alternative to breakable restaurant glasses); a non-breakable plate (to prevent a similar crisis if your toddler decides to use the restaurant plate as a

Frisbee); a small snack (to take the edge off your toddler's hunger in case her dinner is a little slow in showing up); and a couple of toys and activities to keep your toddler entertained until her dinner arrives (for example, an assortment of small toys that you reserve for such occasions). "Take playdough with you," adds Alyson, a 33-year-old mother of two. "It can be a real lifesaver."

- **Don't be afraid to get up and walk around while you're waiting for your dinner to arrive.** "We order and then we take our toddler for a walk around the restaurant," says Kerri, a 36-year-old mother of six. "We go to the bathroom and wash our hands, and sometimes we'll even go out into the parking lot for a bit of a break."

---

tomato cheeks

Do your toddler's cheeks tend to become sore or stained after she indulges in lasagna or other tomato-based foods? Apply a thin layer of petroleum jelly to her cheeks before she dives into her meal (literally!). Not only will it make the after-dinner wipe-down a whole lot easier for the two of you, it will also help to protect her ultra-sensitive skin from the acidic bite of the tomato sauce.

CHAPTER 6

Will the Sandman Ever Come?

"People still have to parent their children at night; it isn't a daytime-only thing. You can't close the door and forget you have kids."

—STEPHANIE, 30, MOTHER OF THREE

S leep deprivation may be a rite of passage for most parents, but that doesn't necessarily mean that we all see eye to eye on the subject of nighttime parenting. Some parents feel the need to be every bit as responsive to their toddler's needs in the middle of the night as they are during the day, while others make the case that it's up to parents to help their toddlers develop healthy sleep habits, even if that means practicing a little after-hours "tough love."

In this chapter, we're going to tackle an issue that may be causing you to lose sleep—both figuratively and literally! We'll start out by looking at what's normal and what's not when it comes to toddler sleep patterns—and the important role that you, as the parent of a toddler, have to play in helping your child to acquire healthy sleep habits. Then we'll talk about naps, bedtime routines, and a range of different sleep challenges—everything from night waking to nightmares to night terrors.

Along the way, we'll cover the always controversial topic of sleep training—and why you might want to reframe this whole issue as "sleep learning" instead.

Toddlers and Sleep

As with anything else toddler-related, there's no such thing as a "one size fits all" sleep pattern. Some toddlers need more sleep in a 24-hour period than the 10 to 13 hours recommended by the Canadian Paediatric Society (or the 11 to 14 hours recommended by the American Academy of Sleep Medicine), while others seem to be able to survive on less. And just as the amount of food your toddler consumes can vary from day to day, the amount and quality of sleep that he clocks can vary from night to night and from naptime to naptime. All that said, most toddlers fall into a sleep pattern that looks at least vaguely similar to this: they head to bed between 7:00 p.m. and 9:00 p.m., they start their day between 6:30 a.m. and 8:00 a.m., and they nap once or twice during the day.

Your challenge, as the parent of a toddler, is to figure out how much sleep your toddler needs right now; and what you can do to help him clock that amount of shut-eye in a way that supports both his long-term development and the health of your relationship.

You can assume that your toddler is getting adequate sleep if . . .

- he wakes up on his own in the morning and after naptime;
- he tends to be in a good mood (as opposed to being irritable) when he wakes up;
- he doesn't have any trouble staying awake in the car or the stroller when you're running short errands around town;
- he's alert and in good spirits in the late afternoon;
- he's calm and happy rather than grumpy and overtired when bedtime rolls around.

whose sleep needs?

Your toddler's need for sleep may be less than your own need for a break from the round-the-clock demands of parenting. While you may need your toddler to take a nap or head for bed early in the evening so that you can enjoy a brief time out, he may not necessarily need that much sleep. As Penelope Leach notes in her book *Babyhood*, "Sleep is . . . a simple biological necessity and, like food, human beings will take it, in varying amounts which are adequate for them, if they are left to 'help themselves.'" Now if only you could convince your toddler to hit the "sleep buffet" a little more often!

To Nap or Not to Nap?

If you rely on your child's naps to catch up on your sleep or to attend to other responsibilities, I've got some bad news for you. Your child's nap is on the endangered species list. At some point between her first and second birthdays (typically at around age 18 months), she'll go from taking two naps a day to one; and at some point the following year, she'll give up that nap, too.

You're not the only one who benefits from your toddler's naps, by the way.

Your toddler benefits, too.

A well-timed nap can help your toddler to function at and feel her best by . . .

- providing her with an opportunity to catch up on any sleep she might have missed out on the night before;
- boosting her mood;
- increasing her attention span and giving her brain the opportunity to mentally file away all the cool things she's been learning over the course of the day;
- helping her to feel comfortably sleepy rather than overtired when bedtime rolls around;

- giving her a bit of a break from you—something that can result in wonderfully happy parent-child reunions after naptime.

But, like all good things, naptime must come to an end. At some point, your toddler will no longer need that nap. So how do you go about deciding when that time has come? By paying attention to your toddler's behaviour, that's how. Specifically, you'll want to note . . .

- **Her mood:** Whether she's in a good mood from dawn to dusk or whether her mood tends to nosedive as the day progresses;
- **Her energy level:** Whether she has enough get-up-and-go to get her through the day or whether she starts to fade after lunch;
- **Her ability to function:** Whether she is able to sustain her usual level of coordination and to stick with challenging tasks through-out the course of the day or whether she starts to lose it (literally) because she's overtired;
- **What kind of difference having a nap makes:** Whether her nighttime sleep is better or worse on days when she takes a nap (is she well rested, overtired, or undertired?).

Here's something else that you need to know: many toddlers go through a difficult period when they get ready to give up one of their naps. They find themselves caught up in a napping no man's land: they sort of do (and sort of don't) still need that nap. If this seems to be what's happening with your toddler, you may find it works well to move her afternoon nap up a little (if she's struggling to adjust to the loss of her morning nap); to schedule quiet time instead of naptime; and to exper-iment with an every-other-day naptime schedule for your toddler (as opposed to trying to get her to go cold turkey when it comes to weaning herself off that final nap).

But don't get fixated on some rigid naptime elimination schedule. Focus instead on how your child is acting and feeling. If you find that your child starts getting up really early in the morning (or is impossible to get up in the morning), that she's grumpy all day long, and that she's not sleeping well at night, she may not be ready to ditch a particular nap quite yet. In this case, simply hit the pause button and remind yourself that the two of you can try again in a couple of weeks or months.

naptime versus nighttime

Here's further proof that you can get too much of a good thing— that "good thing" being your toddler's naps. Research has shown that younger toddlers (ages 11 to 13 months) develop stronger communication and problem-solving skills when they log a greater proportion of their sleep at nighttime versus naptime. The researchers' conclusion? Naps matter, but nighttime sleep matters more, at least when it comes to acquiring these important skills.

Avoiding Bedtime Battles

Bedtime battles are a common problem for parents of toddlers. Studies have shown that approximately 50 percent of children between the ages of one and two resist their parents' efforts to usher them off to bed (something the sleep gurus rather euphemistically refer to as "bedtime refusal"). Unfortunately, these battles get played out at the very time of day when you and your toddler are both running low on energy and patience. So what's an exhausted—and frustrated—parent to do? Why, pull out the ultimate parenting ace card, of course: your toddler's love of routine.

Bedtime routines

We've already talked about how much toddlers thrive on routine—and how freaked out they can be by even the most minute deviation from that routine. (Just try reading your toddler her bedtime story *before* rather than *after* her bath and you'll find out first-hand what I'm talking about! Her searing side-eye glance will tell you in no uncertain terms that you're doing it all wrong.) Anyway, given that toddlers are such creatures of habit, it only makes sense to put that love of routine to work for you at bedtime. Here are a few tips:

- **Come up with a standard bedtime wind-down routine that will signal to your toddler that bedtime is approaching.** Toddlers are so excited about the world around them that they need time to make the transition between playtime and sleep time. You should aim for a gradual wind-down that consists of some sort of predictable series of events—perhaps a snack followed by tooth-brushing, a quiet bath, soothing music, a story, and a quick cuddle. (Tip: You'll want to skip the screen time. Screens don't help kids to wind down: they cause kids to rev up!) Don't feel obligated to devote hours of your evening to carrying out this bedtime routine, by the way; sleep experts have found that a half-hour wind-down will do the trick for most toddlers.

- **When you're trying to decide what sort of snack to serve your toddler at bedtime, zero in on something light that includes both protein and carbohydrates.** The carbohydrates will help to make him sleepy, and the protein will keep him from feeling hungry in the middle of the night. Don't go overboard with the size of the bedtime snack, however, or his digestive system may kick into overdrive, preventing him from getting the shut-eye that he (and you!) so desperately need.

- **If your toddler finds bathtime stimulating rather than soothing, switch it to another time of day.** The last thing you want to end up with at bedtime is a toddler who's wide awake and ready for another hour or two of play! On the other hand, don't be too quick to dismiss the sleep-inducing properties of a nice warm bath. Our bodies are primed to feel extra sleepy about 90 minutes after we step out of the tub. (The post-bath drop in body temperature cues the sandman to show up.)

- **Try to work as many choices as possible into your toddler's bedtime routine.** This will help to elicit her cooperation. While you won't want to flirt with disaster by giving her the choice of whether or not to go to bed, you're probably perfectly okay with letting her decide what toys she'd like to take in the tub, what pyjamas she'd like to wear to bed, and what bedtime stories she'd like you to read to her while you enjoy your pre-bedtime cuddle.

- **Create a sleep-friendly environment for your toddler.** Opt for more subdued light in the evening and try to reduce your household's noise and activity. Ensure that her bedroom is quiet, dark, cool (but not cold), and as distraction-free as possible (which means that she has a few favourite toys at hands, but not her entire toy collection). And while you're doing a comfort check, don't forget to check her pyjamas. It will be hard for her to settle down to sleep if she's being bothered by an irritating tag.

- **Choose a bedtime that works for your toddler.** Don't be afraid to move her bedtime up by a half-hour or so if she's showing signs of being sleepy. If she's yawning, rubbing her eyes or ears, playing with her hair, sucking her thumb, acting bored, or seems a bit clumsier than usual, she may need sleep. Note: It's best to respond to these early warning signals of tiredness rather than allow your toddler to become overtired. If you wait too long before trying to put her to bed, she may end up getting her second wind—which can make it really tough to get her to wind down for the evening. You'll also want to start teaching her to recognize these signs of tiredness for herself; that way, as she gets older, she'll be able to train her body to succumb to sleep as soon as the sandman comes calling (as opposed to stubbornly refusing to heed that call). Some of the signs of overtiredness you'll want to watch for (and ultimately teach your child about) include getting a sudden burst of energy at the very time when you think she should be running on empty; acting "wired," especially if such behaviour is totally out of character for your child at other times of the day; and becoming uncooperative and argumentative or whiny and clingy (a sign that she simply can't cope with the lack of sleep any longer). Of course, if you find that your toddler is having a great deal of difficulty settling down for the night, it could also be because she isn't tired quite yet, in which case you might want to try putting her to bed an hour later and/or to think about eliminating one or both of her naps.

- **Give your toddler the opportunity to learn how to get herself to sleep.** If you rock her to sleep or lie down beside her until she dozes off, she is likely to awaken in a panic in the middle of the night when she realizes that you're no longer right there. Your goal is to allow her to fall asleep in circumstances that she can easily recreate on her own when she wakes in the night: feeling warm and cozy, tucked into her own bed by herself. Note: If you're already in the habit of rocking your toddler to sleep or lying down with her while she's getting to sleep, you'll want to help her to develop other strategies for soothing herself to sleep. Toddlers who aren't able to fall asleep on their own are more prone to night waking than other toddlers because they need to rely on help from a parent in order to fall back asleep.

sleep science

Daylight plays a powerful role in resetting your toddler's circadian rhythms (the body's sleep-wake clock). Exposing your toddler to daylight (as opposed to artificial light) early in the day will cue her body to start feeling sleepy 12 to 13 hours later, when bedtime rolls around. Other things you can do to take advantage of the biological superpower that is your child's circadian rhythm include ensuring that she gets enough physical activity, sticking to regular nap times and bedtimes, and feeding your child at predictable times of day.

- **Accept the fact that your toddler may need a period of quiet play before she's able to settle down for the night.** You may hear her babbling to herself or quietly playing with her toys for a half-hour or even longer. Instead of sweating the fact that she didn't go to sleep right away, applaud the fact that she's mastering the art of getting herself to sleep—a skill that will reap tremendous dividends for her and for you. If your toddler seems panicked at the thought of being away from you (bedtime is, after all, the longest period of separation from you in your toddler's entire day), promise her that you'll come back if she needs you, and then make a point of responding to her right away when she calls. (Note: You may find yourself making a lot of treks to her room at first, but, over time, she'll feel less of a need to test your willingness to deliver on your promise. Or at least that's the theory!) You can also let her know that you'll be back to check on her in a few minutes' time and then again before you go to bed— something that may make it easier for her to go to sleep without you in the room.

Comfort objects

No chapter on toddlers and sleep would be complete without a mention of comfort objects (the term child development experts use to describe teddy bears, blankets, and other "lovies" that, along with mom or dad, may provide an anchor of security for a toddler). Of course, not all experts use the exact same terminology here; others prefer the term "transitional object" or "security object." But whatever you call them, we're all talking about the same thing: inanimate objects to which a toddler forms an exceptionally strong attachment and from which he derives a powerful sense of comfort.

While most parents recognize that bonding with a comfort object is a sign of healthy emotional development, they may worry that their child's dependence on a teddy bear or other object may discourage him from becoming more independent. Actually, quite the opposite is true. Allowing your toddler to turn to his comfort object for reassurance whenever he needs it actually encourages great independence. After all, it's a whole lot easier to go to sleep by yourself if you've got your best friend (a.k.a. "Bunny") tucked under your arm.

Just one quick word of warning with regard to comfort objects. If your toddler needs a special stuffed animal or blanket in order to get to sleep at night, you may want to limit its treks outside your home. After all, if your child becomes distraught waiting for his special blanket to make it through the washer and dryer every now and again, imagine how much worse it would be if that blanket were to be lost forever. Christy has decided that the stakes are simply too high: her toddler's special blanket can never leave the house for any reason! "My son needs to have his blue blanket put over him in a particular way before he'll go to sleep," the 38-year-old mother of two explains. "There have been many nights when we've had to turn the house upside down looking for this blanket. At least I always know it's in the house, however, since we don't allow him to take it anywhere. That would be too risky; we might lose it!"

"Sarah has a bunny that was given to her when she was a newborn. He's almost furless now (he wears a sweater), but I can't even imagine what would happen if he were lost. There has been the occasional night where he's been forgotten at daycare, the dentist, or at a friend's house. Bunny has even been transported by courier on occasion. Oh, the tears we've had about Bunny!"

—JENNIFER, 33, MOTHER OF ONE

By the way, you needn't worry that your toddler will want to take his prized bunny off to university with him or insist that it accompany him down the aisle on his wedding day. The vast majority of children outgrow their dependence on comfort objects before they start school. So don't feel a need to take matters into your own hands by following the advice of well-meaning but misguided relatives who recommend that you "accidentally" drop Bunny over Niagara Falls or otherwise "lose" your child's comfort objects. That's a pretty harsh way to sever a relationship with a much-loved childhood companion. (Just think of how you'd feel if someone suggested this strategy to help you break your attachment to your phone!)

Night Waking

While you may feel like the only parent on your street who's up in the middle of the night tending to the needs of a toddler, you're actually in pretty good company. Approximately 47 percent of toddlers wake in the night at least some of the time and require help from a parent in getting back to sleep.

Misery may love company, but it doesn't necessarily make it easy to cope with the fallout of chronic sleep deprivation, which can include everything from feeling irritable to finding it difficult to think clearly to being zapped of your usual energy and drive. It's not your imagination: sleep deprivation takes its toll on your brain, body, and emotions. While you're helping your toddler to develop the types of sleep habits that will ultimately serve him (and you) well, you'll want to come up with creative strategies for catching up on your sleep. That might mean trading "night shifts" with your partner or asking a friend to take your toddler for a couple of hours so that you can squeeze in a much-needed nap. You'll also find it easier to cope with your toddler's less-than-stellar sleep habits if you remind yourself that sleeping well is a skill that he's trying to master (but hasn't quite managed to master yet) and that there may be some very good reasons to explain his repeated night waking (even if those reasons aren't fully clear to you quite yet). Let's talk about that next . . .

> "My son has been a reluctant sleeper for as long as I can remember. We decided to keep him in our bed so that we could all get some sleep. I don't personally agree with the Ferber method [a rather rigid method of 'sleep training'], so we've stuck with co-sleeping instead. Since my son won't be in our room forever, so what if we end up having him sleep with us for a couple of years? It's just that: a couple of years."
>
> —JULIE, 30, MOTHER OF ONE

The causes of night waking

There are almost as many reasons for night waking as there are night-waking toddlers (which means that there are a *whole lot* of reasons). Here's a quick run-through of some of the most common reasons for night waking—information that can help you to zero in on what's causing your toddler to wake in the night and what you can do to help him to deal with the underlying problem.

Physical discomfort: The physical discomfort associated with such medical conditions as ear infections, allergies, pinworms, urinary tract infections, colds, and fevers can cause a toddler who was previously sleeping through the night to start waking in the night again. The solution to this particular problem is obvious: deal with the underlying health issue and then help your toddler to get back on track with his sleep habits (well, at least until the next health-related curveball comes his way). And, of course, if you're dealing with the physical fall-out from a developmental issue like teething, you'll want to focus on providing comfort while you and your toddler wait for the teething-related sleep disruptions to subside.

Environmental factors: If your toddler wets his bed or becomes uncomfortably hot or cold while he's sleeping, he's more likely to wake up in the middle of the night. Since toddlers are notorious for kicking off the covers midway through the night, you'll want to make sure your toddler gets tucked into bed in suitably warm pyjamas (ones that will keep him warm and cozy, even in the absence of a blanket).

Developmental issues: It's not unusual for a toddler to experience difficulty sleeping when he's just achieved a new developmental milestone like walking. He may be so excited about mastering this new skill that he finds it difficult to wind down at the end of the day, or he may be feeling frustrated if he's unable to immediately achieve a related skill—like climbing! (Who can even think about sleep when you're *this close* to achieving a major breakthrough?) Another developmental issue that can wreak havoc on his—and your—ability to sleep is separation anxiety. If your toddler can't bear being away from you for even 15 seconds during the daytime, he's bound to find it difficult to get through an entire night without you. What your toddler needs, in order to deal with this almost universal rite of passage, is patience and reassurance from you. Not only is this in his best interest, it's in your best interest, too. (Trying to force him to become independent before he's ready is a strategy that tends to backfire; rather than magically morphing into a fiercely independent toddler, he is more likely to become even clingier and even more fearful about being separated from you.)

Emotional issues: A toddler's sleep patterns can be thrown off track by a stressful event like a move to a new house, the birth of a new baby, or a recent hospital stay. The more sensitive your toddler, the more likely he is to have his sleep patterns disrupted by this sort of event.

Sleep problems: If your child has not yet learned how to soothe himself back to sleep if he awakens in the night, he's likely to call for you. He's also likely to call out in the night if he suffers from nightmares or night terrors. (We'll be talking more about these two sleep problems later in this chapter.)

Of course, it's one thing to understand what's causing your toddler to get up in the night, and quite another to know what to do about the situation. After all, it's pretty hard to come up with all kinds of creative solutions when you're suffering from chronic sleep deprivation yourself. Here are a few tips on dealing with this challenging situation.

- **Begin to eliminate nighttime feedings, if you haven't already.** If your toddler is still waking in the night to eat or drink, it's time to start weaning him of the habit. Most healthy toddlers should be able to obtain the nutrition they need via daytime meals and snacks. If you're still bottle-feeding, cut the feeding size back by an ounce a day, start offering water only in the middle of the night, or offer a sippy cup rather than a bottle. If you're breast-feeding, try to cut back on the duration of feedings. Until you've eliminated the nighttime feeding issue, it will be really difficult to deal with the related sleep problem.
- **Give your toddler a chance to settle himself if he wakes up in the night.** If he's tossing and turning and muttering in his sleep, he

may still be half-asleep and—if left undisturbed—may actually manage to get back to sleep on his own. Rushing to his room and picking him up may only add to your nighttime woes: instead of having a half-awake toddler, you'll have a wide-awake toddler on your hands. Of course, if he's really upset (as opposed to just making snuffling noises or talking in his sleep), you'll want to check in on him to try to identify and deal with the underlying need. (The need won't magically disappear on its own, just because it's 3 a.m.!)

• **Remind yourself that sleeping through the night is a skill that needs to be learned.** Expecting your toddler to master this skill overnight will lead to endless frustration for you and for him—and can be damaging to your relationship. "Most adults I know don't sleep through the night, so I decided it was unreasonable of me to expect my children to sleep through," says Joan, a 35-year-old mother of five. "Besides, I remember what it was like when I was a child: how scary it was to wake up in the dark alone, hungry, thirsty, needing to pee, whatever, and I decided that just as an infant awakes with a need, a toddler likely does, too. Just because I don't fully understand what that need is doesn't make it any less important."

• **Don't feel pressured to try a sleep training method that flies in the face of your basic parenting beliefs.** If, for example, you feel quite strongly that it's important to be as responsive as possible to a toddler by day, the "cry it out" method of sleep training may feel very uncomfortable to you. "When my oldest was 18 months, we tried a modified crying-it-out method that consisted of responding after two minutes—the longest period of time she had ever cried without being responded to in her life," recalls Joan, a 35-year-old mother of five. "It worked in just three nights, but it felt wrong, like I was abandoning her and teaching her that she couldn't rely on my being there when she needed me. I decided against taking that approach with my other children." Maria had a similar experience with sleep training: "Ferber didn't work for us," the 32-year-old mother of two explains. "I would just end up sitting outside Talia's door crying while she sat on the other side of the door crying!"

- **When you're considering various options for dealing with your toddler's sleep difficulties,** focus on helping your toddler to develop healthy sleep habits over the long-term as opposed to gravitating toward a quick-fix solution that attempts to eliminate challenging sleep behaviours (like crying in the night) right away. Is it actually possible to teach a child how to sleep through the night without any crying at all? Sure, you may end up with one of those kids who hardly ever cries about anything—and who spontaneously starts sleeping through the night at an early age. But, in most cases, there will be at least a few tears as your child tries to master this new skill (learning how to get to sleep and to get herself back to sleep when she wakes in the night). There don't have to be a lot of tears, and those tears may be shed while you're offering comfort and support, but setting yourself a standard of no tears at all may be setting the bar pretty high for yourself as a parent, to say nothing of robbing your toddler of the opportunity to work on her sleep and self-soothing skills.

- **Don't feel pressured to solve your toddler's sleep problem on your own.** Give her the opportunity to help, too! Talk with her about what's going on and then look for ways to start solving the sleep problem together. You may have to test-drive a couple of solutions before you stumble upon the right one, but tackling this problem together will teach your toddler that it's okay to turn to other people for help in solving a problem—a powerful life lesson. And, what's more, you'll probably find that your toddler is a whole lot more willing to stick with a solution that she had some say in as opposed to one that you simply imposed on her. Hey, it's something to think about . . .

- **Resist the temptation to offer your toddler a sticker or other similar reward to try to bribe her into sleeping through the night.** Sure, the sticker might encourage compliance, but this kind of system of rewards can also exact a considerable price. Your child might feel pressured to "achieve" that sticker night after night, even on nights when she would have benefitted from a little added help or reassurance from you. (Nightmares happen, after all.) There's also a big-picture consideration—one that relates back to our earlier discussions about toddler development and toddler discipline: you want to encourage your child to rely on internal—or intrinsic—rewards as opposed to external—or extrinsic rewards. Not only are internal rewards more motivating: they help to support, and not undermine, her emerging sense of self.

early to bed . . .

Some toddlers have a tendency to get up at the crack of dawn—sometimes even earlier than that! If you've got an early riser in your house, you might try to buy yourself a bit more sleep by pulling down the blind in her room so that it stays dark a little longer, encouraging her to crawl into bed with you for an early-morning snuggle, and/or adjusting your own sleep schedule so that it more closely corresponds with hers. Dealing with an early riser won't feel like such a big deal if you've already clocked adequate zzzzs before your tiny human alarm clock alerts you that it's time to start the day.

- **Remind yourself that this too shall pass—eventually.** "We tried all kinds of things to get Talia to stay in her room when she woke in the night," recalls Maria, a 32-year-old mother of two. "We tried playing a radio, we tried running a fan for background noise, we moved her from a crib to a double mattress on the floor, we put on two layers of pyjamas rather than one so that she'd be warmer at night, we gave her a sippy cup of water in her room in case she was waking up because she was thirsty, we gave her a toy flashlight, we stopped letting her drink water at bedtime in case she was waking in order to empty her bladder. We even tried changing the settings on the thermostat so the furnace wouldn't kick in so frequently, in case that was what was waking her up! In the end, I think she just started sleeping through the night on her own."

From Crib to Bed

As attached to your toddler may be to his crib, at some point he's going to outgrow it—and odds are that day will be arriving sooner rather than later. While 90 to 94 percent of toddlers under the age of 17 months are still sleeping in a crib, only 38 percent of two- to three-year-olds are. Here are some tips that will help you to decide when and how to help your toddler make the shift from crib to bed.

- **Be on the lookout for signs that your toddler may be physically ready to make the move from a crib to a bed**—a move that most toddlers make around the time of their second birthday. Ideally, you will want to make the switch before your toddler gets too tall for his crib. (The crib's side rails should be at the level of your toddler's nipples—something that typically occurs when a toddler is roughly 90 centimetres [35 inches] in height.) If your toddler is a climber and you think it's just a matter of time before he figures out how to hoist himself over the railing or he's toilet trained and starting to want to use the toilet at nighttime, too, you may want to seize the moment and make the move sooner rather than later.
- **Consider where your toddler is at in terms of development.** Let your knowledge of your child guide you in making this decision. Shifting a toddler from crib to bed too soon might force her to cope with freedom she might not be ready for quite yet. Some toddlers feel an overwhelming urge to test the limits of what they are and aren't allowed to get away with under the new rules of the bedtime game! "My son started to climb out of his crib

at about 20 months of age, so we moved him to a toddler bed," recalls Christy, a 38-year-old mother of two. "This just opened a new can of worms. For about three months, he would not stay in his bed. I'd sit in the hallway at the top of the stairs and keep putting him back to bed. I thought it would never end."

- **Ask yourself if this it the best overall timing.** You don't want to boot your toddler out of his crib the same week that you move to a new house or introduce a new sibling. Doing so would simply be making an already tough situation that much tougher for your toddler! Instead, try to pick a time in his life that's relatively stress-free so that he won't have to focus on any other changes while he's busy getting used to sleeping in a new bed. This advice makes sense to Julie, a 30-year-old mother of one. "We're expecting another baby in the summer and have decided to buy another bed for Brandon and put it beside our bed, making a giant bed," she explains. "We didn't want to kick him out of our bed when the baby arrived, possibly causing jealousy. We're going to get him some special sheets and make a big deal out of him having his own bed, but we're still going to keep his bed next to ours until he's ready to move into his own room."

- **Keep safety in mind as you prepare to make the switch.** Steer clear of bunk beds (which aren't considered a safe option for young children) and make sure you choose a safe location for your toddler's new bed (away from windows, heating units, drapery and blind cords, and other hazards). Also, consider using a bed rail to reduce the number of middle-of-the-night tumbles and hold off on giving your toddler a pillow until she's at least 18 months of age (at which point you should look for one that's toddler-sized and firm rather than soft in design).

- **Don't rush to take down the crib.** "We moved Talia from her crib to her bed at 22 months," recalls Maria, a 32-year-old mother of two. "The bed was in her room for about three weeks while she was still sleeping in her crib. At night, we would read in the bed and then put her to sleep in the crib. One night, we asked her if she wanted to sleep in the bed or in the crib, and she said 'bed.' There was no pressure for her to stay in the bed. If she had wanted to go back into the crib, we would have let her."

- **And if you've been co-sleeping all along (in other words, sharing your bed with your toddler)?** You'll probably find that the transition goes more smoothly if you break it down into a series of steps—from "toddler sleeping with parent" to "toddler sleeping in the same room as the parent" to "toddler sleeping in her own room with a parent in the room" to "toddler going solo." You might also measure progress in terms of the percentage of time that your toddler spends co-sleeping versus sleeping on her own: e.g., full-time co-sleeper, part-time co-sleeper, occasional visitor, solo sleeper. This definitely isn't a quick fix or cold turkey proposition. Trust me on this one!

Nightmares, Night Terrors, Sleepwalking, and Sleep Apnea

Now that we've covered most of the garden-variety sleep problems, it's time to zero in on a few of the more exotic types of sleep problems: night terrors, sleepwalking, and sleep apnea.

Nightmares and night terrors

While some parents use the terms "night terrors" and "nightmares" interchangeably, they're actually two entirely different things.

Nightmares (which are less common in toddlers than in older children) tend to occur during the *last* one-third of the night (in the predawn hours, in other words). They happen during a period of light sleep (dream sleep). When a toddler is having a nightmare, he may be crying and screaming, but he can be easily woken up. He may even wake up on his own. All that may be required to get him back to sleep is a cuddle and a bit of reassurance that what happened in his dream wasn't real (admittedly, a difficult concept for a toddler who is still trying to make sense of his fears—see sidebar which follows).

Night terrors, on the other hand, occur during the *first* one-third of the night (within a couple of hours of a child going to bed). They happen when a child is moving from a deep stage of sleep to a lighter stage of sleep. A toddler who is experiencing night terrors may let out a blood-curdling scream and then sit bolt upright in bed with his heart pounding, his body dripping with sweat, and his eyes wide open in a zombielike state. He is completely unaware of his surroundings and—despite the fact that the episode may last as long as half an hour—he will have no memory of it in the morning. It's extremely difficult to wake a toddler who is experiencing night terrors—nor would you want to: waking your child will only serve to prolong the episode. One thing you will want to do, however, is to stay with your child to prevent him from accidentally injuring himself. Night terrors are more common in boys than in girls and they are more likely to occur when a child is stressed and/or sleep deprived. They can occur during both naptime and nighttime sleep.

irrational fears

It's not usual for a toddler to suddenly develop a series of irrational fears that cause her a great deal of distress, like fear of the proverbial monster in the closet. Here's what you can do to help her to cope with her fears:

- Understand that this is a normal stage of toddler development. Toddlers tend to find anything new frightening (hence their deep skepticism of any new food) and they have highly vivid imaginations. Add to that the fact that they have difficulty distinguishing between fantasy and reality and a greater ability than ever before to remember past episodes in which they were frightened, and you can see why fears tend to be so common.
- Don't nag or belittle your child for being afraid or dismiss or laugh at her fears. No matter how bizarre or far-fetched they may seem to you, those fears are very real to your child. "At one point, my husband was in the habit of tossing his bath towel up on the corner of the bathroom door so that it could dry after bathtime," recalls Annie, a 44-year-old mother of one. "This scared our son. He thought it was a monster when he got up to use the bathroom."

- Look for storybooks that deal with whatever type of issue your child happens to be struggling with, whether it's a fear of the dark, a fear of getting lost, or something else entirely. If you can't find a book because your child's fear is a little off the wall—one of my children was deathly afraid of toilet plungers and one of my nieces has an equally deep-rooted fear of pine cones!—you may have to make up a suitable story for your child. You can also encourage your child to work through her fears through art or dramatic play.
- Limit your child's exposure to scary TV shows or movies that other people in the household may be watching. And try to avoid passing along any of your own fears to your toddler. (Your toddler isn't the only one who needs to work hard at being brave.)
- Teach her how to take a slow, deep breath when she's afraid: this will help her to manage the physical manifestations of fear. And remind her that it's okay to turn to you for support. She doesn't have to tackle her fears on her own.

Sleepwalking

While sleepwalking can be a problem at any age, it tends to be particularly common in children ages three through seven years. It is also more likely to occur when a child is sleep deprived. And there's a strong genetic link. Children whose parents were sleepwalkers when they were younger are, in fact, ten times as likely as other children to end up being sleepwalkers.

During an episode of sleepwalking, a child may get out of bed, wander around aimlessly and/or do something odd or irrational (like mistaking a closet for a bathroom), and talk incoherently.

You don't need to wake your child up when she's sleepwalking. Just gently lead her to the bathroom and/or back to bed.

Because sleepwalkers are totally oblivious to danger, you'll want to take steps to keep your toddler safe, should she wake up and start wandering around in the night. You might want to tie a bell to her bedroom door (to alert you to the fact that she's gotten out of bed) and you might want to consider purchasing a door alarm for your front door or activating the door chime system on your security system (to alert you if the front door is opened).

Be sure to mention your child's episodes of sleepwalking to your child's doctor. Sleepwalking is sometimes associated with sleep apnea. (See section which follows.) It is also common in children who experience night terrors.

> "Sarah is a sleepwalker. As near as we can tell, she's getting up to go to the bathroom, but because she's still asleep, she just wanders aimlessly. We keep an ear open and try to grab her and direct her to the right room before an accident happens."
>
> —JENNIFER, 33, MOTHER OF ONE

Sleep apnea

Sleep apnea affects one to three percent of all children, but is most common in preschoolers because this is the age at which the tonsils and adenoids are particularly large in proportion to the airway. It is most likely to occur in children who are obese, who have head and neck abnormalities, or who have exceptionally large tonsils and adenoids.

You should flag your toddler's breathing problems for his doctor if your toddler snores loudly most nights; snores and gasps so loudly in his sleep that he sometimes wakes himself up; is a restless sleeper; sleeps in unusual positions; sweats heavily at night; exhibits behavioural problems during the day (because the symptoms of obstructive sleep apnea, a breathing disorder, can mimic the symptoms of Attention Deficit Hyperactivity Disorder, a disorder that is characterized by impulsivity, high energy, and/or difficulties in paying attention); is difficult to wake in the morning and is either sleepy or irritable when he gets up; and/or has a nasal tone to his voice and breathes through his mouth during the day.

CHAPTER 7

The Maintenance Manual

"Clutter and mess show us that life is being lived."

—ANNE LAMOTT, *Bird by Bird*

Many thousands of years of human evolution have yet to produce anything even vaguely resembling a self-cleaning toddler. Consequently, as a parent of one of these invariably sticky creatures, you can expect to spend a fair bit of your time in cleanup mode. Fortunately, a little soap and water is generally all that's required to remove the latest layer of grime and goo. Thank goodness Mother Nature at least had the foresight to make toddlers fully washable!

In this chapter, we're going to talk about what's involved in keeping a toddler clean from head to toe: bathtime, dental care, hair care, dressing your toddler, and, of course, one of the most controversial issues that you'll have to contend with during the toddler years—toilet training.

Bathtime Basics

It's hard to find a toddler who's ambivalent about bathtime. Most have pretty strong opinions either way. Some toddlers have so much fun during bathtime that they insist on staying in the tub until the water is ice-cold, seemingly oblivious to the fact that their teeth are chattering, while other toddlers are as petrified of water as the Wicked Witch of the West is in *The Wizard of Oz*. (Remember what happened to her when she got wet? She melted!)

---

tub trick

If your toddler hates the feel of cold shampoo on his head, warm up the shampoo a little. Simply float the shampoo bottle in the bathtub for a couple of minutes to get rid of the chill. Take the same approach with the lotion that you slather on his skin after bathtime: float it in the tub for a minute or two before you apply it to his skin.

It's pretty easy to get along with a toddler who positively lives for bathtime—who hops down from the dinner table and sprints to the bathroom because he's so eager to get on with the show. It's a whole lot trickier to deal with a toddler who makes it painfully clear that he doesn't want anything to do with the bathtub—not today, not tomorrow, *not ever*. Here are some tips on helping such a toddler to overcome his fear and/or loathing of all things bathtime:

- **Try to figure out what's fuelling your toddler's bathtub refusal.** Is he actually afraid of the tub or does he simply consider bathtime to be the least interesting part of his day? Once you've identified the root cause of the problem, you can put your parenting skills to good use and start brainstorming some creative solutions.
- **If your toddler appears to be genuinely afraid of the bathtub—** this despite the fact that a fear of water hasn't been a problem for him in the past—try to figure out what may have happened to cause him to suddenly become so fearful. Perhaps he got soap in his eyes, slipped in the tub, or swallowed a mouthful of water the last time he had a bath—experiences that could (understandably) have dampened his enthusiasm for bathtime. Of course, it's also possible that he's developed some strange sort of bathtub-related

fear. While a fear of going down the drain is fairly common, toddlers can come up with all kinds of mysterious fears that may not make any sense at all to you, but that are perfectly logical to them. (My three-year-old developed a huge phobia about black plastic shower heads. Go figure.)

- **If you are able to zero in on the problem, try to come up with an appropriate solution:** e.g., putting a non-slip bath mat in the bottom of the bathtub so that the tub isn't quite so slippery, getting in the tub with your toddler to help him feel more secure, putting a small space heater in the bathroom so that the room doesn't feel quite so chilly when he's wet, or making a deal with your toddler that you'll lift him out of the bath *before* you pull the plug.

- **Load up on some really fun bath toys:** pails, boats, ducks, water wheels, baby dolls that "wet," beach toys (hey, it's a great way to get year-round mileage out of these despite the Canadian climate!), vinyl books, measuring cups, squeeze bottles, plastic containers of various shapes and sizes, sponges (cut into shapes if you're particularly ambitious and/or having a Pinterest moment), and puppet-style washcloths. Note: for additional inspiration in the bath toy department, check out the list of water toys in Chapter 4.

body talk

Don't be surprised if you notice your toddler playing with his penis in the bathtub. Toddlers are naturally curious about anything and everything in their world, including their genitals. Some toddlers fondle their genitals for comfort and others hold their genitals as a way to stop themselves from urinating.

While you're best to ignore his behaviour while he's still quite young, as your toddler gets older you'll want to start talking to him about privacy issues, e.g., "There are some things we do in public and some things we do in private." Obviously, you'll want to choose your words carefully so that you don't inadvertently shame your toddler. You don't want him to feel that what he is doing is bad. It's not. It's perfectly natural.

- **Find other creative ways to make bathtime fun for your toddler, like making hair sculptures while his hair is full of shampoo** (hold up a mirror so that your toddler can admire his wacky 'do' for himself), washing him with animal-shaped or crayon-shaped soap, or treating him to a bubble bath. Note: bubble baths should be an occasional treat because they can be tough on a toddler's tender skin and have been linked to recurrent urinary tract infections in girls.

ear care

Don't worry about trying to clean out the orangey waxy buildup inside your toddler's ears. This waxy buildup helps to waterproof his ears and keep them free of infection. While it's okay to wipe his outer ear with a washcloth to chase away all the day-to-day grime, resist the temptation to start poking around inside his ear with a Q-tip—something that could damage his eardrum.

If, however, your toddler seems to have a lot of excess earwax, you'll want to point out the problem to his doctor. A clogged ear canal can lead to temporary hearing loss, which can interfere with language acquisition in toddlers. Your toddler's doctor can assess the situation through a quick and painless exam and resolve the issue on the spot, if necessary. (In most cases, earwax doesn't cause a problem.)

Hair washing 101

If there's one thing that toddlers hate, it's having their hair washed, whether it's due to the feel of the bubbles on their head or their fear of having soap and water end up in their eyes.

Unfortunately, those all-too-frequent spaghetti-sauce scalp massages make hair washing *de rigueur*. Here are some tips on making the process a whole lot less stressful for you and your toddler.

- Provide your toddler with a snorkelling mask, a set of swim goggles, or a shampoo visor. All three products will help to keep the soap out of his eyes.

- Sit him in the bathtub and wet his hair using a washcloth or (if he'll let you!) a squirt bottle or child-sized watering can.
- Wash his hair with shampoo, making sure to keep the bubbles away from his eyes.
- Rinse his hair thoroughly by either leaning him back in the tub with your hand under his neck while you rinse the shampoo out of his hair or rinsing his hair while he sits in the tub (tilt his head back slightly and hold a face cloth over his eyes while you pour water down the back of his head).

Toddlers and Dental Care

Wondering when you should schedule your toddler's first visit to the dentist? The Canadian Dental Association recommends scheduling that first visit within six months of the eruption of the first tooth (see Table 7.1) or by baby's first birthday (whichever comes first). That way, your baby's first visit to the dentist is likely to involve little more than a quick glance at his teeth—a low-key way to ease him into the routine of dental checkups.

Chances are you're already in the habit of brushing your toddler's teeth. If you're not, you should be: The Canadian Dental Association recommends that parents start brushing their children's teeth as soon as they erupt through the gum. If your child's doctor or dentist believes that your child is at low risk of developing dental decay, you can get away with brushing your child's teeth with water only. If your child is at high risk of developing dental decay, your child's doctor or dentist will recommend using a rice grain–sized amount of fluoride toothpaste on a soft-bristled toddler-sized toothbrush. You should make a point of brushing your toddler's teeth at least twice a day for two minutes at a time, ideally after the first and last meals of the day (to help minimize tooth decay). You'll also want to begin to teach your toddler to spit out rather than swallow the toothpaste. Swallowing too much toothpaste and/or eating toothpaste right out of the tube—as some children like to do—can cause a condition called fluorosis, which can result in white spots forming on your child's teeth. (See the section that follows for more about fluorosis.)

7.1	Tooth Eruption	
Teeth	**Location**	**When They Come In**
Central incisors (lower)	Front of mouth on lower jaw	6 to 10 months of age
Lateral incisors (lower)	Directly beside central incisors on lower jaw	7 to 16 months
Central incisors (upper)	Front of mouth on upper jaw	7 to 12 months
Lateral incisors (upper)	Directly beside central incisors on upper jaw	9 to 13 months
First molars (lower)	Second-last tooth at the back of the mouth on either side of the lower jaw	12 to 18 months
First molars (upper)	Second-last tooth at the back of the mouth on either side of the upper jaw	13 to 19 months
Canines (cuspids, upper)	Between the lateral incisors and the molars on the upper jaw	16 to 22 months
Canines (cuspids, lower)	Between the lateral incisors and the molars on the lower jaw	16 to 23 months
Second molars (lower)	Very back of the mouth on the lower jaw	20 to 31 months
Second molars (upper)	Very back of the mouth on the upper jaw	25 to 33 months

Source: Canadian Dental Association

Here are some other important points to keep in mind when you're brushing your child's teeth:

- **If your toddler has a tendency to want to wriggle away while you're trying to brush his teeth, try standing behind him and leaning his head back against your stomach.** Not only will this position make it more difficult for him to run away, it'll also feel more natural to you because it's similar to the position that you use when you're brushing your own teeth.

- **Give your child a flashlight and ask him to aim the light beam in his mouth while you're brushing his teeth.** Not only will it give him something to do other than trying to wrestle the toothbrush away from you, it'll make it easier for you to see what you're doing.

- **If your toddler insists on brushing his own teeth, make a point of taking turns.** It's great to encourage his toothbrushing skills, but you don't want him to go solo until he's at least six. "What works for us is using two toothbrushes: one for him and one for me," says Julie, a 30-year-old mother of one. Hint: You can sweeten the turn-taking bargain by allowing him to help you brush your teeth, too. It may seem a bit weird at first, but you'll actually be giving your toddler valuable toothbrushing practice because he'll be able to see what he's doing.

- **If your toddler hates anything to do with toothbrushing, look for opportunities to build some choices into the toothbrushing routine** (e.g., would he like to brush his teeth before or after storytime?). And help him to understand why we brush our teeth—to get them sparkling clean! "When I'm brushing my son's teeth, I talk about all the things he's eaten that day: 'Oh, let's brush away that toast. There's some chicken. I have to get that broccoli,'" says Julie, a 30-year-old mother of one.

- **To minimize bacteria growth, rinse your child's toothbrush thoroughly before putting it away.** And make a point of replacing the toothbrush at least three to four times a year—more often than that if the bristles start to look flattened and worn.

- **Don't allow your toddler to run around while he's carrying his toothbrush.** A child can be seriously injured as a result of falling with a toothbrush in his mouth.

- **Try to introduce flossing early.** Ideally, you should try to floss your child's teeth at least once a day. And try to give your toddler's tongue a scrub as often as he'll let you in order to remove some of the bacteria that lives on the tongue.

Finally, don't make the mistake of assuming that you can afford to cut corners when it comes to caring for your toddler's baby teeth. Unrepaired decay in a child's baby teeth (a.k.a. "milk teeth" or "primary teeth") can lead to decay in his permanent teeth as well as to orthodontic problems. This is because your child's baby teeth have an important role to play in guiding the adult teeth into their correct position: they act as space holders for the permanent teeth, which start showing up at around age six.

The baby bottle blues

If your toddler drinks from a bottle, it's important to switch him to a cup as soon as possible. The Canadian Dental Association recommends that parents introduce a cup by a child's first birthday to reduce the risk of tooth decay. (Drinking from a cup doesn't cause liquid to collect around the teeth in quite the same way as drinking from a bottle does, and is consequently less likely to contribute to tooth decay.)

Drinking from a bottle at night or nursing frequently throughout the night can lead to other serious problems with tooth decay. Baby bottle syndrome (taking a bottle to bed and drinking frequently throughout the night) and nursing caries (a unique pattern of dental caries that's caused by nursing at the breast almost continuously) can lead to toothaches, tooth decay, feeding difficulties, and the premature loss of the baby teeth (which can, in turn, result in speech problems, jaw development problems, and the need for orthodontic work).

The most severe tooth damage tends to occur in the areas where liquid can build up in the mouth: around the front and back of the upper front teeth. The earliest warning sign that there could be a problem is the presence of tiny white spots on the upper front teeth. Note: these spots are sometimes so small that they can only be detected by a dentist.

If your toddler absolutely insists on having a bottle within grabbing distance at any time of day or night, fill it with water. At least that way it won't be damaging to his teeth. But don't allow that bottle to kick around indefinitely. You want your toddler to make the transition to a cup by no later than age 15 months.

The facts on fluoride

Something else you need to think about is whether or not your toddler needs a fluoride supplement. Fluoride helps to strengthen tooth enamel to make it more resistant to acids and harmful bacteria—something that helps to stop tooth decay. If your community has fluoridated water, your toddler's fluoride needs are already being fully met, but if your water supply doesn't contain fluoride (for example, your water comes from a well or a spring that contains less than 0.3 ppm of naturally occurring fluoride), your doctor or dentist may recommend that your toddler receive some sort of fluoride treatment or supplement. Not every toddler benefits from such supplementation. Consuming too much fluoride can cause a condition called fluorosis that will cause white spots to appear on his baby and/or adult teeth, permanently damaging those beautiful pearly whites.

Putting the bite on tooth decay

Wondering what you can do to keep the cavities at bay? Here are the key points to keep in mind:

- **Ensure that your toddler is eating a balanced diet made up of a variety of healthy foods.** (See Chapter 5 for practical tips on encouraging toddlers to eat the right kinds of foods.) This will help to promote good dental health.
- **Offer alternatives to sticky, sugary-sweet snacks, since sugar promotes tooth decay.** Note: Sugary and sticky foods (including raisins and other dried fruits) won't do quite as much harm to your toddler's teeth if they're eaten as part of a meal rather than on their own, so if you choose to include these foods in his diet, make sure they're served along with other foods.
- **Don't allow your child to snack nonstop from morning until night** (or to walk around carrying a bottle or sippy cup full of milk or juice). Try to structure his eating into three meals plus one or two snacks. Not only is this better for his teeth, but you'll be promoting healthy eating habits at the same time.

Thumbs and pacifiers

If your toddler hasn't kicked his thumbsucking or pacifier habit by the age of two, you'll want to encourage him to do so as soon as possible in order to prevent orthodontic problems down the road. Sucking a thumb, finger, or pacifier beyond age two increases the likelihood that a child will develop protruding front teeth or a crossbite (a narrowing of the upper jaw relative to the lower jaw). Excessive pacifier use can also interfere with your toddler's speech. Not only will he have fewer opportunities to practice talking, but overuse of a pacifier can also interfere with his articulation skills. He may tend to replace his "t" and "d" sounds (which require that the front of the tongue brush up against the back of the front teeth) with "k" and "g" sounds (sounds produced at the back of the throat).

To discourage your toddler from sucking his thumb during the day, try to come up with creative ways of keeping his hands busy at those times of day when his thumb tends to find its way into his mouth. If, for example, your toddler is in the habit of sucking his thumb while you read to him, give him two small toys to hold on to—one for each hand. This approach tends to be more effective than putting a bandage or a bitter substance on your child's thumb or constantly nagging him about his behaviour—strategies that can actually backfire by reinforcing the thumbsucking habit. Of course, the best way to deal with a thumbsucking issue is by preventing it from becoming a problem in the first place. The sooner you can replace that thumb with a pacifier, the easier the problem will be to deal with down the road. (It's much easier to eliminate a pacifier than it is to disrupt access to a thumb!)

To discourage your toddler from turning to his pacifier each time he's upset (which, by the way, prevents him from learning other methods of managing his emotions), make an effort to keep the pacifier out of sight and your toddler's mind on other things. Better yet, limit pacifier use to nighttime only.

You'll probably find that your toddler's pacifier use will start to decrease as he starts to learn other ways of comforting himself when he's upset, when he's able to communicate more effectively, and when he notices that other children his age no longer have pacifiers. If, on the other hand, your toddler is still extremely reliant on his pacifier by the time his second birthday rolls around, you may have to help him to kick his pacifier habit by going "cold turkey" and tossing the pacifier away.

teeth grinding

Approximately 30 percent of children grind their teeth when they're sleeping and, for whatever reason, teeth grinding is more common in toddlers than in older children. It's most likely to occur when a child is in a very deep sleep. Teeth grinding (bruxism) doesn't generally do any lasting damage to a toddler's teeth (his baby teeth have to last only for a couple of years), but if he continues grinding his teeth as he gets older, your dentist may wish to fit him for a mouthguard to prevent any damage to his jaw or his permanent teeth.

The truth about teething

Some toddlers become miserable while they're teething, while others aren't the least bit fazed. If your toddler seems to be bothered by teething pain, try offering him a rubber teething ring (ideally the water-filled kind that can be put in the fridge or freezer to soothe his tender gums), a cold washcloth, or a frozen bagel to gnaw on. Note: according to the Canadian Paediatric Society, most children who are teething do not require any sort of pharmacological pain relief.

nose picking

Many toddlers get in the habit of picking their nose, either because they're curious about what's inside the nasal cavity, they're looking for relief from cold or allergy symptoms, or their nasal passages are dry and itchy.

The best way to handle the problem is to try to deal with the underlying issue.

If you suspect that an overly dry home environment is making your toddler's nasal passages dry and itchy, you might want to run a room humidifier or squirt a blast or two of saline nasal spray up each of your toddler's nostrils.

continued

nose picking (continued)

If you suspect that your toddler is bothered by a runny nose, let him pick out a box of tissues at the grocery store and then encourage him to use them to wipe or blow his nose.

If you suspect that your toddler is picking his nose as a result of either curiosity or boredom, you might want to give him something else to do with his hands.

Don't get into a power struggle with your toddler over nose picking, or you could make the problem worse. Rather than trying to kick him of this annoying bad habit right now, simply remind yourself that it's unlikely you'll catch him picking his nose 20 years from now as he marches across the stage to pick up his university diploma. Chances are he'll abandon the habit as soon as he starts getting social pressure to stop. (This is one of those times when peer pressure can actually work in a parent's favour!)

Hair Care

Having a hard time convincing your toddler to allow you to run a comb through his hair? You're not alone. Many toddlers make it painfully obvious to anyone within earshot that they hate having their hair combed. Often, this is because a toddler's hair is tangled and matted, which can make it painful to pass a fine-toothed comb through it. Using conditioner on a regular basis can help to detangle your child's hair, and temporarily switching to a wider-toothed comb will make hair-combing easier for him and for you. It's also wise to stick with shorter haircuts during the toddler years. Any parent who lets her toddler go for the long-haired Lady Godiva look is pretty much asking for trouble! (But then again, given the enjoyment most toddlers get out of being buck naked, the hairstyle may actually be kind of apropos.)

Of course, it's one thing to want your child to have short hair. It's quite another to get his hair cut. That first haircut can be a rather hair-raising experience for both you and your toddler.

The first thing you have to do is decide if you'd like to cut your toddler's hair at home or whether it might be wiser to let the pros handle it. If your child is going through a real battle of wills with you at the moment, he might be more cooperative for a complete stranger. But if he's got a major problem with stranger anxiety, being greeted by a scissor-wielding stranger isn't going to make him feel terribly comfortable. Only you can decide what will work best for your toddler.

Here are some tips on making that first haircut less stressful, whether it happens at home or the salon.

At home:

- If you decide to cut your toddler's hair at home, put him in his high chair. You'll find it easier to keep him from wiggling around while you're trying to cut his hair. Note: some parents recommend planting the high chair in front of a mirror so that your toddler will be able to watch, but obviously you'll want to go this route only if you're positive your toddler won't be unduly freaked out by the sight of those scissors approaching his head!
- Dampen your child's hair using a plant mister filled with water and a squirt of hair conditioner. (It'll help to detangle his hair.)
- Cut your toddler's hair with blunt-ended scissors to prevent any accidental nicks and scratches if he suddenly goes into wiggle mode. Be prepared to do the haircut in stages over the course of a day or two if he's at an exceptionally active stage.
- If your toddler is nervous about having his hair cut, try giving someone else a haircut at the same time: perhaps an older sibling or your partner!
- If you think your toddler may be frightened by the sound of the blow-dryer, allow his hair to air dry instead. You don't want to cap off a successful first haircut by freaking him out with a noisy blow-dryer.

At the hairdresser's:

- When you talk with your toddler about his upcoming trip to the local hair salon, use the word "trim" rather than "cut" to describe what's going to happen to his hair. "Trim" is a whole lot less scary.
- Choose your child's hairdresser wisely. You want someone who's comfortable working with toddlers and who will have a whole bunch of creative strategies for eliciting your toddler's cooperation while his hair is being cut.
- Recognize the fact that the first haircut may be a little bit scary for your child. If you can swing it, you might want to ask the hairdresser to cut your hair or another family member's hair first. That way, your toddler will have a better idea of what's actually going to happen and may be a whole lot less fearful as a result.
- Change your child's shirt when the hairdresser is finished cutting his hair. That will help to minimize some of the post-haircut itchiness.
- Last but not least, remember to scoop up a lock of your child's hair—an important memento for his baby book.

Head lice

What discussion of hair care would be complete without a couple of paragraphs on every parent's least favourite topic, head lice?

Head lice are tiny insects that live on the scalp. Their eggs are called nits. Head lice tends to be spread through direct contact between children. According to the Canadian Paediatric Society, there isn't much hard evidence to support the widespread belief that head lice is spread via objects such as hats, combs, and brushes, so there's no need to panic if you happen to catch your toddler trying on another child's hat! (That said, if there's an active lice outbreak at your child's daycare, you'll want to err on the side of caution by discouraging any hat sharing.)

Children don't always become itchy when they contract head lice, so it's a good idea to do periodic spot checks, particularly if you know your child has been in contact with someone else with head lice. Be sure to focus on the area close to the scalp, behind the ears, toward the back of the neck, and on the top of the head. What you're looking for is evidence of a current infestation (a mature insect scampering around your child's scalp or evidence of a recent and not-yet-treated infestation—something that's indicated by the presence of nits, red bumps or scratch marks on the scalp that indicate itching or irritation). Mature insects (one millimetre–long, dark-coloured insects) are harder to spot than nits (greyish-white ovals that resemble dandruff, but that have to be scraped rather than shaken off). Note: Once a lice outbreak has been treated, you don't have to worry as much about the presence of nits. At this point, they are likely to be evidence of an historical infestation as opposed to a current infestation. It's the sight of a live insect that should have you sighing deeply at this stage of the game . . .

To get rid of head lice, your toddler will require two treatments (spaced seven to ten days apart) with a chemical treatment product that is designed to kill lice. According to the Canadian Paediatric Society, this is the only effective method of treating head lice. Because products designed to treat head lice contain heavy-duty chemicals, you should use one of these products only if you're certain that your child has head lice, and you'll want to minimize skin contact beyond the scalp. Once you've administered the treatment, you may want to remove any remaining nits (bearing in mind that you're doing this for cosmetic reasons only, so you don't have to obsess about removing each and every nit). You can remove nits by . . .

- applying a damp towel to your toddler's scalp for 30 to 60 minutes;
- soaking his hair with a solution made up of equal parts of water and vinegar and then applying a towel soaked in the same solution for 15 minutes; or
- washing your child's hair and applying cream rinse containing 8 percent formic acid (a substance that helps to dissolve the "glue" that binds the nit to the hair shaft).

At this point, you can then backcomb the nits off your child's hair by using a fine-toothed nit comb or scrape the nits off your child's hair using your thumbnail. If there are a lot of nits, you may wish to try slathering your child's scalp with a layer of petroleum jelly or hair gel and leaving this layer of jelly or gel in place for approximately 12 hours, to ease the removal.

Finally, soak all combs and brushes in hot water for ten minutes or wash them with a pediculicide ("lice killing") shampoo and then heat dry.

Note: All head lice treatment products require a second treatment seven to ten days after the first treatment, so make a point of doing this important bit of follow-up. Otherwise, your child's head may end up playing host to head lice again. (Nits that were not killed by the first round of treatment can hatch and start the infestation cycle all over again.) Don't feel like you have to keep your toddler at home while you're waiting to administer the second treatment, however. While some daycare centres have "no nit" policies that prevent toddlers from returning to daycare until their heads are entirely nit-free, the Canadian Paediatric Society argues that there's little evidence to support such policies. They recommend instead that a child be allowed to return to daycare as soon as the initial treatment has been applied (with the understanding that a follow-up treatment will be done seven to ten days later).

Clothes Calls

You can't expect your toddler to learn how to dress herself if every item of clothing she owns is tricky to put on and take off. After all, we're talking about a toddler here, not an escape artist! Here are some tips to keep in mind the next time you hit the children's department of your local department store.

- Look for clothing that is comfortable and loose-fitting so that your child will be able to bend, jump, and otherwise go about the business of being a toddler.
- Steer clear of dresses or loose jumpsuits when your toddler is learning how to walk. They may cause her to trip.
- Choose garments that will be easy for your toddler to put on and take off. That means avoiding shirts with overly tight necklines like turtlenecks; clothes with zippers, buckles, and snaps that may

be tricky for her little fingers to manoeuvre; and one-piece gar-ments like overalls and jumpsuits. Instead, look for pants with elastic waistbands, shirts with oversized necklines that stretch as your toddler pulls the shirt over her head, and Velcro-closure shoes that are easy for your toddler to put on and take off. Oh yeah . . . Here's another good reason to "just say no" to pants with zippers until your toddler is a little older—particularly if your toddler is a boy: it's quite common for little boys to acci-dentally catch their penises in the zippers of their pants.

- There are some added advantages to going with two-piece rather than one-piece outfits: you won't have to do as much laundry (you'll have to wash only the half of the outfit that's actually dirty), and your toddler will have a much easier time getting his pants down in time when nature calls.

- For safety reasons, you'll want to look for skid-proof socks and slippers. These will help reduce the number of times your tod-dler slips and falls.

- If your child is easily irritated by the feel of her clothing, look for garments with oversewn seams (they're less irritating) and remove any labels that could end up scratching your child. Then wash the garment a few times to break it in, making a point of using fabric softener in the rinse cycle (unless, of course, your toddler has sensitive skin and/or eczema, in which case you'll want to pass on the fabric softener entirely). Or save yourself all the bother of trying to break in a garment by buying secondhand clothing for your child.

Of course, even more important than having the right wardrobe is having a parent with the right attitude—a parent who is patient enough to give a toddler the chance to try to dress herself, as opposed to rushing in to do everything for that toddler because it may be quicker or easier to do so. Because here's the thing: if you take over entirely, you're telling your toddler that you don't think she can manage this on her own—a message that is likely to be met with feelings of frustration or even outrage and that can both shake your toddler's confidence in herself and thwart her willingness to try new things.

What you want to do is find some sensible middle ground between doing everything for your toddler and expecting her to tackle tasks that she isn't capable of handling on her own quite yet. This sensible middle ground involves scaffolding (supporting her learning in a way that takes into account what she already knows and that allows her to build upon that learning; guiding your toddler in a way that allows her to experience a healthy amount of frustration—enough to challenge her, but not so much that she feels completely overwhelmed).

Working through a tolerable amount of frustration is good for your toddler. It encourages her to be persistent and gives her the opportunity to work at managing those feelings. And, should she be successful in wriggling into that pair of pants, she'll be rewarded with a heady "I did it!" feeling of success that will encourage her to stick with other challenging tasks in future.

So don't be afraid to hit the pause button for a moment when you're toddler is trying to figure out how to put her boots or pants on for herself. The rewards can be considerable for her and for you. "It takes longer to let Morgan do things herself, but it's worth it to see the look of great pride on her face when she has successfully put her shirt on all by herself!" says Kelli, a 32-year-old mother of one.

> "My kids wear rubber boots most of the spring and fall. They can put them on and take them off themselves and there are no laces to tie!"
>
> —MARIA, 33, MOTHER OF TWO

Dollars and sense

While comfort and functionality are obviously the key considerations when you're putting together a wardrobe for your child, you'll also want to consider what all this is going to cost. Here are some tips on getting maximum bang for your clothing buck.

toddler nudists . . .

Convinced that your toddler is a prime candidate for a nudist colony? Relax. Chances are he will have kicked his streaking habit long before he leaves home.

Most toddlers go through a phase—albeit short-lived—where they enjoy taking their clothes off and running around in the buff.

Some toddlers enjoy being naked because they love the feel of the air against their skin. Others are simply eager to put one of their newest talents to good use: the ability to undress themselves. Since they have yet to pick up on any of the social norms governing nudity, they don't see anything wrong with taking their clothes off in the middle of the grocery store.

As with anything else toddler-related, the best way to handle the situation is to remain calm. Simply explain to him that while it's okay to enjoy being naked before, during, and after your bath, it's important to keep your clothes on when you're in public. If that's not enough to convince him to keep his clothes on (well, at least most of the time), you may have to resort to more desperate measures, like dressing him in clothes that are a little more difficult to take off (for example, overalls or playsuits with a zipper up the back) and—if he's not yet toilet trained—putting his diaper on backwards so that it's a little trickier to remove. You'll also want to make sure that his clothes are comfortable so that he'll have less of an incentive to disrobe. (How often have you taken the first opportunity to ditch an uncomfortable pair of shoes?)

• **Don't overshop for your toddler.** He'll be having fewer diaper blowouts than he did as an infant, and as his ability to feed himself improves, he'll be less likely to wear each meal. He probably won't go through more than two outfits in a day, so assuming you're willing to do laundry twice a week, you can probably get away with having eight to ten outfits in his size for each season. Since many of his outfits will end up being splattered with paint, mud, and whatever else happens to catch his interest these days, you'll be better off loading up on clothing at garage sales and secondhand stores or accepting offers of hand-me-downs from family members and friends rather than shopping for designer kids' clothes at high-priced boutiques.

- **Clean out your toddler's closet and drawers at the start of each season.** That way, you'll have a clearer idea of what types of clothing he needs before you hit the stores. If you're planning to visit the consignment stores in search of quality secondhand clothing for your child, bring along some of the garments that your child has outgrown so that you can put them on consignment at the same time.

- **Organize a neighbourhood clothing swap each spring and fall.** You can then donate any leftovers to a charity that collects used clothing.

- **Shop for seconds at manufacturers' retail outlets.** Often the flaw in the clothing is virtually unnoticeable or is something that you can repair easily at home with a needle and thread.

- **When you're shopping for new clothing, try to give your business to stores that offer some sort of wear guarantee** (in other words, they'll replace the item if the outfit wears out before your child outgrows it).

- **Try not to fixate on the price tag.** An expensive pair of jeans that makes it through the toddlerhoods of two or more kids may actually be cheaper than a poor-quality pair that doesn't even survive the toddlerhood of kid number one.

- **Stick to a few basic colours of clothing so that you'll have more mix-and-match possibilities**—something that will help to stretch your clothing dollars and reduce the odds that your child will look like a tacky tourist every time he dresses himself.

- **Make a point of buying patterns rather than solids.** Patterns help to hide stains. And steer clear of anything white unless you want to make stain patrol part of your daily routine. (Actually, steer clear of any light colour, particularly if the fabric is unbleachable.) Note: you can find hands-on instructions for doing battle with the most common types of toddler-related stains in Table 7.2.

- **Invest in durable, easy-care clothing that's designed to grow with your child** (for example, pants and shirts with "grow cuffs" that can be unrolled to add a bit more length to each pant leg or sleeve). While it's a good idea to buy garments that are slightly oversized so that your toddler can get a bit more wear out of them, don't get carried away: you don't want him to trip because his pants are six inches longer than his legs.

Stain removal

The key to removing stains from your toddler's clothing is to act quickly, starting with the least powerful stain-removing agent. If that doesn't do the trick, you may have to up the ante. Be sure to test the stain remover on an inconspicuous part of the garment first if you're not sure how a particular fabric will react to it. It's best to treat the stain from the opposite side of the fabric, placing a paper towel under the stain as you work, and to blot—not rub—the stain. Then pre-treat the stain with a commercial stain remover and launder the garment promptly.

Note: Because heat will set a stain, it's important to treat stains before clothes go through the washer and dryer. Stains can be almost impossible to remove once the heat from the dryer has "baked" the stain in. And if you can't get the stain out? Get creative instead! Your toddler may be able to get some additional mileage out of a stained T-shirt if you tie-dye it, dye it, or allow him to decorate it with fabric paints instead.

7.2 Toddler Stains from A to Z	
Type of Stain	**How to Treat It**
Berries (strawberries, blueberries, etc.)	Apply red-wine stain remover to the stain or pour boiling water on the stain.
Blood	Soak garment in salt water or flush with club soda. If that doesn't work, try making a paste out of meat tenderizer and applying it to the stain or pouring hydrogen peroxide directly on the stain and then flushing with cold water.

continued

7.2 Toddler Stains from A to Z (continued)

Butter or margarine	Remove any blobs of butter or margarine and then work undiluted dish detergent into the stain. If the stain is old, you can reactivate the grease by spraying the spot with WD-40 lubricant and then working in undiluted dish detergent.
Chocolate	Soak garment in an enzyme prewash solution for 30 minutes and then rub liquid detergent into any remaining stain. Rinse well in cold water.
Crayon and coloured pencil	Place the stained area of the garment on a pile of paper towels and spray with WD-40. Turn the garment over and spray the other side of the spot. Allow the garment to sit for 10 minutes and then rub dish detergent into the stain. Launder in hot water.
Crayon, melted	Place the stained area of the garment on a pile of paper towels. Cover with an additional layer of paper towels. Using a hot iron, press the stained area until the crayon has lifted into the paper towels.
Food dye (dyes from flavoured fruit drinks, gelatins, ice pops, for example)	Treat with cold water and ammonia (approximately 25 mL/ 1 tbsp. of ammonia to 250 mL/1 cup of cold water) and then rub salt into the stain. Repeat if necessary. Red, orange, and purple stains can also be treated with red-wine stain remover.
Formula, infant	For white clothing: apply lemon juice and lay garment in the sun or make a paste out of meat tenderizer and apply it to the stain. For coloured fabrics: make a paste out of meat tenderizer and apply it to the stain.
Fruit and fruit juice	Treat the spot with club soda or cold water immediately. Rub in liquid detergent, then flush with hot water. If the stain still remains after this treatment, make a paste out of borax and apply to the stain. Allow the borax to dry and then brush it off. If you discover an old fruit or fruit juice stain, try reactivating the stain with glycerin (available at the drugstore) and then following the same steps for treating fresh fruit or fruit juice stains.
Glue	Soak the garment in warm to hot water and then wash as usual.
Grass stains	Sponge grass stains with rubbing alcohol. If that's not effective at removing the stains, try sponging with vinegar instead or rubbing some non-gel toothpaste into the stains. Rub laundry detergent into the stained areas and launder as usual.

7.2 Toddler Stains from A to Z (continued)	
Ice cream	Sponge the garment with cold water, club soda, or seltzer and then treat any remaining stain with a paste made of cold water and meat tenderizer. (Leave the paste on for 30 minutes or so and then flush with cold water.)
Ink	Sponge a bit of rubbing alcohol onto ink stains. Or try soaking the ink-stained garment in milk. If that doesn't work, try scrubbing the spot with some non-gel toothpaste.
Markers, washable	Believe it or not, washable markers aren't always fully washable. The key is to get to the stain right away and flush the affected area with cold water. Then place the garment on paper towels and saturate the back of the stain with rubbing alcohol, using a cotton ball to blot away the stain. Finally, rub some liquid laundry detergent into the spot and launder as usual.
Milk	Rinse thoroughly and then treat with a paste of meat tenderizer and cold water. Leave the paste on for 30 minutes and then flush with cold water.
Mud	Allow the mud to dry and then brush or vacuum it off. Treat any remaining stains by rubbing them with the cut side of a potato or sponging them with a 50/50 solution of water and rubbing alcohol.
Mustard	Coloured clothing: Scrape off as much of the mustard as possible using a dull knife and then apply glycerin to the stain. Allow the glycerin to sit on the stain for at least an hour before laundering. White clothing: Saturate the stain with hydrogen peroxide or a denture-cleaning tablet dissolved in cold water and allow the solution to soak into the stain for 30 minutes.
Paint, acrylic	Wash the paint out before it has a chance to dry to maximize your chances of getting the stain out. Note: Some acrylic paints are permanent.
Pencil	Use a clean eraser to "erase" pencil marks from your toddler's clothing.

continued

7.2	Toddler Stains from A to Z (continued)
Rust	Saturate the affected area with lemon juice, sprinkle with salt, and then lay the garment out in the sun. If that doesn't do the trick, apply more lemon juice and salt and pour boiling water over the stain. Or make a paste out of water and cream of tartar and apply to the affected area.
Stickers	Apply undiluted heated white vinegar to the affected area, allowing it to soak until the sticker can be peeled away easily.
Tomato (including ketchup, barbecue sauce, tomato sauces, etc.)	Flush the stained area with cold water as soon as possible. Then sprinkle on some white vinegar and flush with cold water. If that doesn't work, try using some red-wine stain remover to get rid of any remaining stains.
Zinc oxide (a common ingredient in diaper creams)	Treat the stain as you would a butter or margarine stain (see above) and then soak the garment in white vinegar for 30 minutes.

Your toddler's sense of style

Your toddler insists on wearing his rubber boots on a hot, summer day. Should you ask him to put on his shoes? Maybe, maybe not. This is one of those battles you can definitely afford to walk away from. Chances are your toddler's new-found love of boots stems from the fact that he finds it easier to step into them than fiddle with the straps on his sandals. So what if your toddler looks like some strange holdover from the go-go boot era?

Of course, if your toddler is determined to try the reverse manoeuvre—insisting on wearing his beach flip-flops in the middle of a winter blizzard—you'll have to come up with a creative compromise: perhaps allowing him to carry his flip-flops in a knapsack on his back while trudging through the snow in his boots or giving him permission to wear his bathing suit under his tracksuit if he's really-and-truly determined to rebel against the Canadian winter.

clothing quick fixes

Here are some clothing tricks-of-the-trade that every parent needs to know about:

- You can firmly anchor buttons that refuse to stay on your toddler's clothing by sewing them on with dental floss rather than thread.
- You can "unstick" a zipper that's hard to zip and unzip by running a bar of soap up and down both sides of the zipper.
- The easiest way to re-thread a drawstring that's come out of the hood of a jacket is by taping the drawstring to a chopstick or knitting needle and then threading it through the drawstring pocket. (Tip: Take this opportunity to double-check that the drawstring doesn't pose a strangulation hazard to your toddler; the drawstring should extend no more than 12 to 15 centimetres [5 to 6 inches] on either side of the hood.)
- When the plastic tips on your toddler's shoelaces wear off, try dipping the ends in nail polish or wrapping them tightly with tape. And if your toddler's shoelaces have a tendency to come undone easily, wet them before you tie them. This will help them to stay tied up.

Perhaps there are some items of clothing in your child's closet that you'd prefer he steer clear of entirely: clothes that are too small, badly stained, or out of season, for example. Simply pack those garments away so that they won't even be an option for him. "I make a point of packing up unseasonable clothing," says Kelly, a 31-year-old mother of three. "That way, I don't have to explain to two three-year-olds why they can't wear shorts in the snow!"

It's Potty Time!

Given all the time and energy some parents put into obsessing about toilet training, you'd think researchers had uncovered a link between the age at which a toddler is diaper-free and his law school entrance exam scores two decades later. But since no study to date has been able to demonstrate that kind of connection, I'd urge you to do yourself and your toddler a favour and chill out about the whole potty training business! Instead of focusing on your child's chronological age, pay attention to his physical and emotional readiness (see Table 7.3). And encourage yourself to make the mental shift from thinking "toilet training" to "toilet learning." (That's the preferred lingo from the Canadian Paediatric Society: a simple yet powerful language tweak that keeps the focus where it should be—on learning a new skill.)

Of course, that's easier said than done if all the other parents you hang out with are potty-mad—and chances are they are! So what's behind this potty mania? A lack of confidence on the part of parents, says Joan, a 35-year-old mother of five: "I think that parents who become competitive about things like toilet training are less confident in their parenting and need to have something measurable to reassure them that their child is on track developmentally and that they're okay parents."

Some of these parents make the mistake of assuming that their toddler is ready just because they are, notes Judy, a 33-year-old mother of one—an assumption that can be misguided, to say the least: "Toddlers can only control a few things in their lives, and one of them is what and when stuff comes out of their bodies."

Sometimes parents rush the process due to a mistaken belief that life will be a thousand times easier once their child is out of diapers. Any experienced parent can tell you that quite the opposite is true: it's a lot more work to mop up puddles and to sprint to public washrooms every 15 minutes than to change a diaper every now and again. Of course, you can't leave your toddler in diapers forever, just because it's a little more convenient for you. One of your jobs as a parent is to teach him the basics of personal hygiene, but in a way that supports his healthy development. So think gentle nudging and encouragement as opposed to signing him up for potty training boot camp . . .

Ultimately, what you're looking for is some sort of sign from your toddler that he's interested in the process. That means recognizing (and accepting) that some kids take longer than others to reach this point. "My daughter ended up being in diapers until she was four," recalls Lisa, a 36-year-old mother of two. "She didn't mind being wet or dirty and—at one point as I rushed madly through a stop sign to get her to the bathroom in time—she calmly pointed out that it would be easier if she wore diapers. Then we wouldn't have to hurry so much!" (Hey, the kid had a point!)

There is, of course, a downside to forging ahead before your child is ready. Anita, a 38-year-old mother of four explains: "When my twins started showing interest in training, I mistook it for readiness, something that led to frustration all around. We experienced many moments of sadness, anger, impatience, and anxiety, and all this was compounded and complicated by trying to train two toddlers at once. I feel a lot of regret, shame, and guilt about the way I handled potty training, so I'm planning to do things very differently this time around; there will be no pressure on my two-and-a-half-year-old at all."

"If you start training too early, then it's the parents who get 'trained,' not the child. For example, if you know that your toddler poops every day after lunch but before naptime, then it's fairly easy to get him to poop in the toilet if you put him on the toilet right after lunch."

—MARIA, 33, MOTHER OF TWO

So how do you go about deciding if your toddler is ready? In addition to considering the signs of physical and emotional readiness (see Table 7.3 below), you'll also want to consider whether this is the best time for all concerned. That means asking yourself if there's anything else going on in your child's life that would make toilet learning a bad idea right now. If, for example, you're about to move, start your child in daycare, or welcome a new baby into your family, you might want to hold off for a while. And it means making sure that the other key adults in your toddler's life are on board, too—especially his daycare provider. Toilet learning should happen at home and daycare at the same time, and you'll want to make a point of using the same language and routines.

And, speaking of readiness, you'll want to make sure that you're ready to embark on the process, too, because it can require a fair bit of time and patience on your part. And, in terms of simple logistics, you'll want to choose a period of time when you're likely to be home a fair bit— perhaps a long weekend. It's not reasonable, after all, to expect a toddler who is just starting to learn how to use the potty to stay dry while you run errands all over town. You might also want to give some thought to the time of year: some parents swear that the secret to success is to start during the summer months, because there are fewer clothes to fumble with when the moment of truth arrives and your toddler needs to make a mad dash for the potty. You might even consider allowing your toddler to run around nude or semi-nude while he's learning the potty-training ropes, something that is much easier to do on a warm summer day than on the coldest day of winter.

While there may be days when you swear you'll be changing diapers for the rest of your life, odds are your child will be graduating from diapers a whole lot sooner than that. Most Canadian kids manage to achieve both bladder and bowel control sometime between 24 and 48 months of age (with girls typically mastering the process a little sooner than boys). That said, it's important to bear in mind that bladder and bowel control don't always happen at the same time; and that there can be a lag in achieving nighttime versus daytime dryness (a lag that can span months or even years).

7.3 The Signs of Readiness

How can you tell when the moment of truth has arrived and it's actually time to start the process of toilet learning? By looking for the following signs of physical and emotional readiness in your toddler.

Physical Readiness:	Emotional Readiness:
• Your toddler is able to recognize the physical sensations that tell him that he needs to pee or poop. He may pause while he's playing and then squat, grunt, or hold on to his genitals. • Your toddler is aware when he's wet or dirty and is starting to show signs that he finds it unpleasant to be wearing a wet or dirty diaper. • Your toddler is able to stay dry for several hours at a time and is capable of emptying his bladder fully rather than just passing a small amount of urine at a time—the typical pattern for younger toddlers. • Your toddler is capable of controlling the sphincter muscles in the anus that hold in stool. • Your toddler is able to pull down his own pants and get himself on and off the potty or toilet.	• Your toddler is showing an interest in the potty or toilet. • Your toddler is willing to sit on the potty or toilet instead of wearing a diaper. • Your toddler understands what a toilet is for and how to use it. • Your toddler is able to communicate effectively with words and gestures—something that makes it easier for you to pick up on the fact that he needs the potty now. • Your toddler is able to tell you when he needs to urinate or have a bowel movement. • Your toddler likes to please you. (Note: this desire to please you tends to rise and fall during the toddler years, so try to time the process to coincide with one of your child's more cooperative phases.)

The right stuff

Once you've determined that the time is right, you'll want to make sure you have all the necessary paraphernalia on hand.

The first decision you'll have to make is whether to start your child on the potty or the big toilet. Here's a quick rundown of the pros and cons.

The potty: A potty tends to be less intimidating to a child. Because it's child-sized, his feet can touch the floor and he'll be less afraid of falling off or falling in. You can also move the potty around so that it's easier for your toddler to get to it in time. (At first, his bladder won't give him a lot of advance warning.) On the other hand, it takes up extra space in the bathroom, it requires additional work on your part (you have to clean and disinfect it), and you may have to take it everywhere with you if your child refuses to use regular toilets at other people's houses. And then there's the fact that it's only a temporary solution; your child will have to start using the toilet eventually, since it would be cumbersome to have to tote his potty back and forth to high school each day!

have potty, will travel . . .

While it's a good idea to stay close to home during the early days of toilet learning, you can't stay home forever. Here are some tips on surviving your toddler's first few trips to the public washroom:

- Keep a spare outfit in the trunk of your car or in your purse in case you can't sprint to the washroom quickly enough or—horror of horrors!—there's a lineup when you get there.
- Be patient. It may take your toddler longer to relax and "let go" if he's using a strange toilet. You might even want to get into the habit of carrying one of your toddler's favourite books in your purse to help him relax.
- Don't be surprised if your toddler has the odd hang-up about using a public washroom. Some children refuse to use toilets that look "different" from the ones at home. "Sarah used to refuse to use any toilet with rust in it," recalls Jennifer, a 33-year-old mother of one. "She insisted that it was dirty. Sometimes we were able to find another toilet; other times we had to just grin and bear it."
- Putting a lot of miles on your toddler's potty because he refuses to have anything to do with any other toilet on the planet? Here's the secret to disposing of all those messes while you're on the road: simply line the potty with a large ziplock bag. That way, when your toddler is finished using the potty, you can simply seal up the bag and deal with the mess when you hit the closest washroom.

The toilet: If you're going to train your child on the big toilet, you'll need to purchase a toilet seat ring to help prevent him from falling in plus a low stepstool to place under his feet so that he feels stable. The advantages of going this route are that it's easier to tote around (and clean) a toilet seat ring than a whole potty, and a toilet seat ring tends to be much less expensive than a potty. On the other hand, some toddlers have fears about using the big toilet because it tends to be a little more difficult to manoeuvre—something that could derail the whole toilet-learning process before it begins. You also have to take the seat on and off so that other people can use the toilet, which can be a bit of a hassle if you have a large family.

"We use a potty because we live in a townhouse with one bathroom and that bathroom is upstairs. It isn't reasonable to expect a child to go that far when they're learning."

—LISA, 36, MOTHER OF TWO

Once you've weighed the pros and cons of potty versus toilet learning, you'll have another decision to make: whether to use cloth or disposable training pants while your child is learning or simply leave him in diapers until he's managing to stay dry most of the time. Personally, I find the diaper method a bit cumbersome, particularly when your toddler is at the stage of dealing with a lot of false alarms. (Despite what the diaper companies claim, those "reusable" plastic tabs on the diapers aren't nearly as reusable as the manufacturers would like us to think. And even if he's wearing cloth diapers, he'll need your help in taking his diaper on and off.) So other than allowing your toddler to run around naked while he's learning to use the potty (a method that works well for a lot of parents, incidentally), you're left with two basic choices: disposable training pants and cloth training pants or underwear.

Disposable training pants: Disposable training pants are basically training pants made out of disposable diapers. They're designed to go up and down with ease as your child uses the potty. While they're highly convenient and can be a lifesaver if you're dining out in a restaurant with a semi-trained toddler, they have two key drawbacks: the price (they're more expensive than disposable diapers) and the fact that they're highly absorbent (your toddler will have a harder time figuring out if his diaper is actually wet). "I think disposable training pants are a bad idea," says Lisa, a 36-year-old mother of two. "They leave kids feeling dry when they're wet. Instead of paying attention to their bodies, they have to depend on disappearing pictures in a diaper to figure out whether or not they've wet themselves." Alyson, a 33-year-old mother of two, has another beef with disposable training pants: "They make such a mess when a child has a bowel movement in them that sometimes I prefer using plain old diapers."

Cloth training pants or underwear: Cloth training pants (those super-thick cotton pants with ultra-tight leg holes) and regular underwear for toddlers are less expensive alternatives to disposable training pants, but they have one key drawback: they aren't great at containing accidents. So if you stick with cloth training pants and underwear, expect to spend a fair bit of time on puddle patrol! Note: When you're shopping for cloth training pants, make sure the pairs you buy are at least a size larger than your child's regular clothes. They tend to shrink a lot in the wash and get very tight around the legs, which makes them difficult and frustrating for toddlers to pull up and down.

> "Some people say that it's easier to train a child who's in cloth diapers. I disagree. Because my daughter was used to feeling wet all the time, it didn't bother her when she peed in her underwear. I actually considered putting her in disposables for a month or two before we started toilet training to see if I could 'teach' her what it felt like to be dry!"
>
> —MARIA, 32, MOTHER OF TWO

And now that we've run through the list of must-have items (some sort of potty or toilet and some sort of training pants), let's talk about the things that you don't need. Believe it or not, there's a whole industry devoted to this process. Some of the goofy products that you can take a pass on include musical potties, talking potties, and potties that change colour when they're peed in. If you're into potty-training gimmicks, at least go with items that can be had on the cheap: a handful of Cheerios for your son to use for "target practice" when he's mastering the art of the stand-up pee and food colouring to tint the toilet water all kinds of colourful shades. (The rationale for dyeing your toilet water? The colour changes after your child pees.)

Getting started

Wondering how to get started with toilet learning? Here's what you need to know to make this particular rite of passage as stress-free as possible for you and your toddler.

- **Start changing your toddler's diaper in the bathroom so that he can begin to make the link between diapers and the potty.** Try emptying the contents of his diaper into the toilet and giving him a chance to flush. (If he's got a major toilet phobia, give him the option of leaving the room before you flush.) Resist the temptation to make negative comments about the contents of his diaper. You don't want him to feel embarrassed or ashamed.

- **Decide which words you intend to use to refer to body fluids, body functions, and body parts.** You'll want to consider which words are used by friends and relatives or at daycare and which words are used in books you've read to your child. Most experts suggest that you stick with the words "penis" and "vagina" for body parts, but that you use other less formal terms for defecation and urination since they don't tend to be used in everyday speech. (Unless, of course, you happen to be attending a convention of urologists!)

- **Make sure that you have the necessary equipment on hand:** either a free-standing potty or a toilet seat ring and a low step-stool. (Even if you lift your toddler on and off, he'll still need the stool to push against when he's having a bowel movement.) Note: If the potty or seat comes with a splash guard, take it off. While these splash guards help to contain the odd spray of urine, your son may end up bumping his penis against it, which could hurt and considerably diminish his enthusiasm for potty training.

- **Put the potty in the bathroom a few weeks or months ahead of time so that your toddler can get used to having it around before he actually starts using it.**

- **Give your child the opportunity to watch a same-sex person use the toilet so that he or she will have a clear idea of how the process works.** (Chances are your child's been following you and/ or your partner to the bathroom for months, so this shouldn't be too hard to arrange!) While some parents suggest having a doll or teddy bear act as a toilet or potty model, this doesn't work nearly as well, unless you happen to own one of those old-fashioned plastic dolls that can really-and-truly pee on demand.

- **Get your toddler involved in the planning process.** Allow him to pick out his training pants and his potty and give him some say about where the potty ends up being stationed in your home. Naturally, you'll want to encourage him to keep the potty on an easy-care floor to minimize the hassle of cleaning up the inevitable near misses.

- **Encourage your child to sit on the potty with his clothes on.** When he's ready, he can try sitting on it with his pants pulled down. Get him used to making a trip to the potty at certain times of day: after he gets up in the morning, after meals and snacks, before his nap, and before bedtime. If he would benefit from a little added inspiration, try running water in the bathtub or the sink to trigger the urge to go.

- **Teach your son to pee in the sitting-down position first rather than the standing position.** That way, he can focus on learning only one new skill at a time. Remind him that he'll have to point his penis downward while he's peeing to avoid spraying everywhere. Once you teach your son how to use the standing position, you'll want to establish some clear ground rules: it's okay to pee in the potty or the toilet, but it's not okay to pee in the potted plant in the living room.

> "I let Joey pee outside when we were playing outdoors and he thought this was great. I found out, however, that doing this can backfire. One day when he was three we were at a public park and he decided to have a bowel movement on the grass—despite the fact that this had never been our practice at home! It was very embarrassing."
>
> —ALYSON, 33, MOTHER OF TWO

- **Teach your daughter to wipe from the front to the back after she's used the bathroom to avoid introducing bacteria or feces from the anus into her vaginal area.** If she finds this too confusing, teach her to pat the area dry rather than wiping. Note: Little girls can be quite susceptible to bladder infections when they're first learning how to use the potty, so you'll want to be on the lookout for the following telltale signs of infection: a more frequent need to urinate, a sudden urge to urinate, pain while urinating, abdominal pain, and/or suddenly having a lot of accidents again after weeks or months of staying dry.
- **Use baby wipes rather than toilet paper for cleaning up bowel movements until your toddler becomes a pro at wiping.** Just make sure that the wipes find their way into the garbage can, not the toilet, or you'll be dealing with a major plumbing nightmare.
- **Teach your toddler good hygiene habits like hand washing right from day one so that they'll become second nature to him.**
- **Accept the fact that accidents are inevitable.** They're part of mastering a new skill. Instead of getting angry with your child if he has an accident en route to the toilet, recognize the fact that he tried to get there on time—and help him to tune into the bodily sensations that might alert him a little sooner next time. Also,

reassure him that *everyone* finds this process tricky at first and that it won't be long before he figures things out.

- **Be encouraging, but don't overdo it with the praise.** Otherwise, your toddler may develop a bad case of performance anxiety. And if you spend too much time talking up the "big boy" thing, your toddler may decide he wants the security of being a baby again—something that could have him back in diapers before you know it. Speaking of which, if your child asks to go back to diapers, let him. Chances are it'll be a temporary phase. Besides, if you refuse his request, you may find yourself embroiled in a huge power struggle with him—something that is hard on your relationship and that could derail the process entirely.

potty training overkill

Think today's generation of parents tends to get a little carried away when celebrating their toddler's toilet-training successes? It's nothing compared with what went on in generations past! In her 1955 *It's Fun Raising a Family* guide, Canadian childrearing expert Kate Aitken told mothers to go a little crazy the first time their child managed to sleep through the night without wetting his bed: "Give him the same treatment you would a hero home from the wars."

- **Once your child is staying dry for prolonged periods of time during the day and during naps, he might be ready to start giving up his nighttime and naptime diapers.** Of course, it will likely be at least a few more months—perhaps even years—until he's reliably able to stay dry all night. (Fifteen percent of five-year-olds continue to wet the bed at night.)
- **Reassure him that this is normal and then minimize the work associated with middle-of-the-night sheet changes by making your child's bed in layers** (waterproof mattress pad, fitted sheet, waterproof mattress pad, fitted sheet). This will save you from having to strip the bed and then remake it in the middle of the night. You'll also want to limit your toddler's fluid intake right

before bedtime and encourage him to use the bathroom right before bed—two other strategies that can help to minimize the number of nighttime accidents.

- **Be patient with your toddler.** According to the Canadian Paediatric Society, it typically takes three to six months to train a toddler, and it may take several attempts before a child is out of diapers for good.

"My third child had a potty fetish. Every time we went someplace new, she would ask if there was a toilet. If there was, she said she had to go. We figured this out quickly. However, the 'helpful' sales staff would hear her and tell us where the toilet was and so off we would go to check out another bathroom. She was really excited the day we went shopping for a new toilet: oh boy, a whole room full of toilets!"

—KERRI, 36, MOTHER OF SIX

Stool toileting refusal

Approximately 20 percent of toddlers between the ages of 18 and 30 months experience an episode of "stool toileting refusal"—a refusal to have a bowel movement on the toilet. The problem usually arises if a child has been splashed while having a bowel movement on the toilet, if he recently had some problems with constipation and has now learned to associate the pain of passing a hard stool with using the toilet, or if he is afraid of allowing part of "himself" to disappear down the toilet. (Yes, some toddlers are nothing short of proprietary when it comes to their poop.)

The good news is that you don't have to pinpoint the underlying issue in order to begin to help your toddler to deal with stool toileting refusal. Here are some tips on dealing with this common but distressing problem.

- **If the problem is being caused by a fear of being splashed while having a bowel movement on the big toilet,** allow your toddler to switch to a potty until he regains his confidence in using the big toilet.

- **If the problem is caused by a fear of parting with his stool,** try to explain to your toddler that it's not a part of his body that's disappearing down the toilet forever; it's just the part of the food that his body no longer needs.

- **If the problem is being caused by constipation, try to increase his fibre intake, moderate his consumption of dairy products** (too much dairy can cause constipation), and ensure that he's getting plenty of liquids. You might also want to talk to your child's doctor about ways of treating constipation. Depending on the severity of the situation, stool softeners may be recommended. Note: Leakage of stool can occur if a large hard mass forms in bowel. This can be an indication that your child is having problems with constipation.

- **Whatever the cause of your child's stool toileting refusal,** be patient. According to Catherine, a 32-year-old mother of four, sometimes your best bet is to back off entirely. "Be prepared to compromise. My daughter could pee in the potty with no problem, but she couldn't bring herself to poop in it. I told her it was her poop and she could do whatever she wanted with it: poop in the potty or poop in a diaper. If she wanted to poop in a diaper, she could ask me to put one on and then I'd change her afterwards. We did that for maybe a week or two, and then she decided to try pooping on the potty." Problem solved!

CHAPTER 8

The Health Department

"Mothers always worry. There's no off switch."

—PRISCILLE SIBLEY, *The Promise of Stardust*

While you won't be trekking off to the doctor's office quite as often now that your child is a toddler, you can still expect to be there on a regular basis. That's because you and your child's doctor make a pretty unbeatable team when it comes to keeping your child's health and development on track.

That, in a nutshell, is what we're going to be talking about in this chapter—the all-important role that you have to play in keeping your toddler healthy and monitoring his development. We'll discuss the importance of "well child" visits (non-emergency visits to the doctor), consider where Canadian health authorities stand on the immunization issue, talk about ways to tell if your toddler is sick, swap strategies for getting medication inside of (as opposed to merely in the general vicinity of) a toddler, look at the causes and treatments of the most common types of pediatric illnesses, swap some "insider tips" on dealing with a toddler's hospital stay, and much more. Here we go . . .

What's Up, Doc?

Your toddler's doctor will probably want to see her at 12 months, 18 months, two years, and three years, and—of course—whenever any sort of health problem warrants an in-between visit. These regular doctor visits play a critical role in helping to keep your toddler healthy by allowing the doctor to keep tabs on her overall health and development and to pick up on any potential problems sooner rather than later.

At each visit, your doctor will check your toddler's height and weight, give her a head-to-toe examination, and provide immunizations at the appropriate intervals (see the material on immunizations below). You'll also want to chime in with any questions of your own, so get in the habit of bringing a list of questions with you to each appointment. (Of course, if it's a burning question, you'll want to call your health unit or your doctor's office in between appointments, as opposed to waiting for the next checkup to roll around.)

autism spectrum disorders

Approximately 1 out of every 68 Canadian children is diagnosed with autism—a developmental disorder that is characterized by motor, sensory, cognitive, and behavioural challenges. You should be alert to the possibility that your toddler may be at risk of having an autism spectrum disorder if you pick up on one or both of the following red flags:

- Your toddler hasn't started to talk (no babbling at all by age 12 months, no words at all by age 16 months, and no meaningful two-word phrases by age 24 months), has low levels of eye contact, and doesn't engage in any back-and-forth sharing of sounds, gestures, and/or facial expressions.
- Your toddler seems to be losing rather than acquiring language and social skills—or your toddler's development appears to have stalled.

If you are concerned with your child's development, it's important to flag your concerns for your child's doctor as soon as possible so that your child can benefit from early treatment.

Here's something else you need to know about doctor visits: not every toddler is a fan of these kinds of checkups. If you find yourself dealing with a toddler who seems well on her way to developing a full-blown case of white-coat syndrome, you'll want to do everything you can to help ease her anxiety. Wondering what that means in practical terms? Here are a few ideas . . .

eye problems

While your toddler's doctor will make a point of screening her for eye problems during checkups, it's important to be on the lookout for evidence of any such problems yourself. You'll want to let the doctor know if, for example, your toddler is prone to red, itchy, or watery eyes; her eyes seem sensitive to light; she has an eye that consistently turns in or out; you notice her squinting, rubbing her eyes, or blinking excessively; she's prone to covering or closing one eye; or she holds objects very close.

- **Schedule your toddler's doctor appointments for her most cooperative time of day**—which means first thing in the morning for most toddlers.
- **Help your toddler to understand why doctor's visits are important and what she can expect from a particular visit to the doctor.**
- **Let the doctor know that your toddler is feeling a little nervous.** She may want to go slow with the examination and involve you as much as possible so that your calming presence can help to calm your child.
- **Do your best to troubleshoot any underlying issues.** It could be that your toddler is put off by the idea of lying on the paper on the examining table—a problem you can easily solve by bringing a blanket or a towel from home. (Some toddlers become frightened by the noise the paper makes as they wriggle around.)
- **Be honest about the fact that certain procedures, like immunizations, do hurt**—but reassure her that they only hurt for a moment and that you'll be there to help her get through it. (By

the way, how you react to your toddler's immunization will help to determine how she reacts, too. "A matter-of-fact, supportive, non-apologetic approach" is what pediatric pain specialists recommend.)

- **Ask your child's doctor whether she still recommends administering pain relief medication to children prior to immunization.** While this used to be standard advice, there's now considerable controversy about the practice. The reason? Medications like acetaminophen and ibuprofen have not been proven to reduce discomfort or pain during injection.

---

on the grow

Toddlers start looking taller and thinner as they head into the preschool years, but this doesn't happen overnight. Most toddlers don't lose their sway-backed stance and potbelly until sometime after their third birthday. A typical toddler grows 5 inches and gains 4 to 5 pounds between ages one and two, and grows 2 to 3 inches and gains 5 pounds between ages two and three.

The Facts on Immunization

Immunizations continue to play a vital role in helping to protect children against disease—so vital, in fact, that both the Canadian Paediatric Society and the National Advisory Committee on Immunization have spoken out strongly in favour of the current practice of routinely immunizing Canadian children against a number of potentially life-threatening diseases.

There are only three specific situations in which an individual definitely should not receive a vaccine (which means that vaccines are strongly recommended for the vast majority of children and adults):

1. Anyone who has had a severe allergic reaction to a vaccine or a component of a vaccine should not receive the same vaccine again. The individual should be referred to an allergist and/or pediatrician so that the specific cause of the allergic reaction can

be determined, along with which vaccines should be avoided and for how long.

2. Individuals with severely compromised immune systems should avoid live viral or bacterial vaccines.

3. Pregnant women should avoid live viral or bacterial vaccines unless the risk from an illness is greater than the potential risk from the vaccine.

How immunizations work

Immunizations help the body produce antibodies against a particular disease. Depending on the type of immunization, it may be injected or given orally. Still, as much as they've revolutionized pediatric health, they aren't always 100 percent effective. (Of people who have been immunized against measles, 99.7 percent will be immune to measles, while 99 percent of people who have been immunized against polio will be immune to polio.) Ensuring that as many people as possible are immunized against a particular disease helps to provide protection to the rest—those for whom immunizations are ineffective or who can't be immunized for health reasons. This group protective effect is known as the herd effect.

Worried that your child might experience a severe allergic reaction following a vaccination? You'll be reassured to know that these types of reactions (which may include breathing problems such as wheezing; swelling and blotchy skin on the body or around the mouth) are extremely rare. Typically these reactions occur within minutes of getting the vaccine, which is why your health care provider will ask you to stay for at least 15 minutes after your child receives a vaccination.

Alarmed by something you've read about immunizations causing autism? A British physician raised this possibility in a much-talked-about 1988 study published in the medical journal *The Lancet* that ended up being thoroughly discredited. Other concerns regarding a possible link between the preservative thimerosal (used in certain types of vaccines, but not in any routine childhood vaccines currently available in Canada) and autism were also investigated, but no such link was found.

8.1 Recommended Immunization Schedule for Canadian Children	2 months	4 months	6 months	12 months	18 months
Diptheria, tetanus, allecular pertussis, and inactivated polio virus vaccine (DTP-IPV)	x	x	x		x
Haemophilus influenzae type b conjugate vaccine (Hib)	x	x	x		x
Measles, mumps, rubella, and varicella vaccine (MMRV)				x	x
Rotavirus vaccine (Rot-5 or -1)	2–3 doses, 4 weeks apart, starting before 15 weeks; this is the only vaccine that is given orally.				
Hepatitis vaccine	3 doses during infancy or preteen/teen years				
Pneumococcal conjugate 13-valent vaccine (Pneu-C-13)	x	x			
Meningococcal conjugate 13-valent (Men-C-C)				x	
Influenza vaccine (Inf)				x (1–2 doses first; then annually)	

Note: Exact immunization schedule varies by province or territory. You can obtain a copy of the most up-to-date immunization schedule for your province or territory by visiting http://healthycanadians.gc.ca/apps/schedule-calendrier/index-eng.php to generate an immunization schedule that is customized to reflect your child's age. Some provinces and territories also offer the bacillus Calmette-Guerin, or BCG vaccine, which protects against tuberculosis.

According to the Centers for Disease Control and Prevention, the misconception that there is a link between vaccination and autism likely persists because of "the coincidence of timing between early childhood vaccinations and the first appearance of symptoms of autism." In other words, no one has been able to demonstrate a definitive link between vaccinations and autism. So that's one worry you can scratch off your list right now.

The vaccination story is a "good news" story. Here's what you need to know about the most common early childhood vaccinations and the 13 devastating and even deadly diseases they prevent. (See Table 8.1 for a schedule outlining when these immunizations typically occur and in which combinations.)

The 5-in-1 vaccine: diphtheria, pertussis, tetanus, polio, haemophilus influenzae type b

The 5-in-1 vaccine provides protection against five different diseases:

- **diphtheria** (a disease that attacks the throat and heart and that can lead to heart failure or death);
- **pertussis or whooping cough** (a disease characterized by a severe cough that makes it difficult to breathe, eat, or drink and that can lead to pneumonia, convulsions, brain damage, and death);
- **tetanus** (a disease that can lead to muscle spasms and death);
- **polio** (a disease that can result in muscle pain and paralysis and death);
- **haemophilus influenzae type b** (Hib) (a disease that can lead to meningitis, pneumonia, and a severe throat infection [epiglottitis] that can cause choking).

Immunization side effects are generally mild. The vast majority of children who experience some sort of reaction to the needle don't experience anything more serious than some pain and redness at the injection site or a low-grade fever.

Measles, mumps, rubella (MMRV) vaccine

This vaccine provides protection against four diseases:

- **measles** (a disease that involves fever, rash, cough, runny nose, and watery eyes and that can cause ear infections, pneumonia, brain swelling, and even death);
- **mumps** (a disease that can result in meningitis—the swelling of the coverings of the brain and spinal cord—and, in rare cases, testicular damage that may result in sterility);
- **rubella** (a disease that can result in severe injury to or even the death of the fetus if it's contracted by a pregnant woman);
- **varicella or chicken pox** (a generally mild and non-life-threatening disease that can, in some cases, lead to a number of potentially serious complications, including pneumonia—an infection of the lungs—and encephalitis—an infection of the brain).

While most children who have the MMRV vaccine experience few, if any, side effects (a slight fever, fussiness, redness or soreness at the injection site), in rare cases, children may develop a fever and/or rash seven to twelve days after the immunization or experience other even rarer complications.

Note: In rare cases, your doctor may recommend that your child receive the varicella portion of the vaccine separately. In this case, your child would be given the two injections one month apart.

Rotavirus vaccine

Rotavirus is a virus in the stool that is spread through person-to-person contact. It is the most common cause of diarrhea outbreaks in child-care centres.

The National Advisory Committee on Immunization is now recommending that healthy infants receive an oral vaccine to protect them against rotavirus, and that they receive this vaccine in two (sometimes three) doses. All doses of the vaccine should be completed by the time the baby is 8 months old.

If your child has a history of anaphylactic reaction to any ingredient in the rotavirus vaccine or its oral applicator (which contains latex), your child should not be vaccinated. Talk to your health care provider.

Hepatitis B vaccine

Hepatitis B is a contagious disease that is spread from person to person via body fluids, including blood and breast milk. Hepatitis B attacks the liver, resulting in liver cancer or other serious liver problems. Side effects of the vaccine are usually very mild. Your child might have a slight fever and there might be redness and soreness at the injection site. These side effects—which typically occur within 12 to 24 hours of the immunization—usually disappear within a few days.

Pneumococcal vaccine

Pneumococcal disease is a bacterial disease that can lead to meningitis (brain infection), bacteremia (bloodstream infection), pneumonia (lung infection), and otitis media (middle ear infection). Complications from pneumococcal disease can result in lifelong damage to the brain, the ears, and major organs. Side effects of the vaccine are usually very mild and include a slight fever and/or redness and soreness at the injection site. These side effects—which typically occur within 12 to 24 hours of the immunization—usually disappear within a few days.

Meningococcal meningitis vaccine

Meningococcal meningitis is a disease that can cause meningitis (an inflammation of the lining around your child's spinal cord and brain). It is spread by the meningococcal germ, a germ carried by one in five healthy teenagers and adults. Side effects of the vaccine are usually very mild. Your child may have a slight fever and/or redness and soreness at the injection site. These side effects—which typically occur within 24 to 48 hours of immunization—usually disappear within a few days. About one in ten older children and adults may experience a headache.

Flu shot (seasonal influenza)

Seasonal influenza (flu) is a common, contagious respiratory infection. It is spread via droplets that are coughed or sneezed by someone who has the flu. It typically starts with a headache, sore throat, and cough. Other symptoms include fever, loss of appetite, muscle aches and fatigue, sweats and chills, throat irritation, plus runny nose and sneezing (although the latter two are more likely to be associated with the common cold).

Children with the flu often experience nausea, vomiting, and diarrhea as well. They are also at risk of developing complications from the flu, including pneumonia. The National Advisory Committee on Immunization recommends that all healthy children over the age of six months receive an annual flu shot to prevent illness and reduce spread of the flu to those who are more vulnerable. If there are children under the age of two in your home, everyone living in your home should receive a flu shot. Note: If your child is less than nine years old and receiving a flu shot for the very first time, two doses are required, spaced about a month apart. From this point onward, a single flu shot is all that is required.

Your child may have a slight fever and/or redness and soreness at the injection site. These side effects—which typically occur within 12 to 24 hours of the immunization—usually disappear within a few days. Once your child reaches age two, your doctor may suggest a nasal spray form of the flu shot (FluMist) as an alternative to the injectable flu shot itself, in order to reduce the number of injections your child receives. FluMist is available across Canada but is not free of charge in all areas.

Note: The best time of year to get a flu shot is in the fall (between October and December) before the number of flu cases in Canada peaks. The shot is still effective, though, even if you get it later in the season. It takes about two weeks after immunization for the flu shot to provide full protection.

How Will I Know If My Child Is Sick?

Most first-time parents live in fear that they'll mistakenly assume their child's runny nose is caused by nothing more sinister than the common cold when, in fact, it's actually a symptom of some life-threatening disease. Just in case this is one of those things that has you tossing and turning in the middle of the night, allow me to reassure you.

Believe it or not, your parent radar is more highly developed than you might realize. Mother Nature has programmed your toddler with a series of symptoms that are designed to tell you if she's developed some sort of illness. (They're not unlike the error messages that show up on your computer screen from time to time, alerting you to the fact that your computer is anything but happy. But unlike that nice, neat little text box, toddler-related error messages tend to be a whole lot messier.) You can expect your toddler to experience one or more of the following symptoms if she's doing battle with an illness.

Respiratory symptoms

Runny nose: Your toddler's nose starts secreting clear, colourless mucus that may become thick and yellowish or greenish within a day or two. A runny nose is almost always caused by a viral infection such as the common cold, but it can also be caused by environmental or food allergies or chemical irritations (although these types of allergies are exceedingly rare in toddlers). Note: Your toddler should be checked by a doctor if the runny nose continues for longer than 10 days in order to rule out these causes and to check for the presence of a sinus infection. Ditto for the presence of a yellow-green discharge that lasts for longer than a week, as that may also be an indication of a sinus infection.

Coughing: Your toddler starts coughing because there's some sort of inflammation in the respiratory tract—anywhere from the nose to the lungs. The most common cause of coughing is the common cold. Other rarer causes include allergies, chemical irritations (such as exposure to cigarette smoke), rare but serious chronic lung diseases like cystic fibrosis, or because she has inhaled and aspirated an object that's causing her to cough.

Wheezing: Your toddler makes wheezing sounds that are particularly noticeable when she's breathing out (exhaling). Wheezing is caused by both the narrowing of the air passages in the lungs and the presence of excess mucus in those major airways (bronchi) or in the lungs, most often triggered by a viral infection. (The more rapid and laboured your child's breathing, the more serious the infection.)

Croup: Your toddler's breathing becomes very noisy (some toddlers become very hoarse and develop a cough that sounds like a seal's bark) and, in severe cases, her windpipe may actually become narrowed. (Typically, the more laboured and noisy your toddler's breathing, the more serious the airway constriction.) Croup is caused by an inflammation of the windpipe below the vocal cords. See the section on treating croup later in this chapter.

Gastrointestinal symptoms

Diarrhea: Your toddler's bowel movements become more frequent and/or their texture changes dramatically (e.g., they become watery or unformed). Diarrhea is often accompanied by abdominal cramps or a stomach ache and is triggered when the bowel is stimulated or irritated (often by the presence of an infection). It can lead to dehydration if it's severe or continues for an extended period of time, so you'll want to monitor your toddler for any possible signs of dehydration. Note: see the section on treating diarrhea later in this chapter.

Dehydration: Your toddler has a dry mouth, isn't drinking as much as usual, is urinating less often than usual, and doesn't shed any tears when she cries. She may also be experiencing vomiting and/or diarrhea. Dehydration is triggered by the loss of body fluids and results in reduced circulating blood volume. It can occur quite rapidly in children with diarrhea, so you'll want to watch your toddler carefully if she's suffering from this problem—especially if she's also experiencing some vomiting. Signs that your toddler's dehydration may be severe include a weight loss of more than 5 percent of her body weight, lethargic or irritable behaviour, sunken eyes, a dry mouth, an absence of tears, pale skin, highly concentrated urine (urine that is dark yellow rather than pale in colour), and infrequent urination. Note: see the section on dealing with dehydration later in this chapter.

Vomiting: Your toddler begins vomiting. Vomiting is more common in children than in adults and tends to be less bothersome to children than adults. It can be caused by specific irritation to the stomach or, more commonly, is simply a side effect of another illness. It's generally only worrisome if your child vomits often enough to become dehydrated or if she chokes and inhales vomit—or if the vomiting is accompanied by a high fever and the child is not drinking well. (This combination of symptoms may indicate that the child has developed pneumonia or a kidney infection.) Note: see the section on managing vomiting later in this chapter.

Skin changes

Change in skin colour: Your toddler suddenly becomes pale or flushed, or the whites of her eyes take on a yellowish or pinkish hue. She may have developed some sort of an infection, whether it be a systemic infection (or example, stomach flu or jaundice) or a more localized variety (pink eye).

Rashes: Your toddler develops some sort of skin rash. It could be the result of a viral or bacterial infection, or an allergic reaction to a food, medication, or other substance. Note: See the section on skin rashes later in this chapter.

Other symptoms

Behavioural changes: Your toddler becomes uncharacteristically fussy and irritable, or sleepy and lethargic. It's possible that some sort of illness or infection is responsible for these changes to her usual behaviour. You know your toddler best, so you may tune into these types of behavioural changes sooner than someone who doesn't know your child quite so well. If you are worried, trust your instincts and get things checked out. You were given those instincts for a reason, after all . . .

Fever: Your toddler's temperature is higher than normal, something that usually indicates the presence of an infection but that can also be caused by a reaction to an immunization or the fact that your toddler is dressed too warmly for the weather. Fever can also be a sign of heat stroke—an important point to keep in mind on a hot day.

More about Fever

Before we move on to our discussion of the most common types of childhood illnesses, let's take a moment to talk about toddlers and fevers—a perennial cause of concern to parents.

Fever isn't the bad guy; the illness is

The first thing you need to know about fevers is that in and of itself it's rarely dangerous. Contrary to popular belief, brain damage due to a high temperature is extremely rare. So that's one fever-related worry you can strike off your list relatively easily.

Fever can, in fact, be a *good* thing, even though it can make your toddler (and consequently you) feel downright miserable for a while. The presence of a fever is usually a sign that your toddler's body is hard at work fighting off an infection (typically a common illness such as a cold, a sore throat, or an ear infection). Most of the bacteria and viruses that cause infections in humans thrive at our normal body temperature, so one of the body's key strategies for defending itself is to elevate its temperature by a couple of degrees. Add the fact that fever helps to activate the immune system, boosting the production of white blood cells, antibodies, and many other infection-fighting agents, and you'll see that there's no need to sweat it when your child gets a fever.

Something else you need to know is that the number on the thermometer is not necessarily directly related to the severity of your child's illness. In other words, even though your child may have a relatively high fever, it's possible that she's only mildly ill. On the other hand, a child with a relatively low fever can, in fact, be quite ill, which is why it's important to pay attention to her other symptoms. Instead of getting hung up on the number on the thermometer—an easy trap to fall into, by the way—concentrate on how sick your child is acting and look for symptoms of any underlying infection. (See Table 8.2.)

8.2 Common Illnesses that Can Cause a Fever	
Symptoms	**What Could Be Causing These Symptoms**
Fever, cough, runny nose	Common cold
High fever, chills, sweats, sore throat, sore muscles (although this last one is tough to spot in a toddler)	Influenza
Fever, earache, discharge from ears, dizziness from pain	Ear infection
Fever, swollen glands, sore throat	Tonsillitis, streptococcal or viral infection, mononucleosis
Fever, nausea, vomiting, diarrhea, cramps	Infectious gastroenteritis (viral or bacterial)

What type of thermometer to use

If you've checked out the thermometer aisle at your local drugstore lately, you already know that there are dozens of different models on the market today—everything from basic digital thermometers to high-tech tympanic (ear) thermometers. But not all of these options are necessarily great choices when it comes to taking your toddler's temperature. You'll want to hold off on using a tympanic thermometer until after your toddler's second birthday, due to concerns about the accuracy of readings they produce with younger toddlers. And you'll want to steer clear of fever strips (strips that are placed on your child's forehead) entirely. According to the College of Family Physicians of Canada, they don't provide accurate results.

Now that we've covered off the gear you'll need to take your toddler's temperature, let's talk about technique. You have two basic choices when it comes to taking the temperature of a young toddler: taking it rectally or taking an axillary temperature (under the armpit). Temperatures of children under four years of age should not be taken orally.

Axillary temperatures (temperatures that are taken under the armpit) tend to be slightly less accurate than rectal temperatures, but they're much easier to take. Here's what's involved:

1. Place the bulb of the thermometer under your toddler's arm so that it's nestled in her armpit, and then hold her arm against her body so that the bulb is thoroughly covered.
2. Hold the thermometer in place until it beeps to indicate that the final temperature reading has been obtained—something that typically takes about two minutes.
3. Clean the thermometer thoroughly using soap and warm water.
4. Keep in mind that axillary temperature readings tend to be about 0.3°C lower than temperatures taken orally: A "normal" range for an axillary temperature is 34.7 to 37.3°C (94.5 to 99.1°F).

Here's what's involved in taking your toddler's temperature rectally (just in case you need to take your child's temperature this way):

1. Place your child on her back with her knees bent over her abdomen.
2. Coat the tip of the thermometer with water-soluble jelly and insert it about 2.5 centimetres (one inch) into your toddler's rectum.
3. Hold the thermometer in place until the digital thermometer beeps to indicate that the final temperature reading has been obtained—something that typically takes about two minutes.
4. Clean the thermometer thoroughly using soap and warm water.

Note: Keep in mind that rectal temperature readings tend to be about 0.5°C higher than temperatures taken orally: A "normal" range for a rectal temperature is 36.6 to 38°C (97.9 to 101°F).

What you need to know about febrile convulsions

Febrile convulsions (seizures) tend to occur when a toddler's temperature shoots up very suddenly or is just about to shoot up. They are more common in one- to three-year-olds than in younger or older children, and are more likely to occur in families with a history of febrile convulsions. They occur in approximately 4 percent of children.

While febrile convulsions are relatively common and generally quite harmless, they can be extremely frightening to watch. If your toddler has a febrile convulsion, she may breathe heavily, drool, turn blue, roll her eyes back in her head, and/or shake her arms and legs uncontrollably.

If your toddler has a febrile convulsion, you should lay her on her back or side (ensuring that she's far away from anything she could hurt herself on) and then gently turn her head to one side so that any vomit or saliva can drain easily. You should note how long the convulsion lasts—anywhere from seconds to minutes. You should call 911 if your toddler's seizure lasts for more than five minutes, she is having difficulty breathing, or another seizure starts shortly after the first one ended. Note: you may want to call for help even sooner if you're not sure what's causing the seizure or if you live in a remote area and it will take longer for an ambulance to arrive.

When to call the doctor about your child's fever

While most fevers are harmless, you should plan to get in touch with your doctor if . . .

- your toddler's fever is very high for a child her age (above 39°C or 102.2°F for a toddler) regardless of whether or not she actually appears to be very ill;
- your toddler has had a fever for a couple of days and her temperature is not coming down;
- she's crying inconsolably or seems cranky or irritable, or she's whimpering and seems weak;
- she's having difficulty waking up or seems listless and confused;
- she's limp;
- she's having convulsions;
- the soft spot (fontanel) on her head is beginning to swell;
- she appears to have a stiff neck or a headache;
- she's acting as if she's experiencing stomach pain;
- she has developed a skin rash;

- she is noticeably pale or flushed;
- she's having difficulty breathing (a possible sign of asthma or pneumonia);
- she's refusing to drink or eat;
- she has constant vomiting or diarrhea;
- she's unable to swallow and is drooling excessively (a possible sign of epiglottitis, a life-threatening infection that causes swelling in the back of the throat);
- you know that she has a weakened immune system, due to a pre-existing condition;
- your gut instinct is telling you that your child is really sick and that she needs to be seen by a doctor.

antibiotics and fever

Don't expect your doctor to prescribe an antibiotic to ward off your child's fever unless there's a specific underlying infection that requires treatment. According to the Canadian Paediatric Society, the vast majority of children with fevers have non-bacterial (viral) upper respiratory infections that don't require antibiotics. That means your first-line of defence against fever is likely to be acetaminophen.

Treating a fever

Of course, it's not necessary to rush off to the emergency ward every time your toddler's temperature shoots up by a degree or two. The majority of fevers can be managed at home. Here's what you need to know.

The best way to treat a fever—assuming, of course, that it actually needs to be treated at all—is by administering acetaminophen, an analgesic that helps to bring down your child's fever while relieving some of her discomfort. (Another option is to treat your child with ibuprofen, but, if you do so, it's really important to ensure that your child is well hydrated. And, of course, you'll want to stick with one or the other. It's dangerous to administer acetaminophen and ibuprofen at the same time, or even to alternate doses of the two medications.) Note: see Table 8.3 for a complete list of items that should be in the family medicine chest during the toddler years.

It's dangerous to exceed the recommended dose of any medication, so make sure that you use a medication syringe or dropper to measure your child's dose and that you stick to the recommended schedule for administering the medication. Studies have shown, for example, that giving a child twice the recommended dose of acetaminophen over a period of days can be toxic. If your child becomes nauseated, starts vomiting, and experiences abdominal pain, you should try to figure out if she might have been given too much acetaminophen and, if there's any chance she has, seek medical attention right away.

If your toddler spits up within minutes of taking her medication, ask your doctor if you should repeat the dose. It generally takes between 30 and 45 minutes for a medication to be absorbed by the intestines. But if the medication has been in your child's stomach for more than a few minutes, don't risk giving her a double dose. It's simply too difficult to determine how much of the original dose she managed to keep down. You can find other helpful tips on administering medication to a toddler in Table 8.4.

8.3   Medicine Chest Essentials

Keep the following items on hand at all times so that you'll have them in the event of illness or injury:

- children's acetaminophen
- adhesive tape
- bandages
- flashlight
- gauze
- ice packs (the instant type that don't require refrigeration)

- infant dropper or medicine syringe
- nail clippers (toddler-safe type)
- scissors (blunt-ended)
- thermometer (digital)
- tweezers

Wondering what else you can do to try to bring down your child's fever? Here's what you need to know.

- Give your toddler plenty of fluids in order to help bring her body temperature down and to help protect against dehydration.
- Avoid overdressing your child. Instead, dress her in loose, light-weight cotton clothing with only a sheet or light blanket for covering.

- Keep your toddler's room cool, but not cold. If she gets too cold her body will start shivering, which will cause her body temperature to rise.
- You can also try to lower your child's temperature by sponging her down with lukewarm water (a sponge bath) or giving her a lukewarm bath. (Don't use cold water or she'll start shivering.) Instead of drying her off, let the water evaporate from her skin. This will help to cool her down. Whatever you do, don't add alcohol to the water in the mistaken belief that this will somehow help to bring down your toddler's temperature. Doing so could lead to serious—even life-threatening—complications.

8.4 Administering Medication to a Toddler

Forget about the spoonful of sugar; what it really takes to get the medicine down is proper technique. Here are tips on administering some of the types of medication that your doctor might prescribe for your toddler.

Oral medications

- Use a syringe or an oral dropper to administer medication. A spoon is too awkward to use; you and your toddler will both end up wearing the medication. Slowly squirt the medication into the area between the toddler's tongue and the side of her mouth, pausing between squirts so that she has a chance to swallow. Otherwise, she'll start to gag and spit the medication out, and you'll be back at square one. Likewise, avoid squirting the medication into the back of your toddler's throat or you'll trigger her gag reflex. And try to avoid hitting the taste buds at the front and centre of your toddler's tongue. (Should the medication not meet with her exacting standards for taste, she'll use her tongue to push it right back out!)
- Avoid adding any sort of medication to a glass of milk or bowl of cereal. If your child wants only part of her milk or her cereal, she'll miss out on some of the medication. If you absolutely have to mix it with some sort of food because she refuses to take it any other way, use only a very small amount of food or liquid—a quantity that you know your child will have no trouble eating or drinking.
- Let your doctor know if your child vomits repeatedly after taking a particular medication or if she has a stomach flu that makes it impossible for her to keep anything down. Your doctor might decide to prescribe an injection or suppository instead.
- If you miss a dose, administer the next dose as soon as you remember. Then add the missed dose to the end of the course of medication. Don't double up on

doses unless your doctor specifically tells you to do so; and be sure to get in touch with your doctor if your child ends up missing an entire day's worth of medication.

- Don't rely on your memory when administering your toddler's medications. It's easy to make mistakes. That's why it's a good idea to get in the habit of noting the time that the medication was given and the dose administered (either using a notebook or a medication tracker app). This is particularly important if more than one person will be responsible for administering the medication. And if you're likely to forget to give your child her medication, set the alarm on your phone to go off the next time she's due for a dose.

Eardrops

- Lay your child down.
- Remove any medication that may have built up on the outer ear as a result of past treatments before you administer the next dose. (Use a damp facecloth as opposed to a Q-tip.)
- Turn your toddler's head to one side and gently pull the middle of the outer ear back slightly. This will allow fluid to enter the ear canal more readily.

Eye drops

- Lay your toddler down on his back.
- Approach your toddler with the eye dropper. He will respond by closing his eyes. While his eyes remain closed, place the drop on the inner corner of the eye. When he opens his eye, the drop will fall in.

Skin ointments or creams

- Apply some of the ointment or cream to a tissue or gauze.
- Using the tissue or gauze, apply the ointment or cream to your child's skin. To reduce the chances of contaminating the ointment or cream, discard the used tissue and use a fresh one if more ointment or cream is required.

Coping with Common Childhood Illnesses and Infections

While there are literally hundreds of illnesses and conditions that can occur during early childhood, we aren't going to be able to touch on each and every one in this chapter. Due to space constraints, I had to limit myself to the more common ones—pediatric medicine's "greatest hits," so to speak! If you'd like to find out about an illness that isn't covered here, you might want to visit one of the many excellent pediatric health websites listed on the website for this book, www.having-a-baby.com.

Here are some important questions to ask your doctor or pharmacist when she prescribes a medication for your child for the very first time:

- How will this medication help my child?
- How necessary is this medication? Is *not* giving my child this medication an option for this condition?
- What is the correct dosage?
- Do I need to shake the bottle before administering the medication?
- How often do I need to give my child the medication? Does it have to be administered at a particular time of day?
- How long does my child have to take the medication? Will the prescription be repeated or is this a one-shot deal?
- Should the medication be taken on a full or empty stomach?
- Are there any foods or drinks my child needs to avoid while taking this medication?
- Should the medication be stored in the refrigerator or at room temperature?
- Is it necessary to wake my child in the night to administer this medication?
- Are there any side effects to this medication that I need to know about?
- Is there any chance that my child could have an allergic reaction to this medication? If so, what warning signs should I watch out for?

Respiratory and related conditions

Condition: Allergies

Cause: Allergies can be caused by pollens, animal dander, moulds, dust, and other substances. Environmental allergies are rare in toddlers, but may begin to emerge between the ages of three and five.

Signs and symptoms: A clear runny nose and watery eyes, sneezing fits, constant sniffing, nosebleeds, dark circles under the eyes, frequent colds or ear infections, a cough that is bothersome at night, a stuffy nose in the morning, and/or noisy breathing at night.

What you can do:

- **Eliminate or limit exposure to the substances that seem to trigger your toddler's allergies.** (In addition to the allergens listed above, you might also want to consider the impact of any wood that is being stored in the home for use in fireplaces or whether your child has developed an allergy to Christmas trees—yes, Christmas trees!)

- **"Allergy-proof" your toddler's room by using allergy-proof zippered covers, purchasing non-allergenic bedding, removing stuffed animals from your toddler's room** (and/or washing them in the washing machine regularly), removing all room deodorizers and baby powders, vacuuming the mattress and washing all of your toddler's bedding at least once every two weeks, avoiding plush carpet (if possible), keeping your toddler's windows closed during allergy season, and vacuuming your toddler's room only when she's out of the room (since vacuuming tends to stir up dust). One final tip: If you haven't done so already, make your home smoke-free. Cigarette smoke aggravates allergies.

- **Keep your child comfortable by treating her symptoms** (for example, using a nasal aspirator to clear her nose), and/or running a cool-mist humidifier in her room. (Be sure to clean the humidifier once or twice a week.) You might also want to think about talking to your child's doctor about the advisability of trying an allergy medication and/or proceeding with allergy testing.

Condition: Asthma (a lung condition that affects the bronchial tubes)
Cause: Most commonly triggered after a viral respiratory infection inflames the lining of the bronchial tubes in the lungs. Asthma can also be caused by an irritant such as cigarette smoke or paint fumes; allergens such as pollens, mould spores, animal dander (particularly from cats), house dust mites, and cockroaches; and inhaling cold air. In some older children, exercise may also be a trigger for asthma.

Signs and symptoms: Coughing and/or high-pitched wheezing or whistling as your toddler breathes. The cough typically gets worse at night or if your toddler gets a cold. In cases of severe asthma, your toddler's breathing may become very rapid, her heart rate may increase, and she may vomit; or she may become very tired and slow-moving and cough all the time (in which case she requires immediate medical attention).

What you can do:
- **Try to eliminate anything that could be triggering your toddler's asthma problems, including any irritants or allergens.**
- **Work with your doctor to come up with a game plan for preventing and treating future asthma attacks through medication and/or lifestyle modifications.**

Condition: Bronchiolitis (an infection of the small breathing tubes of the lungs; not to be confused with bronchitis, which is an infection of the larger, more central airways)

Cause: Caused by a virus (frequently the respiratory syncytial (RSV) virus) that results in swelling of the small bronchial tubes. It is typically picked up as a result of being exposed to someone with an upper respiratory tract illness. Bronchiolitis is much more common in infants than in toddlers and is most likely to occur during the winter months.

Signs and symptoms: Triggered by a virus that results in swelling of the bronchioles, which in turn leads to reduced air flow through the lungs. It initially starts out like a normal cold with a runny nose and sneezing, but after a couple of days, a child with bronchiolitis starts coughing, wheezing, and having trouble breathing. Your child may also be irritable and may experience difficulty eating due to the coughing and breathing problems.

What you can do:
- **Keep your toddler comfortable by using a nasal aspirator or a cool-mist humidifier.** (Just make sure that you clean the cool-mist humidifier on a regular basis—ideally once or twice a week—to prevent it from becoming a breeding ground for bacteria.)

- **Watch for signs of dehydration, since toddlers with bronchiolitis can become dehydrated.**
- **Get in touch with your doctor to find out whether any additional treatment may be required.** Some toddlers who have a lot of difficulty breathing may require medication to open the bronchial tubes. A few will also need to be hospitalized so that oxygen and fluids may be administered until the toddler's breathing improves.

Condition: Common cold

Cause: Spread from person to person via airborne droplets containing the cold virus or via contaminated hands and/or objects (such as toys). It is most contagious from one day before to seven days after the onset of symptoms, which helps to explain why your toddler managed to pick up a cold at playgroup even though every child in the room appeared to be the absolute picture of health! According to the Canadian Paediatric Society, there are more than 200 viruses that cause colds. Unfortunately, being infected by a particular virus once doesn't provide you with any protection against getting that virus again—something that goes a long way toward explaining why the common cold is so, well, common!

Signs and symptoms: Runny nose, sore throat, cough, decreased appetite. May be accompanied by a fever, in which case your child may also experience a headache (although it can be pretty tough to diagnose a headache in a toddler). While a cold typically lasts for five to seven days in an adult, children's colds tend to drag on a little longer—bad news, I know, if your toddler is waking up every hour on the hour, frustrated because her nose is clogged up!

What you can do:

- **Keep your toddler comfortable.** You might want to clear out her runny nose by using a nasal aspirator or—if her nose is really stuffed up—by placing a cool-mist humidifier in her room. (Note: be sure to clean the cool-mist humidifier frequently to prevent it from becoming a breeding ground for bacteria.)

- **Keep your toddler's face clean.** Infections of the face can occur as a result of prolonged exposure to nasal secretions, and your toddler could end up with yellow pustules or wide, honey-coloured scabs (impetigo).
- **Don't be surprised if your toddler ends up eating and drinking less than usual.** She may have difficulty eating or drinking if her nose is really stuffed up, and her appetite may be off, too. There's generally little cause for concern, provided she's consuming enough liquids to avoid becoming dehydrated.
- **Watch for signs that your child's cold could be developing into something more serious.** You'll want to get in touch with your doctor if she develops an earache or a fever over 39°C (102.2°F); if she becomes exceptionally sleepy, cranky, or fussy; if she develops a skin rash; if her breathing becomes rapid or laboured, or if her cough becomes persistent or severe.

Condition: Croup, or laryngotracheitis (an inflammation of the voice box or larynx and windpipe or trachea)

Cause: Usually caused by a viral infection in or around the voice box. Children are most susceptible to croup between six months and three years of age. As children get older, their windpipe gets larger, so swelling to the larynx and trachea is less likely to result in breathing difficulties. There are two types of croup: spasmodic croup (which comes on suddenly, is caused by a mild upper respiratory infection or allergy, and keeps occurring repeatedly over time) and viral croup (a one-time occurrence triggered by a viral infection in the voice box and windpipe and which may be accompanied by noisy or laboured breathing—a condition known as "stridor").

Signs and symptoms: A cough that sounds similar to a seal-like bark and/or a fever.

What you can do:

- **Keep your toddler comfortable by using a cool-mist humidifier in her room;** by filling your bathroom with hot steam from the shower and then letting her breathe in the moist vapours; or by taking her outside so she can breathe in some cool night air.

• **Get in touch with your doctor if the croup seems to be particularly severe or if your toddler shows the following types of symptoms:** fever higher than 39°C (102.2°F), rapid or difficult breathing, severe sore throat, increased drooling, refusal to swallow, and/or discomfort when lying down.

Condition: Ear infections (otitis media)

Cause: Caused by a virus and/or bacteria, and typically occur in the aftermath of a cold. Because a child's Eustachian tube (the tube that connects the middle ear to the back of the nose) is very short and very narrow, children are highly susceptible to ear infections. (Half of children will require treatment for at least one ear infection by the time they turn three.) Of course, some toddlers are more susceptible to ear infections than others. According to the College of Family Physicians of Canada, a toddler is more likely to develop an ear infection if he is exposed to cigarette smoke, has had one or more ear infections in the past (particularly if those infections occurred before his first birthday), uses a pacifier, attends daycare, was born prematurely or was of low-birthweight, and/or is male.

Signs and symptoms: Fussiness and irritability, difficulty sleeping (because lying down tends to increase ear pain), and difficulty hearing (for example, your toddler stops responding to certain types of sounds). You may also notice fever and cold symptoms and you may detect fluid draining from your toddler's ear. Note: If there is pus coming from your toddler's ear, this means that her eardrum has burst—something that is not serious, but that may require treatment with antibiotic drops and/or oral antibiotics.

What you can do:

• **Keep your toddler comfortable by treating her fever and cold symptoms** (see earlier sections of this chapter) and by offering her acetaminophen to treat her earache.

- **Get in touch with your doctor to arrange for your toddler's ears to be checked.** Your doctor may want to prescribe an antibiotic to clear up the infection. Note: Not everyone agrees that antibiotics should be prescribed for children with uncomplicated ear infections (although doctors still tend to err on the side of caution when it comes to children under the age of two). Research has shown that nearly two-thirds of children with garden-variety ear infections recover from pain and fever within 24 hours of diagnosis without any treatment and that over 80 percent recover spontaneously within one to seven days. (When children are treated with antibiotics, 93 percent recover within the first week.) If an antibiotic is prescribed, give it a chance to do its job. Don't be surprised if your child's temperature remains high for the first day or two after she starts antibiotic treatment. It takes time for the antibiotics to start working their magic, which will, in turn, start to bring that fever down.

antibiotic alert

Antibiotics are powerful medications that can be used to treat life-threatening illnesses like meningitis as well as less serious infections such as impetigo. Because they're so effective, they tend to be used widely, which has unfortunately led to the emergence of antibiotic-resistant strains of bacteria. You can do your bit to prevent these strains of bacteria from becoming more of a problem by ensuring that you follow your doctor's instructions for antibiotic use carefully and that your child finishes taking any antibiotic she starts (unless, of course, your doctor tells you otherwise).

- **In most cases, there's no need to rush off to the emergency ward in the middle of the night to seek treatment for an ear infection.** Simply treat your toddler's pain with acetaminophen during the night and then call your doctor's office in the morning to set up an appointment.

swimmer's ear

Some toddlers develop a painful infection known as "swimmer's ear." It occurs in the delicate skin of the outer ear canal. The condition is caused when frequent exposure to water allows bacteria and fungi to grow. A toddler will typically experience itching followed by a swelling of the skin of the ear canal and then some drainage. Sometimes a toddler with "swimmer's ear" will experience extreme pain when the earlobe or other outside parts of the ear are touched. The condition is treated with eardrops containing antibiotics and/or corticosteroids to help fight infection and reduce the amount of swelling in the ear canal. Your child's doctor may also recommend that you give her an over-the-counter pain relief medication to help relieve her discomfort.

- **Even if your toddler's ear infection has already been diagnosed by a doctor, you should call your doctor's office again if she develops one or more of the following symptoms:** an earache that worsens even after she's on antibiotics, a fever that's greater than 39°C (102.2°F) after treatment begins or a fever that lasts more than three days, excessive sleepiness, excessive crankiness or fussiness, a skin rash, rapid or difficult breathing, or hearing loss.
- **Your child's doctor may want to check her ears again after she's finished the antibiotic to ensure that there's no fluid remaining in her ear**—although it may take a couple of weeks for the fluid to clear. (Fluid in the ear can lead to further infections and/or hearing problems down the road.) Not all doctors recommend a routine follow-up visit. Others simply advise you to get in touch if you're concerned about your child's ongoing symptoms. Note: If your child has recurrent problems with ear infections (for example, five or six ear infections requiring five to six treatments with antibiotics during a 12-month period), your doctor may recommend that myringotomy tubes be inserted in your child's ears to help balance the pressure between the middle ear and the ear

canal and allow the fluid that accumulates in the middle ear to drain. These tubes are inserted while your child is under general anaesthetic and generally stay in place for one to two years, at which point they typically fall out on their own. Some children need a second set of tubes.

Condition: Influenza

Cause: Caused by the influenza virus (a virus that is spread from person to person via droplets or contaminated objects).

Signs and symptoms: Fever, chills, and shakes; extreme tiredness or fatigue; muscle aches and pains; and a dry, hacking cough. (It's different from the common cold in that a toddler with the common cold only has a fever, a runny nose, and a small amount of coughing.)

What you can do:

- **Keep your toddler comfortable by treating her fever and cold symptoms** (see relevant sections above).
- **Better yet, prevent the flu from happening by ensuring that your toddler receives a flu shot.**
- **If you happen to pick up on your child's flu symptoms early** (within a day or two of the onset of symptoms), it may be possible to minimize the severity of the flu by having your doctor prescribe an antiviral medication called Tamiflu. This is good to know in the event that there's a flu outbreak in your community and your toddler begins to exhibit symptoms.

Condition: Pink eye (conjunctivitis)

Cause: Spread from person to person as a result of direct contact with secretions from the eye. It is caused by viruses or bacteria. Pink eye is contagious for the duration of the illness or until 24 hours after antibiotic treatment has been started.

Signs and symptoms: Redness and discharge from the eye.

What you can do:

- **Get in touch with your doctor to see if antibiotic eye drops should**

be prescribed (if your child's eye discharge is yellowish and thick, indicating a bacterial infection that will respond to antibiotics).

- **Keep your child away from other people until the antibiotic eye drops have been used for at least one full day.**
- **Make a point of washing your hands really, really well after coming into contact with your child.** Thorough hand washing is the key to preventing pink eye from spreading.

Condition: Pneumonia (infection of the lung)

Cause: Spread from person to person via droplets or by touching contaminated objects. The infectious period varies according to the cause. Pneumonia can be caused by both viruses and bacterial infections.

Signs and symptoms: Rapid or noisy breathing, possibly accompanied by a cough and/or flaring of the nostrils; pale or bluish skin colour; shaking or chills; high fever; decreased appetite and energy; vomiting.

What you can do:
- **Get in touch with your doctor so that the cause of the pneumonia can be determined and an appropriate course of treatment can be mapped out.** Unless there is high fever and vomiting, pneumonia in toddlers is generally viral in origin and doesn't require antibiotics. Viral pneumonias are typically treated with acetaminophen (for fever) and bronchodilators (to minimize wheezing). Bacterial pneumonias, on the other hand, require treatment with antibiotics.
- **Monitor your child's symptoms carefully if she's being cared for at home and report any changes in her condition to her doctor.** Your child may require emergency assistance if she's having difficulty breathing.

Condition: Respiratory syncytial virus (RSV)

Cause: A virus with an incubation period of five to eight days.

Signs and symptoms: A raspy cough, rapid breathing, and wheezing (particularly common in children under the age of two).

What you can do:
- **Keep your toddler comfortable by using a nasal aspirator or a cool-mist humidifier.**
- **Watch for any signs of dehydration.**
- **Get in touch with your doctor to talk about treatment options.** Some toddlers who have a lot of difficulty breathing may require medication to open the bronchial tubes. A few will also need to be hospitalized so that oxygen and fluids can be administered until the toddler's breathing improves. In general, a child who is drinking well and who doesn't have a fever can be cared for and monitored at home.

Condition: Sinusitis (sinus infection)

Cause: The mucus in your child's sinuses becomes infected with bacteria, usually as the result of a lingering cold.

Signs and symptoms: Persistent nasal discharge (especially yellow-green discharge that has been present for more than a week), fever, a cough that gets worse at night, tenderness in the face, dark circles under the eyes, puffy lower eyelids, bad breath, and fatigue.

What you can do:
- **Get in touch with your doctor to talk about whether your toddler should be on some sort of an antibiotic.**
- **Keep your child comfortable.** (See the tips in the section above on treating the common cold.)

Condition: Strep throat

Cause: Strep throat is a bacterial infection. It is transmitted via droplets or by touching contaminated objects and is contagious until 24 to 36 hours after the start of antibiotic treatment. Strep throat is more common in children over the age of three than in younger children, so hopefully this is one infection your child will be able to sidestep during the toddler years.

Signs and symptoms: Sore throat, fever, swollen glands in the neck. (Note: if a skin rash is also present, the condition is known as scarlet fever.) Typically, a child with strep throat does *not* have a cough or a runny nose.

What you can do:

- **Get in touch with your doctor to arrange to have a throat swab taken to determine whether or not your toddler has strep throat.** If she does, an antibiotic will be prescribed to help kill off the strep germ. If left untreated, strep throat can result in kidney disease or rheumatic fever (a serious condition that can cause heart damage and joint swelling). It can also lead to skin infections, bloodstream infections, ear infections, and pneumonia.
- **Offer plenty of liquids plus whatever foods happen to appeal to your toddler;** and watch for signs of dehydration.

Condition: Tonsillitis (infection of the tonsils)

Cause: Tends to be viral in origin. (When bacteria causes a sore throat, that sore throat is typically diagnosed as strep throat.)

Signs and symptoms: Fever, swollen glands under the jaw, a very sore throat, cold symptoms, and abdominal pain.

What you can do:

- **Treat your toddler's fever and cold symptoms.** (See earlier sections of this chapter on treating a cold or fever.)
- **Have your toddler examined by your doctor to see if a throat swab should be taken and/or an antibiotic should be prescribed.**

Condition: Whooping cough

Cause: Caused by a bacterial infection. The incubation period is seven to ten days.

Signs and symptoms: Cold-like symptoms that linger. About two weeks into the illness, the cough suddenly worsens. When the toddler coughs, thick mucus is dislodged, causing her to gasp for her next breath (the "whoop" in whooping cough). She turns red in the face during the cough and may vomit afterwards. Whooping cough typically lasts for three to four months.

What you can do:

- **Offer your toddler plenty of fluids.**
- **See if a cool-mist humidifier will help with your toddler's cough.**
- **Seek immediate medical attention if your child becomes exhausted or is having difficulty breathing.** Many young children end up being hospitalized so that they can be treated with oxygen (and antibiotics in the hope of preventing the illness from spreading—although the antibiotics have to be administered right away to be effective). A nasal swab may be taken early on to confirm the diagnosis.

Skin and scalp conditions

Condition: Boils

Cause: Usually caused by staphylococcus bacteria from an infected pimple.

Signs and symptoms: Swellings on the skin that are raised, red, tender, and warm. Most commonly found on the buttocks.

What you can do:

- **Apply hot compresses to the boils three to four times daily in order to bring them to a head, and then continue applying them for a few days after the boils pop and drain.** Avoid picking at or squeezing at your toddler's boils, as this may result in scarring and spreading.
- **Get in touch with your doctor.** If the boils don't drain on their own, they may need to be incised and drained by your doctor. A topical antibiotic or systemic antibiotics may also be required.

Condition: Cellulitis

Cause: Usually caused by a bacterial infection such as staphylococcus or streptococcus.

Signs and symptoms: Swollen, red, tender, warm areas of skin that are usually found on the extremities or the buttocks. They often start out as a boil or a puncture wound but then become infected. They're typically accompanied by a fever and swollen and tender lymph glands.

What you can do:
- **Give your toddler acetaminophen to help control the fever and pain.**
- **Contact your doctor.** This condition will need to be treated with antibiotics (oral, injected, or intravenous, depending on the severity of the case).

Condition: Chicken pox

Cause: Caused by a viral infection that is spread from person to person. The incubation period is two to three weeks. It is very difficult to control the spread of chicken pox because it can be transmitted through direct contact with an infected person (usually via fluid from broken blisters), through the air when an infected person coughs or sneezes, and through direct contact with lesions (sores) from a person with shingles (a possible complication of chicken pox). Outbreaks are most common in winter and in early spring. The good news is that chicken pox has largely been eradicated since the varicella virus immunization started to be administered routinely.

Signs and symptoms: A rash with small blisters that develops on the scalp and body and then spreads to the face, arms, and legs over a period of three to four days. A child can end up with anywhere from less than a dozen to more than 500 itchy blisters that dry up and turn into scabs two to four days later. Other symptoms of chicken pox include coughing, fussiness, loss of appetite, and headaches. Chicken pox is contagious from two days before to five days after the rash appears.

What you can do:
- **Ensure that your child has received the MMRV vaccine, which protects against chicken pox.**
- **Keep your toddler's nails trimmed so that she'll be less able to scratch at her chicken pox.** If that doesn't seem to do the trick, you might want to consider providing her with a set of hand puppets or mittens to wear around the house.
- **Try to minimize the amount of itching your toddler experiences by giving her colloidal oatmeal or baking soda baths or by dabbing**

calamine lotion on her spots. (Note: Don't apply calamine lotion to the spots in her mouth. Calamine lotion is for external use only.)

- **Give your child acetaminophen to help bring down her fever and eliminate some of her discomfort.** Note: Do not give children Aspirin or drugs containing salicylate at any time, since Aspirin use during certain illnesses, including chicken pox, has been linked to Reye's syndrome—a potentially fatal disease that affects the liver and the brain.

- **Be sure to get in touch with your doctor if your child's fever lasts longer than four days;** if it remains high after the third day after the spots appear; if your child shows signs of becoming dehydrated; or if your child's rash becomes warm, red, or tender. Note: some doctors choose to prescribe an antiviral medicine to make the chicken pox less severe, but, in order to be effective, this medication must be administered within the first 24 hours of the onset of chicken pox.

Condition: Eczema

Cause: Unknown, but it tends to be worse in winter when your toddler's skin is driest. There is a demonstrated link between eczema, allergies, and asthma. Eczema is not contagious.

Signs and symptoms: Extreme itchiness that results in a rash in areas that are scratched, especially the cheeks, wrists, elbows, knees, and belly.

What you can do:

- **Keep your toddler's skin well moisturized by applying a non-allergenic moisturizing lotion a couple of times each day.**
- **Dress your child in cotton and other breathable fabrics.**
- **Keep your toddler's nails trimmed so that she'll be less likely to infect her skin through scratching.**
- **Give your toddler an oatmeal bath.** (Don't open the cereal cupboard; you need colloidal oatmeal, a product that can be purchased in the drugstore.)
- **Your doctor may prescribe a steroid cream if your toddler's eczema is particularly severe.**

*Condition: **Fifth disease*** (erythema infectiosum)

Cause: Caused by a virus known as parvovirus B19. Once the rash appears, the disease is no longer likely to spread—important information to have if you or someone else you know is pregnant. (In rare cases, exposure to fifth disease can be harmful to the developing baby.)

Signs and symptoms: A "slapped cheek" rash on the face accompanied by a "lacey" red rash on the trunk and extremities. The child may also have a fever and sore joints. Fortunately, this illness is more common in school-aged children than in younger children.

What you can do:

- **There is no treatment for fifth disease, nor is there any vaccine available.** This is one of those diseases that you simply have to "wait out."
- **Fifth disease may heighten anemia in children who are already anemic**—you'll want to get in touch with your doctor as soon as possible if your child has sickle-cell anemia or some other form of chronic anemia.

*Condition: **Hand, foot, and mouth syndrome***

Cause: Caused by the Coxsackie virus—a contagious virus with an incubation period of three to six days. The virus is most active during the summer months.

Signs and symptoms: Tiny blister-like sores in the mouth, on the palms of the hands, on the soles of the feet, and on the buttocks. These are accompanied by a mild fever, a sore throat, and painful swallowing. Lasts approximately seven to ten days and is contagious from one day before until one day after the blisters appear.

What you can do:

- **Give your toddler plenty of liquids and soft foods as well.** Note: ice pops can ease some of the discomfort of the sores in the mouth while ensuring that your child remains well hydrated.
- **Keep your toddler comfortable by treating her with acetaminophen until her symptoms start to subside.**

Condition: Impetigo (an infection of the skin)

Cause: Caused by a bacterial infection.

Signs and symptoms: A rash featuring oozing, blister-like, honey-coloured crusts that may be as small as pimples or as large as coins. Outbreaks of impetigo typically occur below the nose or on the buttocks or at the site of an insect bite or scrape.

What you can do:

- **Have your toddler seen by a doctor so that the rash can be diagnosed and an antibacterial ointment and/or an oral antibiotic can be prescribed.**
- **Trim your toddler's nails to prevent her from scratching the rash.** Keep the sores covered to minimize the chance that they'll spread to other parts of the body and other people.

Condition: Measles (rubeola)

Cause: Spread by a virus that has an incubation period of 8 to 12 days. Measles are now extremely rare, except in areas where there are low vaccination rates.

Signs and symptoms: Cold, high fever (40°C or 104°F), cough, bloodshot eyes that are sensitive to light. Around the fourth day of illness, a bright red rash erupts on the face and spreads all over the body. (Even the inner cheeks will have spots, which will be white in colour.) At around the time that the spots break out, the child starts feeling quite ill. The infectious period lasts from three to five days before the rash appears until after the rash disappears (typically four days after the rash appears).

What you can do:

- **Have your child vaccinated against measles** (this is part of the MMRV vaccination).
- **Have your toddler seen by your doctor so that the illness can be properly diagnosed and any complications (pneumonia, encephalitis, ear infections, etc.) can be treated.**
- **Give your child acetaminophen to manage her fever and plenty of fluids to keep her well hydrated.**

Condition: Ringworm

Cause: Caused by a fungus that is spread from person to person through touch.

Signs and symptoms: An itchy and flaky rash that may be ringshaped and have a raised edge. When the scalp is affected, a bald area may develop. Ringworm is highly contagious until treatment has commenced.

What you can do:

- **Take your toddler to see the doctor so that oral medications and/ or topical ointments or creams may be prescribed to treat the outbreak.**

Condition: Roseola

Cause: Caused by a virus with an incubation period of five to ten days. Roseola is very common in toddlers under the age of two.

Signs and symptoms: High fever that arises suddenly in a previously well toddler, and which may occasionally result in febrile convulsions. The fever breaks on the fourth or fifth day and is then followed by a faint pink rash that appears on the trunk and the extremities and lasts for one day.

What you can do:

- **Treat your toddler's fever and give her plenty of fluids to prevent dehydration.**

Condition: Rubella (German measles)

Cause: Caused by the rubella virus—a virus that has an incubation period of 14 to 21 days and that is contagious from a few days before until seven days after the rash appears.

Signs and symptoms: A low-grade fever, flu-like symptoms, a slight cold, and a pinkish red, spotted rash that starts on the face, spreads rapidly to the trunk, and disappears by the third day. Also accompanied by swollen glands behind the ears and in the nape of the neck.

What you can do:

- **Have your child vaccinated to prevent rubella** (this is part of the MMRV vaccination).

- **Have your child examined by a doctor to confirm that she has developed rubella.** Sometimes only a blood test can confirm that the rash and other symptoms have been caused by rubella as opposed to some other illness.
- **Keep your child away from women who are or could be pregnant.** Rubella can be very dangerous to the developing fetus.

Condition: Scarlet fever

Cause: Caused by streptococcus bacteria. Has an incubation period of two to five days.

Signs and symptoms: Sunburn-like rash over face, trunk, and extremities, including a moustache-like gap of unaffected skin around the mouth; sandpaper-like skin; fever; tonsillitis; and vomiting. The rash usually disappears in five days. Despite its scary name, it's usually no more serious than strep throat, but it's contagious until one to two days after antibiotic treatment has begun. It's more common in school-aged children than in toddlers.

What you can do:
- **Have your toddler seen by your doctor so that antibiotic treatment can be started.** (Note: other members of your family may also be treated at the same time, even if they haven't actually developed the illness.)
- **Offer liquids and bland foods** (if your toddler is old enough for solid foods) and watch for signs of dehydration.

Gastrointestinal conditions

Condition: Campylobacter

Cause: Source of infection may be poultry, beef, unpasteurized milk, or other food. The bacteria that causes this condition is excreted in the stool, so your child is infectious while she has symptoms.

Signs and symptoms: Fever, diarrhea, blood in stool, and cramps.

What you can do:

- Get in touch with your doctor to see if a stool sample is required in order to confirm that your toddler has been infected with campylobacter.
- Keep your toddler away from other children while you treat the illness.
- Give your child acetaminophen to reduce her discomfort and treat her fever. Also, see tips under diarrhea (below) for advice on managing your child's diarrhea.

Condition: Constipation

Cause: Too little water in the intestines and/or poor muscle tone in the lower intestines and rectum. The problem can also be triggered by a change in diet (for example, excessive consumption of high-fat dairy products).

Signs and symptoms: Abdominal discomfort and hard, dry stools that may be painful for your toddler to pass and that may be streaked with blood when they finally emerge.

What you can do:

- Up your toddler's intake of water, prune juice, prunes, pears, plums, peaches, and grapes—nature's stool softeners! Warmed fruit compote (for example, three to four dried apricots warmed or stewed with a small amount of water) can really help to get your toddler's bowels moving. If these home remedies don't provide your toddler with adequate relief, your doctor may recommend using non-prescription stool softeners.
- Limit the number and quantities of constipating foods that your toddler eats (high-fat dairy products tend to be a particular problem) while adding fibre to your toddler's diet. Good sources of fibre include bran cereals, whole-grain breads and crackers, and fibre-rich vegetables such as peas and beans.

Condition: Diarrhea

Cause: Caused by gastrointestinal infections (especially gastroenteritis), colds, food intolerances, and antibiotic treatments. A common cause of diarrhea in toddlers is excessive juice consumption. It's so common, in fact, that it's got its own name: "toddler's diarrhea."

Signs and symptoms: Frequent watery, mucusy, foul-smelling, explosive, and occasionally blood-tinged stools. Diarrhea is frequently accompanied by a bright red rash around the anus.

What you can do:

- **Because each child's pattern of bowel movements is different, what you're looking for is a change in your toddler's bowel movements.** Start tracking the frequency and quality of your toddler's stools and note whether she's vomiting or not, how much food and liquid she's been taking in, and how ill she seems. This information will help your doctor assess whether your toddler is at risk of becoming dehydrated. Note: Call your doctor or go to the hospital immediately if your toddler is having bloody or black stools, has been vomiting for more than four to six hours, has a fever of 38.5°C (101.3°F) or greater, or is showing some signs of dehydration. (See the section on dehydration earlier in this chapter.) Diarrhea can throw your toddler's balance of salts (called electrolytes) and water out of whack—something that can affect the functioning of her organs.

- **Try to figure out what may have triggered the diarrhea:** illness, a change in diet (a common culprit being too much fruit juice), or the result of antibiotic treatment for an ear infection, for example.

- **Make sure that you apply a barrier cream at each diaper change to prevent your toddler from developing a diarrhea-related rash.** (These rashes can be incredibly painful.)

- **If your toddler is becoming dehydrated,** consult your doctor about the advisability of offering her an oral rehydration solution such as Pedialyte.

- **Don't give your toddler any diarrhea medication unless you're told to by your doctor.** These medications—which slow down *oral rehydration solutions*

While mothers a generation ago were told to treat diarrhea by giving their children ginger ale, juice, and sugar water, doctors no longer recommend that these beverages be given because their salt content is too low and their sugar content is too high—something that can actually aggravate the child's diarrhea. Add to this the fact that certain types of fruit juices can have a laxative effect—the last thing your toddler needs when she's battling diarrhea—and that many types of soda pop contain caffeine (a diuretic that can cause your toddler to become dehydrated) and you can see why oral electrolyte solutions (also known as oral rehydration solutions) are becoming the first-line defence against diarrhea.

Believe it or not, even plain water isn't recommended for a toddler who's becoming dehydrated because it can lead to low salt and sugar levels in the body.

One thing you *may* want to consider, assuming that your toddler is only mildly ill, is offering your toddler diluted apple juice instead of oral rehydration solution. A recent study published in the *Journal of the American Medical Association* concluded that "the use of diluted apple juice and preferred fluids as desired may be an appropriate alternative to electrolyte maintenance fluids in children with mild gastroenteritis and minimal dehydration."

the action of the intestines—can actually worsen diarrhea by allowing the germs and infected fluid to stagnate in the gut.

• **Once the vomiting and diarrhea stops, offer small quantities of non-irritating foods.** (Your best bet is to stick to the so-called "brat" diet at first: bananas, rice, applesauce, and toast, but if there's another food that appeals to your toddler right now, you might want to offer that food instead—unless, of course, that food is high in sugar.) Ideally, you want to start feeding solids to your toddler again as soon as possible. Keeping your toddler on a clear fluid diet for too long may itself produce diarrhea (aptly named "starvation stools"). So the sooner you can get back your toddler's "normal" diet, the better. Note: if your toddler is drinking cow's milk, your doctor may recommend that you offer a non-lactose, soy-based beverage for the next little while, because sometimes a toddler's recently out-of-whack intestines may have difficulty tolerating lactose for up to six weeks.

- **Don't be alarmed if your toddler has more frequent bowel movements once you reintroduce these foods.** It may take seven to ten days or even longer for her stools to go back to normal again. The bowel is relatively slow to heal.

- **If you notice the diarrhea starting up again, you might want to back off and stick to foods that you know she can tolerate well.** If the diarrhea continues to be a problem, get in touch with your doctor: she may want to order stool cultures to see if there's a parasite such as giardia responsible for your toddler's misery.

---

when to call the doctor

According to The College of Family Physicians of Canada, you should call your doctor (or seek emergency treatment) if your toddler . . .

- has diarrhea and a fever of over 38.5°C (101.3°F);
- is exhibiting some of the signs of dehydration (irritability, decreased appetite, less frequent urination, more concentrated urine, weight loss, dry mouth, thirst, sunken eyes, lack of tears when crying, skin that isn't as "springy" as usual);
- has stools that are bloody and slimy or has blood in her vomit;
- is bloated, listless, unusually sleepy;
- has had abdominal pain for more than two hours; and/or
- hasn't passed urine in eight hours.

Condition: *Escherichia coli* (E. coli)

Cause: Can be picked up from poultry, beef, unpasteurized milk, or other food sources. Undercooked hamburger is the classic source of E. coli: hence, its nickname, "hamburger disease."

Signs and symptoms: Fever, diarrhea, blood in stool, cramps. The germ that causes this condition is excreted in the stool, so your child is infectious while she has symptoms.

What you can do:
- Get in touch with your doctor to see if a stool sample is required to attempt to confirm that your toddler has been infected with E. coli.
- Keep your toddler away from other children while you treat the illness.
- Give your child acetaminophen to reduce her discomfort and treat her fever and ensure that she's consuming plenty of fluids. (See the tips on managing diarrhea that you'll find elsewhere in this section.)

Condition: Food poisoning

Cause: Caused by eating contaminated food.

Signs and symptoms: Severe diarrhea and vomiting that starts suddenly and unexpectedly within hours of eating the offending food. Not infectious, but symptoms may be shared by all members of the family who ate the same food.

What you can do:
- **Contact your doctor if your child's symptoms are severe.** Otherwise, offer plenty of fluids and follow the tips on treating vomiting and diarrhea that you'll find elsewhere in this section.

Condition: Giardia (a parasite in the stool that causes bowel infections)

Cause: Spread from person to person or may be picked up by drinking contaminated water.

Signs and symptoms: Most children have no symptoms, but some may experience loss of appetite, vomiting, cramps, diarrhea, very soft stools, and excessive gas. This condition is infectious until cured.

What you can do:
- Get in touch with your doctor to see if a stool sample is required to attempt to confirm that your toddler has been infected with giardia.
- Keep your toddler away from other children while you treat the illness.

- **Give your child acetaminophen to reduce her discomfort and treat her fever.** Also, see the tips on managing diarrhea that you'll find elsewhere in this section.

Condition: Hepatitis A (a liver infection)

Cause: A virus in the stool that can be spread from person to person or via food or water.

Signs and symptoms: Most children exhibit few symptoms. Where symptoms are present, they include fever, reduced appetite, nausea, vomiting, and jaundice (a yellowish tinge to skin and eyes). Hepatitis A is infectious from two weeks before to one week after the onset of jaundice.

What you can do:

- **Get in touch with your doctor.** She may want to order an immune globulin vaccine for all members of your family, including your toddler.

Condition: Norwalk virus

Cause: Spread from person to person.

Signs and symptoms: Vomiting and diarrhea for one to two days. Contagious for the duration of the illness.

What you can do:

- **Get in touch with your doctor to see if a stool sample is required to attempt to confirm that your toddler has been infected with Norwalk virus.**
- **Keep your toddler away from other children while you treat the illness.**
- **Give your child acetaminophen to reduce her discomfort and treat her fever.** Also, see the tips on managing diarrhea that you'll find elsewhere in this section.

Condition: Rotavirus

Cause: Caused by a virus in the stool that is spread through person-to-person contact. Rotavirus is the most common cause of diarrhea outbreaks in child care centres.

Signs and symptoms: Fever and vomiting followed by watery diarrhea. Contagious for duration of illness.

What you can do:

- **Get in touch with your doctor to see if a stool sample is required to attempt to confirm that your toddler has been infected with rotavirus.**
- **Keep your toddler away from other children while you treat the illness.**
- **Give your child acetaminophen to reduce her discomfort and treat her fever.** Also, see the tips on managing diarrhea that you'll find elsewhere in this section.

Note: The rotavirus vaccine is now routinely recommended to prevent this illness. See the immunization section of this chapter.

Condition: Salmonella

Cause: Acquired mainly by eating food that has been contaminated with salmonella. Such foods typically include eggs, egg products, beef, poultry, and unpasteurized milk.

Signs and symptoms: Diarrhea, fever, blood in stool. Infectious while symptoms persist.

What you can do:

- **Contact your doctor if your child's symptoms are severe.** The doctor may want to confirm the presence of salmonella via a stool and/or blood test. Otherwise, offer plenty of fluids and follow the tips on treating vomiting and diarrhea that you'll find elsewhere in this section.

Condition: Shigella

Cause: Caused by a virus in the stool that can be spread from person to person.

Signs and symptoms: Diarrhea, fever, blood and/or mucus in stool, cramps. Highly contagious for the duration of the illness.

What you can do:

- **Get in touch with your doctor to see if a stool sample is required** to attempt to confirm that your toddler has been infected with shigella.

- **Keep your toddler away from other children while you treat the illness.**
- **Give your child acetaminophen to reduce her discomfort and treat her fever.** Also, see the tips on managing diarrhea that you'll find elsewhere in this section.

Condition: Vomiting

Cause: Vomiting can be caused by a viral infection, food poisoning, or gastroesophageal reflux (a condition in which stomach acids are regurgitated into the esophagus, frequently resulting in forceful regurgitation through the nose).

Signs and symptoms: Vomiting can be accompanied by diarrhea or other symptoms depending on the underlying cause.

What you can do:

- **Offer small, frequent servings of fluid to prevent dehydration.** Tip: try making ice pops out of the oral electrolyte solution to see if this makes it easier for her to keep the fluid down.
- **If you are unsure what is causing your toddler's vomiting** or you are otherwise concerned about her vomiting, seek medical attention.

Other conditions

Condition: Meningitis

Cause: Can be bacterial or viral in origin. Meningitis can be fatal. The incubation period is usually 10 to 14 days. Fortunately, bacterial meningitis—the most deadly kind—is very rare in preschool children who have been fully immunized.

Signs and symptoms: Bacterial meningitis (spinal meningitis) may begin like a cold, flu, or ear infection, but the child becomes increasingly ill and very lethargic; and develops a fever of 38.9 to 40°C (102 to 104°F) and a stiff neck. With viral meningitis, the toddler exhibits similar symptoms but isn't quite as ill.

What you can do:

- **Contact your doctor immediately.** She'll want to do a spinal tap to determine whether the meningitis is bacterial or viral in origin. The sooner the illness is diagnosed and treated, the better the outcome.

- **If the meningitis turns out to be bacterial in origin, your doctor will want to treat the illness with intravenous antibiotics for at least seven days.** Your child will need to be hospitalized during this time.

- **If it turns out to be viral in origin, the illness will be treated like the flu.**

Condition: Mumps

Cause: Spread by a virus that has an incubation period of seven to ten days.

Signs and symptoms: Flu-like symptoms and an upset stomach initially; then tender swollen glands beneath the earlobes two or three days later. Your child may look as if she has "chipmunk cheeks" and may find it painful to open her jaw. She may also have a low-grade fever. Mumps typically last for seven to ten days, and the illness is contagious until the swelling is gone.

What you can do:

- **Ensure that your child has been vaccinated against this illness** (by receiving the MMRV vaccine).
- **Feed your child liquids and soft foods.**
- **Apply cool compresses to the neck.**
- **Administer acetaminophen to relieve discomfort and pain.**
- **Call your doctor's office immediately if your child becomes drowsy,** starts vomiting repeatedly, becomes dehydrated, or develops a stiff neck.

Condition: Pinworms

Cause: Caused by a parasite (intestinal worms).

Signs and symptoms: Night waking and restlessness; intense itching around the anus or in the vagina; and the presence of thread-like, one-centimetre-long worms that travel out of the rectum to deposit eggs around the anus or the vagina.

What you can do:

- **Use a flashlight at night to try to detect worms coming out of your toddler's anus** (they're more visible in the dark) and/or place sticky tape around your toddler's anus so that you can capture some eggs and take them to your doctor's office for identification.
- **Keep your toddler's fingernails trimmed short to discourage scratching.**
- **Each member of the family will have to be treated with a medication to eradicate the parasite.** The good news is that treatment is simple: take one tablet now and a second tablet in two weeks' time.

Condition: Tetanus (lockjaw)

Cause: Caused by bacteria in a deeply contaminated wound. The incubation period can be anywhere from 3 to 21 days. Tetanus is extremely rare in individuals who have been vaccinated.

Signs and symptoms: Muscle spasms, particularly in the jaw muscles; convulsions.

What you can do:

- **Contact your doctor immediately.** Your toddler will need to be treated with antibiotics.

Condition: Urinary tract infections (UTIs)

Cause: Can be difficult to diagnose. If your child suffers from recurrent urinary tract infections, your doctor may need to order an ultrasound or other test to determine the cause of the recurrent infections.

Signs and symptoms: Fever, painful and frequent urination, vomiting, abdominal pain. Note: A persistent fever with no obvious cause may be the only symptom of a urinary tract infection. Your child's doctor is particularly likely to suspect a UTI if the unexplained fever is accompanied by vomiting.

What you can do:

- **Get in touch with your doctor so that the urinary tract infection can be diagnosed** (usually through the collection of a urine sample) and antibiotic treatment can be started. A urine sample is typically collected by taping a clear plastic bag to a toddler's diaper area but it's also possible to collect a "clean catch" (uncontaminated) sample via the potty if your toddler is toilet trained.

Making a Trip to the Hospital

Unless your guardian angel happens to offer round-the-clock care and a bullet-proof guarantee, you're bound to have to take your child to the hospital at some point in her life—assuming, of course, that you haven't already.

Whether you end up making a spur-of-the-moment trip to the emergency room with a sick or injured toddler or providing bedside comfort and reassurance to a toddler who is in hospital, awaiting surgery, you're bound to find the experience stressful. Here are some tips on minimizing the stress for her and for you.

Emergency room visits

- **Make sure that you know where your toddler's health card is at all times.** That way, you won't have to waste valuable time looking for it if you have to make an impromptu trip to the emergency room. Consider taking a photo of your child's health card and storing the image on your phone as a backup. Just remember that health cards expire, so you'll want to remember to update the image at the appropriate time.
- **Get in the habit of keeping a fully stocked diaper bag in the trunk of your car.** In addition to including all the essentials—diapers, wipes, a spare outfit or two, and a change pad—you'll also want to ensure that it's equipped with enough drinks, snacks, and enough toys to keep your toddler entertained for a couple of hours.

- **Don't forget to bring your stroller.** It can serve as a portable storage bin (you can put your change bag and all your other stuff inside) or a bed or chair for your toddler.

Overnight stays

- **Find out what services are available to you while your child is staying in the hospital.** Some hospitals provide meals to parents of patients. Others provide roll-up cots and access to shower facilities. (Gone are the days when parents were expected to restrict their visits to "visiting hours." Most hospitals today recognize that parents will want to stay by their toddler's side as much as possible—and support this practice fully, knowing how much their young patients benefit from this kind of round-the-clock parental support.)

- **If you weren't able to pack a lot of your toddler's favourite things before she was checked into the hospital,** ask a friend or relative to go home and scoop up her favourite blanket, her pillow, and some of her favourite books. The more familiar objects she has around her, the more "at home" she'll feel. Just be sure to put her name on all of her personal possessions. It would be nothing short of disastrous to have her favourite blanket accidentally go AWOL in the hospital laundry!

- **If you're having difficulty understanding what the medical staff are telling you about your child's condition,** ask a friend or family member to stay at the hospital with you so that they can help you to obtain the answers you need. You may find it difficult to process complex medical information if you're feeling anxious and/or exhausted.

Preparing your child for surgery

- **If you know ahead of time that your toddler will be having surgery,** you'll want to take steps to prepare her for what will happen before, during, and after her surgery. But because toddlers don't have a particularly clear concept of time, you'll probably want to hold off on having "the big talk" until a day or two before her operation.

- **Make sure that you understand hospital policies about eating and drinking restrictions prior to surgery.** Most hospitals will require that your toddler stop eating solid foods at midnight the night before surgery. She may be allowed to consume clear liquids up until two hours before her scheduled surgery, however, so make sure you're crystal clear about the rules.
- **To give your toddler a bit of control over the situation, allow her to make some choices, where appropriate.** For example, she might want to decide which pair of pyjamas or which stuffed animal gets to accompany her to the hospital.
- **Expect some behavioural changes during and after your toddler's hospital stay.** Most toddlers find it difficult to adjust to such dramatic changes to their normal routines. You may find that your toddler is extra-clingy, hyperactive, and/or that she's developed some new fears. The best way to handle the situation is to be patient and give your toddler plenty of extra reassurance and love.

Up until now, we've been focusing on keeping your toddler healthy. Now it's time to zero in on an even bigger challenge: keeping your toddler safe!

CHAPTER 9

The Safety Department

"Toddlers are curious by nature and have no inhibitions! I think that's the biggest challenge about keeping them safe. They just want to explore and haven't yet had the experience of hurting themselves or being faced with danger."

—JUDITH, 32, MOTHER OF ONE

"If the hospital awarded frequent flyer miles for each of my son's visits to the hospital, I would have been around the world by now."

—TERRI, 34, MOTHER OF THREE

While it's a rare toddler indeed who manages to get through the toddler years without ending up with at least a few bumps and bruises, it's up to you to do what you can to keep your toddler safe. Of course, as any veteran parent will tell you, this is definitely one of those things that's easier said than done. At this stage of his development, your toddler is hungry to explore his world, but almost oblivious to the dangers that surround him—a pretty risky combo!

Adding to the challenge is the fact that some toddlers demand considerably more vigilance from their parents than others, in which case you could find yourself on high alert from dusk to dawn and beyond. That's how things played out for Alyson, a 33-year-old mother of two. "My daughter, Maggie, constantly has me on my toes," she explains. "She loves to climb, has no fear of the water, and picks up on new things—like how to unscrew lids!—very quickly. I find her a real challenge, since I'm not really able to take my eyes off of her at all."

If, like Alyson, you're looking for the lowdown on what you can do to keep your curious and fast-moving toddler at least a little safer, this is the chapter for you. We're going to talk about toddler-proofing your home, keeping your toddler safe in the car, and other things you need to know in order to reduce your toddler's risk of injury. We'll wrap up the chapter with a crash course in the basics of emergency first aid: information that I hope you'll never need, but that you definitely need to know just in case.

Babyproofing: The Sequel

You've spent the past year babyproofing your child's world. Now it's time to make sure that your home is toddler-proof as well. That means training yourself to see your home through the eyes of an ultra-curious, extremely high-energy one- or two-year-old. (Trust me, you'll never look at a kitchen chair the same way again. Rather than a place to sit down, you'll see it as a launching pad to all sorts of incredible adventures.)

While it's unrealistic to think you can prevent every conceivable type of accident from occurring, there's plenty you can do to encourage your toddler's passion for discovery *and* keep him safe at the same time. ("We have to balance our desire to keep our toddlers safe against our desire to let them learn," explains Anita, a 38-year-old mother of four.)

Here's what that means in practical terms.

Every room

- **Keep a set of emergency telephone numbers on the front of your refrigerator or in another prominent place in your home** (so that anyone caring for your child in your home can find them immediately) and enter these numbers into your smartphone, too. That way, you'll be able to access this information quickly and easily in the event of an emergency. One thing you don't want to do, of course, is to add "911" as a smartphone contact. The potential for pocket dials is simply too great.

- **Keep curtain and blind cords out of your toddler's reach to reduce the risk of strangulation.** Or, better yet, opt for curtains and blinds that are completely cord-free.

- **Keep high chairs, cribs, and furniture away from windows, appliances, and other potential hazards.** Note: If some of these pieces of furniture are easily pushed or dragged around by a toddler (for example, kitchen chairs or stepstools), you may have to store them in a closet or some inaccessible area to prevent your toddler from using them to climb up on things. (One of the parents I interviewed for this book confessed to stashing her kitchen chairs in the bathroom!)

- **Ensure that all windows in your house are lockable and that the screens in all of your windows are secure and backed with screen guards** (safety devices designed to catch the screen and your toddler if he starts to fall out the window).

- **Keep your toddler away from baseboards and portable heaters and other heating appliances like gas fireplaces and wood stoves.** In some cases, a physical barrier may be required.

- **Use plastic safety covers on door handles and cord locks on electrical outlets.** Get in the habit of unplugging electrical appliances and putting away extension cords when they're not in use.

- **Install toddler-proof latches on drawers and cupboard doors.**

- **Anchor bookcases and tall dressers to the wall to prevent tipping,** and avoid placing heavy items like televisions on top of these pieces of furniture.

- **Keep a fire extinguisher near each exit to your home.**

- **Store lighters and matches out of your toddler's reach and insist that visitors do the same.**

- **Don't use space heaters when you have young children** (due to both the fire risk and the potential for burns).

- **Ensure that there's a smoke detector on each level of your home and that there is a smoke detector close to the bedrooms.** Change the batteries in your smoke detector at least twice a year (whenever you move your clock forward or backwards) and test the alarm at least once a month, using the battery test button. Ensure that there is a carbon monoxide detector in the bedroom area, too.

- **Check that any extension cords in use in your home are in good condition and that they meet current safety standards.**
- **Store medications and cleaners in their original containers so that you'll be able to identify which products your child has consumed in the event of a poisoning.** Keep medications in a locked medicine cabinet or lockbox and store cleaners out of reach of your toddler.
- **Wipe up spills promptly and avoid decorating with area rugs, which can pose a tripping hazard.**
- **Avoid leaving your toddler and your pet alone in the same room.** Keep your pet's toys and food away from your toddler. And keep your cat's litter box in a part of the house that is off limits to your toddler.
- **Keep coins, marbles, pen or marker caps, button-sized batteries, and other small items safely out of your toddler's reach.** This may mean clearing out the family junk drawer and/or locking the desk in your home office until your child is considerably older. Nearly all (95 percent) of deaths from choking occur in the home environment; and for every actual death that occurs, approximately 110 children are treated in hospital emergency rooms for non-fatal choking. The presence of older siblings in the home increases a young child's risk of choking—both because older siblings have toys with smaller pieces and because older siblings are sometimes involved in feeding or supervising toddlers (and may not be fully aware of all that's required to keep a toddler safe from choking).

"Childproofing for a toddler is difficult when you have an older child because the older child may leave toys around that a toddler shouldn't have."

—KAREN, 36, MOTHER OF THREE

- **Make sure that every plant in your home is toddler-safe.** Call your local poison control centre if you're not sure which house-plants are and aren't dangerous if ingested. (You can find a list of provincial and territorial poison control centres at http://capcc.ca.)

Halls and stairways

- **Hang a hook or a shelf near the front door so that visitors can keep their bags and/or briefcases out of your toddler's reach while they're visiting.**
- **Install wall-mounted baby gates at the top (and, if necessary, the bottom) of each set of stairs.** Ensure that each set of stairs is equipped with a handrail that's firmly attached to the wall or the floor, and that the carpet on the stairs is tacked down securely to prevent tripping. Keep the stairs free of objects, including toys. Stairs are responsible for roughly one in six falls requiring hospitalization in children between the ages of one and four.
- **Get rid of your dry cleaning bags as soon as you bring your dry cleaning into the house.** Tie them in knots and toss them in the recycling.
- **Install door alarms on all exterior doors.**

Your toddler's room

- **If your toddler is still sleeping in a crib, make sure that it's still in good condition.** Tighten the screws and ensure that the sides of the crib are still firmly locked in place. Replace the crib mattress if it's too soft, too worn, or it doesn't fit the crib snugly.
- **Make sure that your toddler's crib mattress has been dropped to the lowest setting to prevent him from tumbling out.** If the crib rail is at his mid-chest level when the mattress is in its lowest position, it's time to shift him from a crib to a bed. See Chapter 6 for tips on helping your toddler to make this transition.
- **Remove any large toys from your toddler's crib.** He may use his toys as a stepstool to climb out of the crib.

- **Don't allow a child under the age of six to sleep on the top bunk of a bunk bed.** The risk of falls and/or suffocation is simply too great.

- **Make sure that your toddler wears fire-retardant sleepwear rather than regular clothing at bedtime.**

- **Remove any drawstrings or cords from your toddler's clothing in order to reduce the risk of strangulation.**

- **Keep the diaper pail out of reach of your toddler or purchase a model with a childproof latch.**

- **Avoid using decorative plug covers in your toddler's room.** They'll only encourage him to touch the electrical outlets, so stick with plain plug covers instead.

- **Move rocking chairs and gliders to another part of the house.** They can pinch fingers or otherwise injure a toddler.

- **If your toddler is still using a pacifier, regularly inspect it for signs of deterioration.** According to Health Canada, pacifiers should be changed at least every two months, before they show any signs of deterioration.

- **If your toddler likes the security of having a night light in his room,** choose a simple night light that doesn't look like a toy. If it looks too much like a toy, your toddler may try to play with it and could end up with an electrical burn. Because night lights can pose a hazard to curious toddlers, some parents prefer to hook the main light in the room up to a dimmer switch instead.

- **Tie a small parts tester (a plastic cylinder that is the same size and shape of a small child's throat) to your toddler's change table.** That way, you'll know where it is whenever you want to find out whether a particular toy contains parts that are small enough to pose a choking hazard.

Bathroom

- **Check the temperature on your hot water heater.** Most water heaters are set at 60°C (140°F) or higher rather than the 49°C (120°F) that most safety experts recommend.

- **Fill your toddler's bath with a few inches of cold water and then add hot water until the bath has reached the appropriate temperature.** Finish up with a bit of cold water so that the last water to come out of the tap is cold water. (That way, if your toddler manages to turn on the tap, the first splash of water will be cold, not hot.)

- **Place your toddler as far away as possible from the taps and faucet,** both to prevent him from reaching for the taps and accidentally scalding himself and to reduce the likelihood that he'll bang his head on the faucet.

- **Use bath mats in the bathtub to reduce the risk of slipping.**

- **Avoid using bath seats as they can provide you with a false sense of security.** (It is easy to let your guard down and become momentarily distracted, assuming that your toddler is safe in the seat.)

- **Never leave a toddler unattended in the bathtub.** The peak risk period for drowning is age one through four. And don't rely on school-aged siblings to provide bathtub supervision. A toddler in a bathtub requires the mindful attention of an adult.

- **Empty the tub as soon as you're finished bathing your toddler to reduce the risk of an accidental drowning after the fact.**

- **Lock all medications (including vitamins and herbal remedies) in a lockable medicine cabinet or,** even better, store them in a small cash box or medium-sized fishing tackle box that can be locked and then stashed on the top shelf of your bedroom closet.

- **Keep all medications in their original containers and ensure that the products you buy are equipped with child safety caps.** Then, to reduce the number of products that are available to a toddler on the loose, weed out the out-of-date and obsolete medications on a regular basis.

- **Keep mouthwash, shampoo, cosmetics, nail polish remover, and other toiletries out of your toddler's reach,** along with scissors, razor blades, blow-dryers, flat-irons, and other potentially hazardous objects.

- **Equip the toilet seat with a childproof latch** and leave it in place until your toddler starts using the toilet.

Kitchen

- **Check that the base of your toddler's high chair is wide enough to be stable, and that the chair's safety harness is still functional.** If your toddler has graduated to a booster seat, you'll want to ensure that it's firmly strapped to the chair so that the booster seat doesn't slide off when your toddler starts squirming around.

- **Be mindful of where you place your toddler's high chair.** You want to make sure that it's clear of walls or other objects that your toddler could push against, potentially tipping the high chair, and far away from hazards such as stoves.

- **Use placemats rather than a tablecloth at your kitchen table.** Otherwise, your toddler could tug on the tablecloth, causing everything on the table to come tumbling down on him.

- **Keep cords for kettles, toasters, and other electrical appliances out of the reach of children,** and get in the habit of leaving appliances unplugged unless they're actually in use.

- **Turn pot handles toward the back of the stove and cook only on the back burners.**

- **Be aware that oven doors can become hot enough to burn children.** Be sure to supervise your toddler carefully the entire time he's in the kitchen and to turn off the oven immediately after you're finished using it to reduce the odds of his being burned. Consider installing a child safety lock on your oven door. Toddlers have been known to open the oven door, crawl on it, and use it as a stepladder to access the stovetop.

- **Organize your kitchen cupboards so that the items that are of the greatest interest to your child** (for example, the cupboard where you keep the cookies) are the farthest distance from the stove. And make sure that your toddler has a safe play area. When he starts exploring the cupboards, give him his own cupboard full of plastic containers, measuring spoons, and other treasures that he can dump on the floor.

- **Keep knives, can openers, and other sharp items out of the reach of children.**

- **Learn which foods pose a choking risk to toddlers,** and either chop the foods into very small pieces or avoid them entirely until your child is older. Never leave your toddler unattended when he's eating. (See Chapter 5 for other valuable tips on minimizing the risk of choking.)
- **Use caution when you are heating your toddler's food in the microwave.** Microwave cooking produces hot spots in foods. To avoid burns, stir the food thoroughly and check the temperature carefully before serving it to your toddler.
- **Use cups with lids when you're drinking hot beverages like coffee or tea,** to reduce the likelihood of spills and burns.
- **Keep household cleaners—including dishwasher detergent—out of reach of children.** Better yet, stick to non-toxic cleaners and avoid pod-style cleaning products entirely to reduce your child's exposure to toxins in the home. (They look too much like candy.)
- **Keep plastic wrap and plastic bags out of your toddler's reach.**

Family room

- **Make sure that the toys you buy for your child are age appropriate.** (See Chapter 4 for more about toddlers and play.)
- **Steer clear of toys that have sharp points or edges that could injure your toddler or that contain smaller pieces that could be removed and swallowed** (eyes on stuffed animals or wheels on toy cars, for example). Discard any broken toys that have developed sharp edges or that could present a choking hazard. You'll also want to get rid of any toys that feature drawstrings and other dangling strings that are any longer than 20 centimetres (7 inches). If your toddler inherits any such toys from an older cousin, take scissors to any offending strings.
- **Ensure that the packaging that came with the toy is disposed of appropriately to avoid any choking or suffocation hazards.**
- **Ensure that any toys that require batteries have child-safe battery compartments** (ones that can be opened only with a screwdriver).

- **Help your toddler to put his toys away when he's finished playing with them to prevent trips and falls.**
- **If you have a toy box, make sure that it's safe.** The toy box should have a safety hinge to prevent the lid from closing too quickly and ventilation holes to ensure that your toddler will be able to breathe if he happens to get trapped inside. Note: you'll find all kinds of other suggestions for storing your child's toys in Chapter 4.
- **Ban latex balloons from your home while your child is young.** They pose a significant choking hazard for babies, toddlers, and pre-schoolers. Stick with shiny foil balloons instead.

Living room

- **Use a fireplace pad on your hearth and keep your child far away from the fireplace while it's being used.** It's also important to keep children away from gas fireplaces. The glass doors on a gas fireplace can reach 200°C (400°F) while the fireplace is on, and it can take up to 45 minutes for the glass to cool to a safe temperature after the fireplace has been turned off.
- **Put your vacuum cleaner away when it's not being used so that your child won't accidentally hurt his fingers or toes with the beater bar.**
- **Position floor lamps so that they're out of your toddler's reach or pack them away entirely.**
- **Place table lamps toward the back of the table and wrap the cord loosely around the table leg for added stability.**

Laundry room

- **Store laundry products out of your toddler's reach.** Laundry pods (which can look a lot like candy to a toddler) are more toxic than traditional liquids and powders and should be avoided until your youngest child is six years of age or older.
- **Never allow your toddler to play in or around the washer or dryer,** and ensure that the washer and dryer doors are kept closed.

The Canadian Partnership for Children's Health and Environment (www.healthyenvironmentforkids.ca) encourages Canadian parents to think about "environmental childproofing" as well as traditional childproofing. Not only are babies and toddlers more vulnerable to environmental toxins than adults are because their bodies are still developing; they come into contact with toxins more than adults do because they explore the world with their mouths and their hands and because they live their lives closer to the ground, where toxins tend to accumulate. Fortunately, there's a lot we can do to reduce the levels of toxins in our homes, according to the CPCHE. They recommend that parents act on these five key tips:

1. **"Bust the dust."** Cleaning with a good-quality vacuum, a wet mop, or a damp mop will remove dust (one of the main sources of children's exposure to toxic chemicals) from the environment. Plan to vacuum or damp-mop twice a week if you have a child who is at the on-the-floor, crawling stage. And minimize the amount of dust in your environment by removing your shoes when at the door (use mats to trap dirt from outdoors) and eliminating clutter (store toys in closed containers).

2. **"Go green when you clean."** Use non-toxic cleaning products. Avoid antibacterial soap. Steer clear of air fresheners, dryer sheets, and scented laundry detergent. If your clothes require dry cleaning, choose a dry cleaner who uses a non-toxic process.

3. **"Renovate right."** Choose less toxic paints, finishes, and glues (those labelled VOC-free [for volatile organic compounds free], zero-VOC, or low-VOC); and ensure proper ventilation when using these products. Use plastic sheeting and duct tape to seal off the portion of your house that is being renovated, and be sure to close off heating and cooling vents. Keep your work clothes separate from other household laundry. Keep pregnant women and young children away from the area being renovated.

continued

environmental childproofing (continued)

4. **"Get drastic with plastic."** Don't use plastic wrap or plastic containers in the microwave, even if the products claim to be microwave-safe. Heat and store food in glass rather than plastic containers. Eat fresh or frozen foods as much as possible (to minimize exposure to BPA, a chemical used in the lining of most food and drink cans). Avoid products manufactured from PVC or vinyl. They may contain phthalates, harmful chemicals that were banned from children's toys in 2011.

5. **"Dish safer fish."** Choose varieties of fish that are lower in mercury: Atlantic mackerel, herring, rainbow trout, wild or canned salmon, and tilapia. If you eat canned tuna, choose light rather than white. And follow provincial and territorial guidelines regarding eating any fish you catch.

Basement

- **Store paint thinners and other harmful substances out of your toddler's reach**—ideally in a locked cabinet.
- **Ensure that woodworking tools are kept in a locked room or cabinet.**
- **Keep your toddler off unfinished basement stairs.** Not only may the stairs be lacking a toddler-safe railing, but they may also lead down to a rock-hard cement floor—not exactly the type of surface you want your toddler to be landing on if he happens to take a tumble.

Garage

- **Store your toddler's ride-on toys and other outdoor playthings somewhere other than the garage so that he learns the garage is off limits to children** (unless, of course, you plan to use your garage as a storage spot for children's things only, in which case you would want to store tools, pesticides, automotive products, and other items that could be hazardous to children in a locked backyard shed or other secure location).

- Ensure that the garage door is equipped with a safety feature that will cause it to go back up if it comes into contact with a person or object.

Backyard

- **Ensure that your pool area is properly fenced** (the fence should be at least 1.2 metres (4 feet) high and should surround the entire pool) and that the gate on the fence is both self-closing and self-locking.
- **Check that any playground equipment is safe and well anchored.**
- **Empty your toddler's wading pool whenever it's not in use.**
- **Ensure that your toddler's sandbox has a lid to keep neighbourhood cats out.** Cat feces is more than just a nuisance: it can be highly toxic for pregnant women and young children.
- **Keep your toddler away from any poisonous plants or weeds that are growing in your yard**—or, better yet, plant something else until your toddler is a little older.
- **Keep the barbecue away from your child's play area.**
- **Get in the habit of putting your garden hose away when you're finished using it;** otherwise, the water in the hose may become hot enough to scald a curious toddler.
- **Don't even think about trying to mow the lawn or using any electrical garden tools while your toddler's underfoot.** It's simply too risky.
- **When you're choosing ride-on toys, keep your child's age, size, and abilities in mind.** Ensure that your child's riding toys feature wheels that are spaced wide enough apart to promote maximum stability. Use riding toys in a safe area that is away from stairs, traffic, swimming pools, and other dangers. And supervise your toddler closely when he's using a riding toy.
- **Help your toddler to understand the rules of the road** (why we stop and look both ways before we cross the street, for example), but don't expect him to be able to apply or remember these rules without your help for quite some time. According to child safety

experts, most children don't acquire the skills required to safely cross the road on their own until they are about nine years of age.

- **Stay in the know about juvenile product recalls by visiting the recalls and safety alerts page of healthycanadians.gc.ca.**

safety on the go	Be extra-vigilant when you're visiting other people's homes. You have no way of knowing whether their house is toddler-proofed to the same degree as your own. (Unless they have a toddler the same age, odds are it's not.)

Safety on the Road

While most parents assume that they've done their bit for safety by buckling their child into his car seat, studies have shown that as many as 88 percent of car seats are installed incorrectly or improperly used. Here's what you need to know to prevent a needless tragedy.

Toddler car seats

Your toddler is ready to graduate from a rear-facing car seat to a forward-facing car seat when his weight reaches 10 kilograms (22 pounds). He'll stay in his car seat until he reaches 22 to 29 kilograms (40 to 65 pounds), at which point he'll be ready for a booster seat. (Don't be in a rush to move to a booster seat. A forward-facing car seat provides better protection than a booster seat because it spreads the force of a sudden stop or crash over the strongest parts of your child's body.)

Here are some important safety tips to keep in mind when it comes to using a forward-facing car seat safely:

Check for correct installation. Make sure that the seat is facing forward, not backwards, and that a tether strap is used to anchor the car seat in place; and ensure that a locking clip is used to hold the seat belt in place if you are using a shoulder belt/lap belt combination.

Check for positioning. Make sure that the harness straps pass through the slots in the back of the car seat at the appropriate level (in other words, at or just above your child's shoulder height). And the chest clip should be positioned at the level of your toddler's armpits.

Check for fit. Make sure that the harness straps are snug enough to protect your child. (You should be able to insert one finger between your toddler's collarbone and the car seat harness.)

Plan to replace your child's car seat if you're involved in an automobile accident, even if it was just a minor fender bender. Car seats are designed to withstand the impact of only a single car accident. Likewise, make a point of discarding your child's car seat if it is past its expiry date (generally six to ten years after the date of purchase, depending on the manufacturer). Plastic deteriorates due to exposure to sunlight; labels become difficult to read; parts may wear and stop working properly; safety standards and regulations may change; and—if you're purchasing a car seat secondhand (which, quite frankly, is not recommended)—instruction manuals may be misplaced and subsequent owners may not receive product safety alerts, should problems arise.

Other car safety tips

- **Always use a Canadian government—approved car seat** (apparently our standards are a bit more rigorous than those of our neighbours to the south, so that means sticking to "homegrown" car seats rather than trying to bring one across the border). And don't attempt to use any other sort of juvenile product (for example, a kitchen booster seat) as a substitute for a real car seat.
- **Never allow your toddler to ride in your arms when the car is moving, no matter how unhappy he may be about being strapped in his car seat.** (Hint: You're likely to have a happier toddler if you're realistic about the length of the car trips you plan at this stage of his life. It's a rare toddler who can stand spending more than a couple of hours in the car at once.) If you have to make a

longer trip because you're travelling to visit far-flung friends and relatives, schedule frequent breaks. Your toddler will need them.

- **Don't place groceries or other objects near your toddler, since they may end up becoming dangerous projectiles in the event of an accident.** Store them in your trunk or luggage compartment instead. A can of pop, flying at 100 kilometres an hour, can do a lot of damage to a toddler or young child.

- **Eliminate the temptation to text when you drive by turning your phone off and/or placing it out of reach.** According to the Canadian Automobile Association, you're 23 times as likely to have a car accident when you're texting as you are when your cell phone is securely stashed away. And recognize the fact that your toddler can also be a significant source of distraction when you're driving—which is why you'll want to anticipate your toddler's needs as much as possible, before you hit the road, and to be prepared to pull over, if necessary. (That way, you can meet his needs without jeopardizing his safety or your own.)

- **Plan to take your toddler's car seat with you if you're travelling by air.** While airlines currently allow parents to hold young children in their laps rather than buckling them into a car seat, doing so leaves them vulnerable to injury or even death in the event of severe turbulence or a crash.

Summer Safety

It's summertime and the living is easy—but that doesn't mean you can afford to give safety a vacation. If anything, parents need to be more vigilant about keeping their toddlers safe during the spring and summer months. With the warmer weather comes an increased risk of injuries. Here are the key areas you'll want to focus on in order to keep your toddler safe.

Drowning: According to the Canadian Red Cross, drowning is one of the leading causes of death for Canadian children between the ages of one and four, second only to motor vehicle accidents. Children can drown in less than 4 centimetres (1 1/2 inches) of water—just enough water to cover the nose and mouth—and the majority of drownings occur when an adult's attention is momentarily distracted. Take appropriate precautions with your own backyard pool: Use pool alarms and ensure that the pool area is enclosed inside a 1.2-metre (4-foot-high) fence with a self-closing, self-latching gate, and turn wading pools upside down when they're not in use. You'll also want to give some thought to other water hazards near your home, such as ponds, your neighbour's backyard hot tub, and so on. And you'll want to make it a family rule that your child wears a life jacket whenever he's around water.

Sun safety: It's also important to protect your children from the harmful effects of the sun. Make sure that your child is wearing sunglasses, a sunhat, and a cover-up (ideally dark-coloured clothing made from tightly woven fabric). Choose a sunscreen with a sun protection factor (SPF) of at least 30, and ensure that your child avoids the sun around midday, when the sun's rays are strongest. For maximum protection, apply sunscreen 30 minutes before your child heads outdoors, paying particular attention to the areas of the body that are most often overlooked (the ears, the nose, the lips, and the top of the feet). You'll also want to remember to reapply your child's sunscreen throughout the day.

Playground safety: More than 28,000 Canadian children are injured on playgrounds each year. The three biggest culprits are slides, monkey bars, and swings. Because the majority of injuries result from falls, it's a good idea to remember the rule of five (keep children under age five off any piece of equipment that's higher than 1.5 metres, or 5 feet) and to teach children the basic rules of playground safety (for example, the importance of waiting your turn, going down the slide feet first, and steering clear of moving swings and the bottoms of slides). It's also important to choose age-appropriate equipment; to check playground equipment for signs of wear and tear; to ensure that the equipment conforms with current safety standards; and to look for a loose-fill surface that is at least 15 centimetres (6 inches) deep under swings, climbers, and slides to cushion falls. You'll also want to be on the lookout for any related hazards that could result in injury or illness, like puddles of water that could pose a drowning hazard, animal feces, broken glass, and garbage.

Garage injuries: Garages play host to some of the most hazardous items in our homes: gasoline, antifreeze, paints, solvents, pesticides, power tools, lawnmowers, and so on. That's why it's a good idea to designate them as kid-free zones and to store bicycles and other outdoor play equipment in a shed or other location. That way, your toddler will never have any reason to step foot in the garage.

Dog bites: Dog bites are yet another hazard of the season. While nearly half of dog bites are caused by the child's own pet, it's important to teach your toddler how to behave around other people's dogs and to supervise him closely whenever he's around animals. Teach your child to stand still if he is approached or chased by a strange dog. Make sure that he understands the importance of not running, kicking, or making threatening gestures toward the dog, no matter how frightened he may feel. (A better strategy is to face the dog and back away slowly until he's out of the dog's reach.)

Winter Safety

Of course, safety is a year-round responsibility, so you'll need to take steps to keep your toddler safe during the fall and winter months, too. That means avoiding frostbite. Skin that is exposed to extreme temperatures will freeze quickly if it's left exposed. That's why it's important to bundle up your toddler during cold weather, dressing him in several layers of warm clothing (for example, a coat or snowsuit that is both water and wind resistant; mitts and boots that are neither too small nor too tight; a warm hat; and a scarf). Your toddler's cheeks, ears, nose, hands, and feet are most vulnerable to frostbite. Affected skin initially becomes red and swollen and feels as though it's stinging or burning. If the skin continues to be exposed to the cold, it will tingle and turn greyish, and then turn shiny and white and lose all sensation. If your toddler complains of a sore body part—the key warning symptom of frostbite—you should gently remove any clothing that's covering the frostbitten area and slowly rewarm the area using body heat. Do not massage or rub snow onto the frostbitten skin or use heat or warm water to warm the skin. Instead, call your child's doctor to discuss treatment.

the safety generation gap

While some grandparents do a terrific job of getting up to speed on modern child safety practices, some seem determined to stick with the practices that were in vogue a generation earlier.

While Kelli's parents respect her wishes when it comes to child safety, they make it clear that they think she's being overly protective of her child. "They find our use of technology (baby monitors) and fancy accoutrements (bouncy chairs and swings) superfluous," the 32-year-old mother of two explains. "When I ask my parents to do things for my child in a certain way, they say things like, 'How did we ever raise three children without you and your baby books?'"

Dealing with this kind of safety generation gap in your family? Make it as convenient as possible for your parents or in-laws to be safety conscious. ("When my children go out in cars with relatives, I simply ask for their car keys so that I can go install the seats myself," explains Sandi, a 31-year-old mother of two.) But, at the same time, don't be afraid to take a hard line when it comes to your child's safety. This is one of those situations where there's quite simply no room for compromise.

First-Aid Essentials

Serious accidents can and do occur in the home, which is why it's important to receive training in both first aid and cardiopulmonary resuscitation (CPR). Organizations such as the Canadian Red Cross (www.redcross.ca) and St. John Ambulance (www.sja.ca) offer such training on a regular basis. But even if you *have* received proper training in emergency first aid, it can be easy to draw a blank when your child starts choking or gets a bad burn. That's why I decided to include a quick reference chart outlining some basic infant first-aid procedures (see Table 9.1). Please note that I was barely able to scratch the surface here, due to space constraints, so don't make the mistake of considering this chart to be a substitute for proper training (and regular recertification) in first aid and CPR.

9.1 Emergency First-Aid Procedures

Type of Emergency	What to Do
Allergic Reaction	• If your toddler is exhibiting the symptoms of an allergic reaction (for example, swollen hands and eyelids, wheezing, and a hive-like rash), take him to your doctor's office or the hospital emergency ward immediately. (If the reaction is severe and/or you're not sure what triggered it, err on the side of caution by seeking emergency medical assistance right away.) • Talk to your doctor about how to handle future allergic reactions, which, by the way, are likely to be more severe. You might want to carry a kit with injectable adrenalin (an EpiPen with measured doses of epinephrine) in order to buy your toddler enough time to get to the hospital for emergency treatment.
Bleeding	• If your child starts bleeding and the cut appears to be fairly deep, place a clean piece of gauze or cloth over the site of the bleeding and apply firm pressure for two minutes. If that stops the bleeding, you should attempt to clean the wound by running it under cold water. If the bleeding continues, apply more gauze and wrap tape around the cut to keep pressure on the bleeding. • Position your toddler so that the area that is bleeding is above the level of his heart. This will help to reduce the amount of bleeding. • If the bleeding still won't stop, the wound is gaping, and the cut appears to be quite deep, you'll need to take your toddler to the hospital or your doctor's office for stitches. You'll also need to seek medical attention for your toddler if the cut has dirt in it that won't come out; the cut becomes inflamed; your child starts running a fever; the cut begins oozing a thick, creamy, greyish fluid; red streaks form near the wound; or the wound is caused by a human or animal bite.

continued

Breathing, stopped	• Call 911 or have someone else make the call for you immediately. Try to figure out why your toddler isn't breathing if you discover that he's pale or turning blue. Look for any foreign objects in the mouth and clear out any vomit, mucus, or fluid that could be making it difficult for him to breathe by turning him on one side.
	• Place your toddler on his back. Note: if there's any chance that your toddler's back could be injured, you will need a second person to help you move him—to keep his head and neck from twisting. Check for signs of breathing.
	• If he is not breathing, perform 30 chest compressions in rapid succession (using the heel of one hand, but make sure that the heel of your hand is not at the very end of the breastbone). Open the airway by pushing your toddler's chin up with one hand and his forehead back with your other hand. Watch for chest movements and feel for his breath on your cheek. If he is still not breathing, cover his mouth with your mouth, pinching his nose closed, and deliver two rescue breaths (roughly one second each). Repeat rescue breathing and chest compressions until help arrives.
Burns	• Assess the severity of the burn. First-degree burns (such as sunburns) cause redness and minor soreness and can be treated with cool water. Second-degree burns cause blistering, swelling, and peeling, are very painful, and may require medical treatment. Third-degree burns damage the underlying layers of the skin and can lead to permanent damage; medical treatment is a must.
	• Submerge the burned area in cool water for at least 20 minutes (or, in the case of a burn to the face, apply a cool, water-soaked face cloth to the burn). This will help to ease your toddler's pain as well as lessen the amount of skin damage. Note: do not apply ice to a burn, as this can cause damage to the tissues.
	• If the skin becomes blistered, white, or charred, cover the wound before heading to your doctor's office or the hospital. Note: you'll also want to give your toddler a dose of acetaminophen to help control the pain.
	• If your child gets a chemical burn as a result of coming into contact with a caustic substance, immerse the burned area under cool, running water for 20 minutes. Gently wash the affected area with soap. (Vigorous scrubbing will cause more of the poison to be absorbed into the skin.)

9.1	Emergency First-Aid Procedures (continued)
Type of Emergency	**What to Do**
Burns (continued)	If the substance was also inhaled or swallowed, get in touch with your local poison control centre immediately. If a caustic substance was splashed into your toddler's eyes, flush the area for 20 minutes. (Swaddle your toddler in a towel to keep his arms out of the way and lay him on his side. Then pour water into his eye and onto a towel below. If your toddler closes his eyes tightly, pull down on the lower lid or put your index finger on the upper lid just below the eyebrow and gently pry your toddler's eyes open. Once you've finished flushing your toddler's eyes, call for medical advice.)
Choking	• Quickly determine whether your toddler is able to breathe. If your toddler can cough, cry, or speak, the airway is not completely blocked, and your toddler's built-in gag and cough reflex will help to dislodge the object. In this case, your best bet is to do nothing other than to reassure your toddler that he's going to be all right. • If your toddler does not appear to be breathing, he will likely be gasping for air or turning blue, losing consciousness, and/or looking panicked (wide eyes and mouth wide open). In this case, you should perform a Heimlich manoeuvre (abdominal thrusts administered while you stand behind and wrap your arms around your toddler). If your toddler is still small, you have the option to kneel on the floor with one knee raised, lean your child across your raised leg with his head pointing down, and administer five quick, forceful blows between your toddler's shoulder blades using the heel of your hand. If you are in a public place, shout for help; if you're at home alone, run with the toddler to the phone and dial 911 while you attempt to resuscitate him. • If the back blows don't dislodge the object and your toddler still isn't breathing, immediately flip your toddler over and deal four quick, forceful chest thrusts to the toddler's breastbone (about one finger's width below the level of the toddler's nipples, in the middle of the chest). To administer a chest thrust, you quickly press the breastbone to a depth of 1.5 to 2.5 centimetres (1/2 to 1 inch). You keep your fingers in the same position between thrusts but allow the breastbone to return to its normal position. • If your toddler is still not breathing, hold his tongue down with your thumb and forefinger, lift the jaw open, and check if you can see the object that's causing the blockage. (The mere act of holding your toddler's tongue away from the back of his throat may relieve the blockage.) If you see the object, carefully sweep it

out. If you can't see it, don't poke your finger down your toddler's throat or you may accidentally cause an object that's out of sight to become further lodged in your child's throat.

- If the tongue-jaw lift doesn't work, begin mouth-to-mouth resuscitation on your toddler. Cover his mouth with your mouth, pinching his nose closed, and give two quick breaths. If your toddler's chest rises with each breath and the airway is clear, you should continue administering mouth-to-mouth resuscitation until help arrives or your child starts breathing on his own.
- If your toddler still isn't breathing, repeat all of these steps until help arrives.

Convulsions (seizures)	<ul><li>Assess the severity of the convulsion. Convulsions can range from localized muscle shakes to full-body shakes (grand mal seizures), which may involve falling and writhing on the ground, the rolling back of the eyes, frothing at the mouth, tongue biting, and a temporary loss of consciousness. If you're unsure what it is you're dealing with, seek medical attention for your child.</li><li>Place your toddler safely on the floor, either face down or on his side to allow the tongue to come forward. This will also help to drain secretions from the mouth. Note: you don't have to try to manipulate your toddler's tongue or stick anything in his mouth.</li><li>Keep your toddler away from furniture so that he won't injure himself during the convulsion.</li><li>Don't give your toddler any food or drink during or immediately after a convulsion.</li><li>If your toddler's lips start to turn blue or he stops breathing, clear his airway and give mouth-to-mouth resuscitation. Cover his mouth with your mouth, pinching his nose closed, and give two quick breaths. If his chest rises with each breath, the airway is clear and you should continue administering mouth-to-mouth resuscitation until help arrives or your child starts breathing on his own.</li><li>Have your toddler seen by a doctor. Note: if the seizure lasts longer than two to five minutes or you live a considerable distance from a hospital, call 911 to access emergency medical assistance.</li></ul>
Head Injury	<ul><li>Try to assess the seriousness of the situation. If your toddler is unconscious but is still breathing and pinkish in colour rather than blue, lay him on a flat surface and call for emergency assistance.</li></ul>

continued

9.1 Emergency First-Aid Procedures (continued)

Type of Emergency	What to Do
Head Injury (continued)	Note: do not attempt to move him if you suspect that his neck may be injured. • If he's not breathing, follow the steps outlined above on dealing with a child who isn't breathing. • If your toddler is acting like himself (he's alert and conscious and seems to be behaving normally), apply an ice pack (wrapped in a sock or face cloth) or a bag of frozen vegetables to the cut or bump and monitor your toddler closely over the next 24 hours—checking him every two hours around the clock to see if his colour is still normal (pink rather than pale or blue), that he's breathing normally (there may be cause for concern if your toddler's breathing becomes shallow, irregular, he's gasping for air, or he periodically stops breathing altogether), and that he's rousable with gentle stimulation. If he seems well, you can let him continue sleeping. If you're concerned that there could be a problem, sit or stand your toddler up and then lie him back down again. Normally this will cause the toddler to react. If you don't get a suitable reaction, seek medical attention immediately. • You should seek medical attention immediately if you notice any signs of disorientation, crossed eyes, pupils that are unequal sizes, persistent vomiting (as opposed to just a one-time occurrence), oozing of blood or watery fluid from the ear canal, convulsions, or any signs that your toddler's sense of balance has been thrown off by the fall.
Poisoning	• Seek emergency medical attention from your local poison control line if your toddler seems to be exhibiting any signs of severe poisoning-related distress (e.g., severe throat pain, excessive drooling, difficulty breathing, convulsions, and/or excessive drowsiness). The person handling the call will want to know the name of the product that was ingested and what its ingredients are, so be sure to have this information handy. You'll also be asked the time of the poisoning and approximately how much of the poison your toddler ingested, the age and weight of your toddler, and whether he's exhibiting any symptoms (for example, vomiting, coughing, behavioural changes, and so on). • Do not attempt to induce vomiting. Inducing vomiting under the wrong circumstances (for example, if a caustic substance was ingested) could lead to severe tissue damage. In some cases, you'll be instructed to give your toddler a particular antidote—sometimes something as simple as a couple of glasses of water or a glass of milk.

Parting Thoughts

The toddler years are amazing, but they fly by all too quickly. It won't be long before that wriggly little toddler has morphed into a practically civilized preschooler. In the meantime, you'll want to seize the moment and savour it.

Consider these words of wisdom from Helena, a 33-year-old mother of one: "Living with a toddler can be compared to a rollercoaster ride. Not only do you have your ups and downs, but there are times of quiet anticipation and times when you cannot help yourself from screaming! But most of the time it's an exciting, ever-changing, and thrilling ride. Enjoy the ride."

"I definitely felt more confident as Sarah got older. That first bump on the head, the first flu, the first unexplained rash—each milestone built my confidence as a parent."

—JENNIFER, 33, MOTHER OF ONE

Glossary

Associative play: Very loosely organized play (e.g., a group of preschoolers are sharing a box of blocks, but each is making his own block tower).

Asthma: A lung disease that causes the air passages to become narrowed as a result of muscular spasms and swelling of the air-passage walls.

Authoritarian parenting: A parenting style that is based on parental control, that is, "I'm the one in charge." *See also* permissive parenting *and* authoritative parenting.

Authoritative parenting: A parenting style that is based on communication and flexibility. *See also* authoritarian parenting *and* permissive parenting.

Axillary temperature: A temperature reading that is taken by placing a thermometer in the armpit.

Boils: Raised, red, tender, warm swellings on the skin that are most often found on the buttocks.

Bronchiolitis: A viral infection of the small breathing tubes of the lungs.

Bronchitis: An infection of the central and larger airways of the lungs.

Bruxism: Teeth grinding.

Campylobacter: A common bacterial cause of intestinal infections.

Cellulitis: Swollen, red, tender, warm areas of skin that are typically found on the extremities or the buttocks and that often start out as a boil or puncture wound prior to becoming infected.

Conjunctivitis: Pink eye.

Cooperative play: When preschoolers play together and have a common goal in mind (e.g., "Let's play house!").

Co-regulation: Managing your thoughts, feelings, and behaviour with the help of another person.

Co-sleeping: Sleeping with your baby or toddler.

Croup: A respiratory condition in which your toddler's breathing becomes very noisy. In some cases, his windpipe may become obstructed.

Diphtheria: A disease that attacks the throat and heart and that can lead to heart failure or death.

E. coli: Escherichia coli: A dangerous and even life-threatening type of bacteria that can be picked up from poultry, beef, unpasteurized milk, or other food sources.

Eczema: Extreme itchiness that results in a rash in areas that are scratched.

Encephalitis: An infection of the brain.

Epiglottitis: A life-threatening infection that causes swelling in the back of the throat.

Febrile convulsions: Seizures that may occur when a toddler's temperature shoots up very suddenly.

Fifth disease: A common childhood disease that is characterized by a fever and a "slapped cheek" rash on the face plus a red rash on the trunk and extremities.

Fontanel: The so-called "soft spot" on a baby or young toddler's skull. The area of the skull where the cartilage has not yet hardened into bone (something that typically happens by the age of two).

Functional play: Play that involves imitating real-world activities like using a cell phone or pushing a vacuum cleaner around the house.

Gender: Characteristics associated with being male or female in a particular culture or society. An individual's own concept of his/her gender is described as gender identity.

German measles: *See* rubella.

Giardia lamblia: A parasite in the stool that causes bowel infections.

Haemophilus influenzae type b (Hib): A disease that can lead to meningitis, pneumonia, and a severe throat infection that can cause choking (epiglottitis).

Hand, foot, and mouth disease: A common childhood disease that is characterized by tiny blister-like sores in the mouth, on the palms of the hands, and on the soles of the feet. The sores are accompanied by a mild fever, a sore throat, and painful swallowing.

Head lice: Tiny insects that live on the scalp and that are spread through direct contact between children.

Herpangina: An inflammation of the inside of the mouth.

Impetigo: An infection of the skin that is characterized by yellow pustules or wide, honey-coloured scabs.

Laryngotracheitis: An inflammation of the voice box or larynx and windpipe or trachea.

Loose parts play: Refers to play using materials and spaces that can be enjoyed in any number of ways and that put children (rather than adults) in charge of their own play.

Meningitis: An inflammation of the membranes covering the brain and the spinal cord.

Mumps: An illness that is characterized by flu-like symptoms and an upset stomach followed by tender swollen glands beneath the earlobes two or three days later.

Myringotomy tubes: Tubes that are inserted in the middle ear to help balance the pressure between the middle ear and the ear canal and to allow fluid that has accumulated in the middle ear to drain.

Onlooker play: When young toddlers observe others at play rather than participate themselves.

Otitis media: An ear infection.

Parallel play: When two toddlers play side by side but without actually interacting.

Parent burnout: Burnout that is directly related to the task of parenting. It is characterized by feelings of exhaustion, a sense that you're parenting on autopilot (as opposed to making conscious and deliberate parenting decisions), and feelings of hopelessness and cynicism about parenting (for example, you start to believe that you're a bad parent and that nothing you do makes a difference for your child).

Pediculosis: *See* head lice.

Permissive parenting: A parenting style that involves few rules for children. *See also* authoritarian parenting *and* authoritative parenting.

Pertussis: *See* whooping cough.

Pinworms: Intestinal worms.

Pneumonia: An infection of the lungs.

Polio: A disease that can result in muscle pain and paralysis and/or death.

Renal disease: Kidney disease.

Respiratory syncytial virus (RSV): A respiratory infection that results in a raspy cough, rapid breathing, and wheezing.

Rheumatic fever: A serious disease that can result in heart damage and/or joint swelling.

Roseola: A common childhood illness that is characterized by a high fever followed by the appearance of a faint pink rash on the trunk and the extremities. Lasts for one day.

Rotavirus: A virus in the stool that is spread through person-to-person contact.

Rubella: A disease that is characterized by a low-grade fever, flu-like symptoms, a slight cold, and a pinkish-red spotted rash that starts on the face, spreads rapidly to the trunk, and then disappears by the third day. Rubella can be harmful—even fatal—to a developing fetus. Also known as German measles.

Salmonella: An illness that is typically acquired by eating food such as eggs, egg products, beef, poultry, or unpasteurized milk that has been contaminated with salmonella bacteria.

Scaffolding: Supporting your toddler's learning in a way that takes into account what she already knows and helps her to build upon that earlier learning. It's about guiding your toddler in a way that allows her to experience a healthy amount of frustration—enough to challenge her, but not so much that she feels completely overwhelmed.

Scarlet fever: *See* strep throat.

Self-regulation: Learning how to manage your thoughts, feelings, and behaviour in ways that work for, not against, you.

Separation anxiety: A baby or toddler's fear of being separated from the person or persons he cares most about.

Sepsis: A serious infection caused by bacteria that has entered a wound or body tissue. Commonly known as blood poisoning.

Shigella: An illness that is caused by a virus in the stool that can be spread from person to person.

Shingles: A disease that is characterized by a rash with small blisters that begin to crust over, resulting in itching and intense and prolonged pain.

Sinusitis: A sinus infection.

Soft spot: *See* fontanel.

Solitary play: When a toddler plays by herself.

Stranger anxiety: A baby or toddler's fear of strangers.

Strep throat: A bacterial infection that is characterized by a very sore throat, fever, and swollen glands in the neck. If a skin rash is also present, the condition is known as scarlet fever.

Swimmer's ear: An ear infection caused by frequent exposure to water.

Toilet learning: The Canadian Paediatric Society's preferred term for "toilet training." It keeps the focus where it should be—on helping your toddler to learn a new skill.

Tympanic temperature: A temperature reading that is taken using a tympanic (ear) thermometer.

Varicella zoster immune globulin: A type of immunization that is given to prevent or minimize the severity of the chicken pox.

Whooping cough: A disease that is characterized by a severe cough that makes it difficult to breathe, eat, or drink. Whooping cough can lead to pneumonia, convulsions, brain damage, and death.

Recommended Readings

Looking for some additional resources to help guide you through the toddler years? The following titles were helpful to me during the research and writing of this book.

Barbre, Jean. *Foundations of Responsive Caregiving: Infants, Toddlers, and Twos*. St. Paul, MN: Redleaf Press, 2013.

Bjordlund, David F., and Carlos Hernandez Blasi. *Child and Adolescent Development: An Integrated Approach*. Belmont, CA: Wadsworth, 2012.

Cowie, Helen. *From Birth to Sixteen: Children's Health, Social, Emotional and Linguistic Development*. New York: Routledge, 2012.

Douglas, Ann. *Mealtime Solutions for Your Baby, Toddler, and Preschooler*. Toronto: John Wiley and Sons Canada, 2006.

———. *Sleep Solutions for Your Baby, Toddler, and Preschooler*. Toronto: John Wiley and Sons Canada, 2006.

———. *Parenting Through the Storm: How to Handle the Highs, the Lows, and Everything in Between*. Toronto: HarperCollins Canada, 2015.

Galinsky, Ellen. *Mind in the Making: The Seven Essential Life Skills Every Child Needs*. New York: HarperCollins, 2010.

Gopnik, Alison. *The Gardener and the Carpenter: What the New Science of Child Development Tells Us About the Relationship Between Parents and Children*. New York: Farrar, Straus, and Giroux, 2016.

Greene, Ross W. *Raising Human Beings: Creating a Collaborative Partnership with Your Child*. New York: Scribner, 2016.

Greenspan, Stanley I., and Serena Wieder. *Infant and Child Mental Health: A Comprehensive Developmental Approach to Assessment and Intervention.* Washington, DC: American Psychiatric Publishing Inc., 2006.

Hoffman, Kent, Glen Cooper, and Bert Powell with Christine M. Benton. *Raising a Secure Child: How Circle of Security Parenting Can Help You Nurture Your Child's Attachment, Emotional Resilience, and Freedom to Explore.* New York: The Guilford Press, 2017.

Klein, Tovah. *How Toddlers Thrive: What Parents Can Do Today for Children Ages 2-5 to Plant the Seeds of Lifelong Success.* New York: Touchstone, 2014.

Kohn, Alfie. *The Myth of the Spoiled Child: Challenging the Conventional Wisdom about Children and Parenting.* Philadelphia, PA: Da Capo Press, 2014.

Langworthy, Sara E. *Bridging the Relationship Gap: Connecting with Children Facing Adversity.* St. Paul, MN: Redleaf Press, 2015.

Lansbury, Janet. *No Bad Kids: Toddler Discipline Without Shame.* Los Angeles, CA: JLML Press, 2014.

Lapointe, Vanessa. *Discipline Without Damage: How to Get Your Kids to Behave Without Messing Them Up.* Vancouver, BC: LifeTree Media/ Greystone Books Ltd, 2016.

MacNamara, Deborah. *Rest, Play, Grow: Making Sense of Preschoolers (Or Anyone Who Acts Like One).* Vancouver: Aona Books, 2016.

McClelland, Megan M., and Shaura L. Tominey. *Stop, Think, Act: Integrating Self-Regulation in the Early Childhood Classroom.* New York: Routledge, 2016.

North, Joanna. *Mindful Therapeutic Care for Children: A Guide to Reflective Practice.* London: Jessica Kingsley Publishers, 2014.

Senior, Jennifer. *All Joy and No Fun: The Paradox of Modern Parenthood.* New York: HarperCollins, 2014.

Summers, Susan Janko, and Rachel Chazan-Cohen. *Understanding Early Childhood Mental Health: A Practical Guide for Professionals.* Baltimore: Paul H. Brookes Publishing Co., 2012.

Wilson, Bee. *First Bite: How We Learn to Eat.* New York: Basic Books, 2015.

Van der Zande, Irene, with Santa Cruz Toddler Care Center staff. *1, 2, 3… The Toddler Years: A Practical Guide for Parents and Caregivers.* Third Edition. Santa Cruz, California: Toddler Center Press, 2011.

Acknowledgements

While my name may be the one that's splashed on the front cover of this book, *The Mother of All Toddler Books* was truly a team effort from start to finish. Writing a book of this size and scope requires assistance from a huge number of people—people I'd like to take a moment to pause and thank right now.

First Edition

First of all, I'd like to thank the parents who agreed to be interviewed for the book. It's your stories and words of wisdom that truly bring this book to life. I owe each and every one of you a huge thank you: Molly Acton, Rita Arsenault, Aubyn Baker, Christina Barnes, Sue Beaulieu, Debbi Beiko, Candice Bianic, Brandy Boissonneault, Janet Bolton, Vicky Boudreau, Elisa Brook, Kelli Cale, Karen Chamberlain, Laura Ciarallo, Jennifer Clarke, Brandy Conlin, Stacey Couturier, Marguerite Daubney, Brenda J. Davie, Kara Doerksen, Julie Dufresne, Stephanie Estabrook, Jane Fletcher, Anne Gallant, Julie Gardiner, Leslie Garrett, Danielle Gebeyehu, Yvonne Gilmour, Jo-Anne Gomes, Joyce Gravelle, Julie Grimaldi, Sandra Grocock, Sue Guebert, Terri Harten, Karen Hayward, Monica Hecht, Andrea Illman, Debbie Jeffery, Cathy Jones, Trish Kennedy, Cindy Legare, Sharon Louie, Stephanie MacDonald, Catherine Marion, Heather Martin, Jennie Maynard, Lori Mcgonigle, Melanie McLeod, Joan MacNeil, Robin MacNeil, Colleen MacCuaig, Sidney Ellen Mckay, Colleen Mielen, Alyson Miller, Jedidja Nawolsky, Tami Overbeck, Kerri Paquette, Anita Paradis, Diane Pepin, Maria Phillips, Catharine Piuze, Bernadette Pratt, Cynthia Pugh, Kerri Quirt, Rose-Marie Racine, Myrna MacDonald Ridley, Lisa Roberts, Lisa Rouleau, Caroline Rosenbloom, Jeannine St. Amand, Loree Siermachesky, Rochelle Simon, Cathy Smale, Kimberlee Smit, Janice Smith, Janie Smith, Jennifer Smith, Christy Sneddon, Sherry Sollows,

Helena Steinmetz, Susan Stilwell, Elizabeth Taylor, Lynda Timms, Melinda Tuck, Lise Van Beilen, Kristina Vienneau, Lori Voth, Kelly Wall, Cathy Watson, Tanya Weiner, Judith White, Stephanie Whyte, Joanne Wilson, Julia Wolst, Lynn Woodford.

I'd also like to thank the book's technical reviewers for the time and effort they put into reviewing various portions of the manuscript:

Richard Whatley, M.D., a brilliant and compassionate family physician whose insightful comments contributed a great deal to the book.

Laura Devine, R.N., a caring and committed nurse who also happens to be one of the most "together" parents I've ever met!

Lorrie Baird, a faculty member in the early childhood education program at Sir Sandford Fleming College and home daycare provider extraordinaire whose insightful comments on the chapters on child development, play, and creative discipline contributed tremendously to the book.

Cathy L. Kerr, M.A., psychologist and early childhood consultant, who suggested some excellent additions to the chapters on child development and play.

Brenda Wines-Moher, R.D., a dietitian and metric conversion whiz kid whose comments on the nutrition chapter were extremely helpful and who saved me from making a grievous error (encouraging parents to serve their toddlers "chopped children" as opposed to "chopped chicken").

As always, I am grateful to my husband, Neil, and my children, Julie, Scott, Erik, and Ian, for putting up with the usual book deadline insanity (think takeout, takeout, and more takeout!), and my research assistant and friend Diane Wolf for going above and beyond the duty on many occasions while I was busy researching and writing this book. (How can you say a proper thank you to someone who will drop everything to make an emergency run to Tim Horton's on your behalf?)

I also owe a huge debt of gratitude to Canada's most patient editor, Susan Girvan, who never let on how crazy I was making her when I needed to request a month-long extension for this book. Susan, a career in the theatre and/or the diplomatic service awaits you!

And as for the rest of the unsung heroes at the now-defunct CDG Books—Joan Whitman, Robert Harris, Jennifer Smith, Tom Best, Jamie Broadhurst, Scott Mitchell, and countless others—what can I say except, "Thanks for the memories." It's been a privilege and pleasure working with you.

Second Edition

Updating this book proved to be a rather Herculean task. Not only did I have fourteen years of child development research to catch up on, I also found myself sideswiped by a minor health crisis. (As I was heading into the home stretch on this project, I was diagnosed with a balance-and-dizziness disorder that forced me to drastically cut back on screen time—no small task for an author in the midst of book revisions). I wouldn't have been able to make it through the process at all if it hadn't been for the unwavering support of my agent, Hilary McMahon of Westwood Creative Artists, and my editor, Brad Wilson of HarperCollins Canada. Thank you both for your faith in me and your commitment to the books we create together.

Thanks also to my two technical reviewers for their extraordinary patience during what proved to be a long and drawn-out process. Yes, I'm looking at you, Michael Dickinson and Cathy Kerr.

I also need to thank all the readers who have been in touch over the years to suggest ways to make this book more helpful and relevant to the up-and-coming generation of Canadian parents. You'll find your fingerprints all over the book, alongside my own. I so appreciate your wisdom and your passion for all things The Mother of All.

Finally, I need to acknowledge the invaluable support of my husband, Neil Douglas, who has more than earned the moniker "The Father of All." Thank you being by my side on this, our latest journey.

Index